Sports Illustrated

The Baseball Book

1971 | THE PLATE Willie Mays touched to score his 1,950th run.

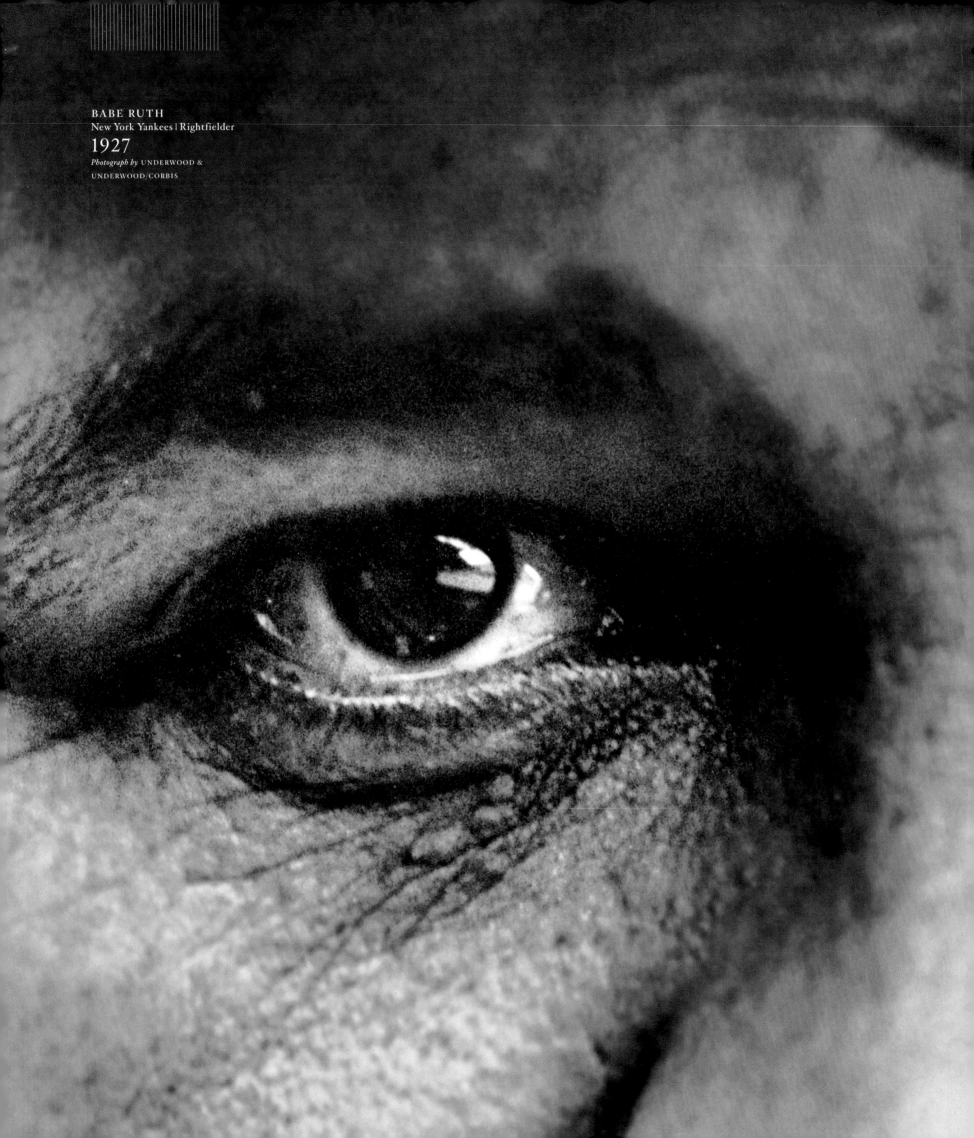

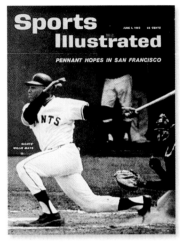

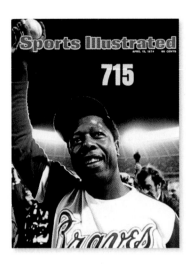

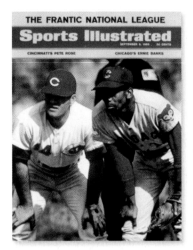

The Baseball Book

ROB FLEDER
Editor

STEVEN HOFFMAN
Designer

BOB ROE *Senior Editor*   DAVID SABINO *Associate Editor*

NATE GORDON *Photo Editor*   MICHELE BREA *Assistant Photo Editor*

KEVIN KERR *Copy Editor*   MELISSA SEGURA *Reporter*

JOSH DENKIN *Associate Designer*

THE NATIONAL BASEBALL HALL OF FAME
Archives and Historical Reference

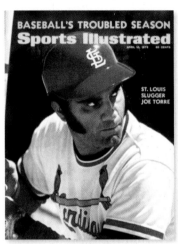

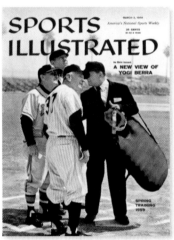

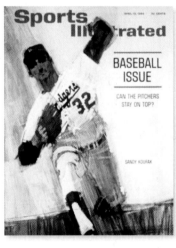

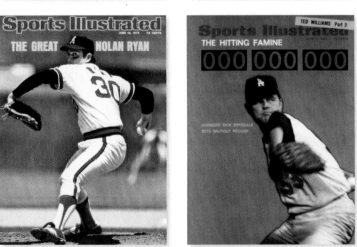

Sports Illustrated Contents

2006 TIME INC. HOME ENTERTAINMENT PUBLISHED BY SPORTS ILLUSTRATED BOOKS • TIME INC. 1271 AVENUE OF THE AMERICAS, NEW YORK, N.Y. 10020 • ALL RIGHTS RESERVED. NO PART OF THIS BOOK MAY BE REPRODUCED IN ANY FORM OR BY ANY ELECTRONIC OR MECHANICAL MEANS, INCLUDING INFORMATION STORAGE AND RETRIEVAL SYSTEMS, WITHOUT PERMISSION IN WRITING FROM THE PUBLISHER, EXCEPT BY A REVIEWER, WHO MAY QUOTE BRIEF PASSAGES IN A REVIEW • SPORTS ILLUSTRATED BOOKS IS A TRADEMARK OF TIME INC. • ISBN 13: 978-1-933405-23-0 ISBN 10: 1-933405-23-6 • LIBRARY OF CONGRESS CONTROL NUMBER: 2006929293

NATIONAL BASEBALL HALL OF FAME

INTRODUCTION
{ BY TOM VERDUCCI }

IN YOUR HANDS YOU HOLD A FAMILY ❧ PHOTO ALBUM. ❧

IT IS AN ALBUM OF YOUR FAMILY. OF MY FAMILY. OF ALL OF US WHO SHARE A LINKAGE NOT BY BLOOD BUT BY THE RAPTURE WE FEEL FOR THIS MOST FAMILIAR—IN THE WORD'S PUREST DERIVATIVE SENSE, THE LATIN *FAMILIA*—OF GREAT AMERICAN PASTIMES. BASEBALL IS THE GAME OF OUR FATHERS, AND IT IS THE GAME OF OUR SONS (AND, YES, DAUGHTERS), AND IT WILL BE THE GAME OF THEIR SONS AND DAUGHTERS. AND ALL THOSE WHO HAVE PLAYED IT OVER THESE MANY GENERATIONS—EVEN THE DISTANT ONES—HAVE BECOME PART OF OUR FAMILY TOO.

ALL OF BASEBALL said its last goodbye to Ruth at Yankee Stadium on June 13, 1948, two months before his death.

FROM THESE pages, as if from a wellspring of memory, come images that are more comfortable and familiar than awe-inspiring. Baseball photographs evoke an intimacy unmatched in sports, partly because the ballplayers, without masks, padding or oversized bodies, and often captured in the honest warmth of broad daylight, *look* like members of the family. Nagurski, Butkus, LT, Wilt, Kareem . . . who among us ever had such fierce, massive company at our Thanksgiving table?

But here is droopy-drawered Grandpa Casey, enthralling us with that rubbery face as much as with his nonsensical stories, and Uncle Babe, the favored relative who makes you fish around the pockets of his camelhair coat to find the hidden treasure he'd always bring, and cousin Mickey, forever brightening the room with his laughter so that he was forgiven if he threw back one or two too many; and big brother Jackie, always the gentleman, teaching us, without having to say a word, how to conduct ourselves. In these family photos we almost always see the subject at eye level. He is of us.

Baseball was *the* game long ago, as America grew its muscles on the world's schoolyard, and so the trove of familiar baseball faces and photographs is far richer than those of other sports. To this very day, 58 years after his death, is there a more recognizable mug in sports than Babe Ruth's? The faces of Hogan, Tilden, Baugh, Louis and Mikan, meanwhile, have receded or blurred.

Consider the world of 1948, a world that had just escaped calamity and was moving hopefully into an uncertain era. Truman signed the Marshall Plan to salve a war-ravaged Europe, and ground was broken for the United Nations; Tojo was hanged for his war crimes and Gandhi was assassinated. And yet the Pulitzer Prize for the best news photograph taken that year was awarded to Nat Fein

for a picture of Ruth at Yankee Stadium on June 13.

Ruth, wracked by cancer, would be dead in two months, and he looked and sounded like a condemned man. That afternoon he put on his Yankees uniform one last time, for Babe Ruth Day ceremonies, at which his number 3 would be retired. Fein, a photographer for the *New York Herald-Tribune*, broke from the pack of newsmen and shot Ruth from behind as he stood before his teammates and the throng at Yankee Stadium. With a snap of the shutter he created one of the most familiar images in the history of America. The dying Ruth, bent at the waist, leans on his bat in the manner of a cane just to stay upright. His teammates stand at attention, caps removed. The leaden sky and the neoclassical frieze ringing the upper reaches of the cavernous stadium frame the solemn tableau of a man attending his own funeral.

The image is such an indelible part of our album that by now it seems as if we were there. We can smell the rain in the air, see Ruth's old teammates from the 1923 team stumble stiffly through a two-inning exhibition and hear the gravelly voiced Ruth croak into the microphone as he had a year earlier at another ceremonial appearance at the Stadium, when he said in already faint tones: "You know this baseball game of ours comes up from the youth. That means the boys. And after you've been a boy, and grow up to know how to play ball, then you come to the boys you see representing themselves today in our national pastime."

The essayist Susan Sontag, writing about photography in 1977, declared that in image-obsessed industrial societies, "Ultimately, having an experience becomes identical with taking a photograph of it." In baseball it is as if the reverse is true; that the photograph ultimately confers upon the viewer a kind of phantom experience.

Seen often and long enough—a word of advice: If you don't

ROBINSON MADE opponents sweat any time he got on base, as in the '55 World Series against the Yankees.

linger over the images on these pages, order up an EKG for yourself immediately—the photographs do seem to mirror our memories. You remember with the clarity of an eyewitness the bravado of Robinson, supreme ruler of the base paths; the boundless joy of Yogi Berra and Don Larsen locked forever in perfect embrace; the midflight, hair-raising intensity of an iron-willed Pete Rose, letting nothing get in his way. So familiar are the images that you somehow believe you were there.

In that sense I saw Willie Mays make the greatest catch there ever was. The familiar photograph—there are two versions of it, snapped from nearly identical vantage points—takes me back to Sept. 29, 1954, ignoring the small detail that the day predates my birth. It is Game 1 of the World Series, with the mighty Cleveland Indians visiting the New York Giants in their huge oblong ballpark, the Polo Grounds. I walk up to the ticket window and fork over $2.10 for a seat in the bleachers.

This is the same year that a Parisian-born Columbia professor, Jacques Barzun, published one of the most famous testimonials to the game, writing, "Whoever wants to know the heart and mind of America had better learn baseball." The centerfield bleachers at the Polo Grounds would have been a good place to start such learning. Here most of the men wear their shirts open at the neck instead of the starched white collars clenched by ties that are found in the lower seating bowl around the bases. Some wear fedoras, though not as many as you see in the better seats. And there are colored men out here, still only seven years after Jackie Robinson first changed the unwritten rules about who could or couldn't be a ballplayer, and by extension, a truly vested major league fan.

In these centerfield bleachers we sit almost 500 feet from home plate, pushed to such an outpost by the goofy

shape of a ballpark better suited for the range and speed of horses than outfielders. Dead centerfield, where the second-floor clubhouses were located in a 60-by-60 foot building accessible by a stairway *on the field*, measures 483 feet from home plate. In the 59 combined seasons the ballpark would be used in this incarnation (the fifth version of the Polo Grounds) by the Giants, Yankees and Mets, no batted ball ever reached the building.

The bleachers extend about 30 feet toward the diamond on both sides of the building. Sitting there that day, I know only two men have ever homered into these seats: Luke Easter in a Negro league game in 1948 and Joe Adcock in '53. It was not the place to sit if you had designs on a souvenir that you could hold in your hand.

By the eighth inning shadows begin to stretch over the ballpark, adding a theatrical lighting to the already suspenseful story told on the scoreboard. The score is tied at 2 and the Indians have chased New York starting pitcher Sal Maglie by putting the first two batters on. (Maglie, a kind of baseball Zelig, would start the 1951 game in which Bobby Thomson won the pennant with the Shot Heard 'Round the World, this '54 Mays Catch game and the '56 Larsen perfect game.) Giants manager Leo Durocher summons lefthander Don Liddle to pitch to the lefthanded-hitting Vic Wertz.

What happens next is as familiar to me as my parents' wedding portrait or the group pictures (first black-and-white, then Kodachrome) of my brothers, sisters and me with which my parents carpet-bombed friends and family every Christmas. Wertz so thoroughly crushes a pitch from Liddle that just for a moment we consider the ridiculous idea that the baseball might actually carry into our hands. While we try to comprehend its trajectory, Mays wheels and runs, his mind instantly mastering

LARSEN had to catch Yankees catcher Berra after tossing a perfect game against the Dodgers in the '56 Series.

the calculus needed to know, based on its speed and launch angle and the air currents, where it will land. He is pleased with how the calculations come out. The ball, according to his mental math, will wind up in his glove. Not too much later, not too far from his centerfield position, Mays will say in the clubhouse, "I had it all the way. There was nothing too hard about it."

The Polo Grounds outfield, besides including that stairway and being a vast swath of greenery, presents various other challenges for a centerfielder in 1954. The bullpens, for instance, are located in the power alleys—*on* the field. For drainage purposes, the outfield slopes down 18 inches to drains about 20 feet beyond the infield, then rises again, but very gradually, so the entire expanse is below the level of the infield. Durocher, in the Giants' dugout, cannot see Mays's legs churning as he goes after Wertz's drive. Mays is visible to him only from about the waist up, the 24 on the back of his uniform growing smaller, like the taillights of a car speeding away. Mays is headed smack toward the batter's eye on the rightfield flank of the clubhouse, a 14¼-foot high wooden wall atop a 4¼-foot high concrete wall.

Mays, his legs still pumping in the manner of pistons in a well-oiled race engine, suddenly throws up both hands, palms skyward, in the way a man might catch a baby tossed from the second floor of a burning building. At precisely that moment, with the baseball only inches above Mays's glove, Matty Zimmerman clicks the shutter on his 70mm sequence camera with the 20-inch lens. Zimmerman is an Associated Press photographer shooting from an elevated vantage point behind home plate (a position shared by Frank Hurley of the New York *Daily News*).

It has been quite a year for Zimmerman. Six months earlier, on March 16, while shooting an NBA playoff game between the Knicks and the Celtics at Madison Square Garden, Zimmerman captured the great Boston guard Bob Cousy and future Marquette basketball coach Al McGuire both knocked off stride by a collision as Cousy manages to fling the basketball toward the hoop.

Then, just 20 days before he snapped the shutter on Mays, Zimmerman was sent on assignment to Lexington and 52nd Street in the middle of the night to shoot a movie publicity stunt in front of the Trans-Lux Theater. The featured star was the wife of another famous New York centerfielder, Joe DiMaggio, who had been retired from the Yankees for three years now. Marilyn Monroe, in the midst of filming *The Seven Year Itch,* looked stunning in all her blondness and a pleated white halter-top dress.

A crowd of 1,500 gawkers practically drooled and howled at the sight. When Monroe stepped atop a subway grate on the sidewalk, an electric fan placed below it by the movie's enterprising publicity agents clicked on. The skirt of Monroe's dress billowed upward in the blast of air, revealing those famous legs all the way up to her panties as, with great flirtatious cheer, she used her hand to anchor the skirt to her legs.

A smoldering DiMaggio watched the scene, enraged. Monroe, of course, loved the attention. Later that night the two of them would engage in a heated argument in which DiMaggio hit Monroe, according to biographer Richard Ben Cramer. They would start divorce proceedings in a matter of weeks.

Hoots from the crowd rose with the hem of Monroe's skirt as flashbulbs popped like fireworks from the scores of professional and amateur photographers, but it was Zimmerman who got the definitive shot, the one that to this day is the ultimate image of Monroe's playful sexiness at the height of her beauty.

TED WILLIAMS got a warm greeting from DiMaggio (5) after his three-run homer won the '41 All Star Game for the American Leaguers.

Less than three weeks later at the Polo Grounds, Zimmerman did it again; Monroe and Mays defined on film in perpetuity just 20 days and five miles apart on the island of Manhattan.

Like his Monroe, Zimmerman's Mays is forever young and graceful, the ball floating above his glove in that last instant of doubt—at least for all of us except Mays—about where it would land. Reporters would estimate in their breathless accounts that Mays had to be 450, 460, even 470 feet from home plate when he made the catch, though a more reasoned estimate would be about 430 feet. We hardly have time to marvel at the catch before Mays spins and fires a missile of a throw back to the infield, keeping the runner at first base from advancing. The Indians never did score, losing 5–2 when Dusty Rhodes hit a walk-off homer that, in a cruel twist of irony for Cleveland, traveled only about 270 feet.

"Does this guy Mays make catches like that all the time?" a shocked Wertz said in the clubhouse later.

Liddle, who was replaced by a righthander after the catch, caught sight of Durocher in the clubhouse after the game and cracked, "Well, I got my man."

Like the Mays catch, the classic baseball photographs stir our heart and our senses. You can practically smell that oddly sweet aroma of beer and popcorn from the catacombs of Tiger Stadium and the virtual mustard that emanates from the stylin', corkscrew-swingin' Reggie Jackson. You feel the cold beer shower upon the head of crestfallen White Sox leftfielder Al Smith. You hear the clicks and pops of the old box cameras, manned by nattily dressed photographers perilously close to home plate, that capture the timeless beauty of DiMaggio's silky batting stroke.

I'm not sure the modern photographs, despite the leaps in technology, move us like that. The modern game, for one thing, is made for TV and played under the klieg lights of the ballpark-cum-soundstage. No World Series game has been played in sunshine in 22 years. The artificial light does not flatter the ballplayer or the moment. (Notice as you travel through these pages how many of the great photographs were snapped during day games.)

Can you recall a truly iconic contemporary picture—the Mays Catch for our children—from the all-night World Series era? Where is the definitive shot of Kirk Gibson in 1988? Joe Carter in 1993? Edgar Renteria in 1997? Luis Gonzalez in 2001? Maybe, starting with Carlton Fisk waving his World Series home run fair in 1975, moving pictures have replaced the photograph as our favored means of transportation. We are the mobile video generation, staring into our cellphones and video iPods and laptops at motion that doesn't ever stop. Neither, though, do we. We don't *linger* on these images. We don't need to imagine the roar of the crowd because it is provided in full-range digital audio.

Maybe such a shift has indeed taken place, or maybe all that is missing from the next generation of baseball iconography is the passage of time and the patina that only nostalgia can provide. I hope so.

Not long after Mays's catch, Durocher, the salty Giants manager, filmed a commercial for Schlitz beer in which he said of Mays, "And he caught it, like a ballet dancer." The pages of this album you hold display time and again the balletic nature of baseball—an outfielder's leap, a pitcher's follow-through, the pas de deux of fielder and runner at a base—though it is better than ballet because there is no choreography and there is the added complication of a ball in motion. But even more than that these pages are filled with the familiar: The dancer's grace of Mays is immutable in that photograph. He is forever 23. And we are there with him. ❧

MAYS TURNED turned his back on Wertz to chase down his long drive at the Polo Grounds in the '54 Series.

The Baseball

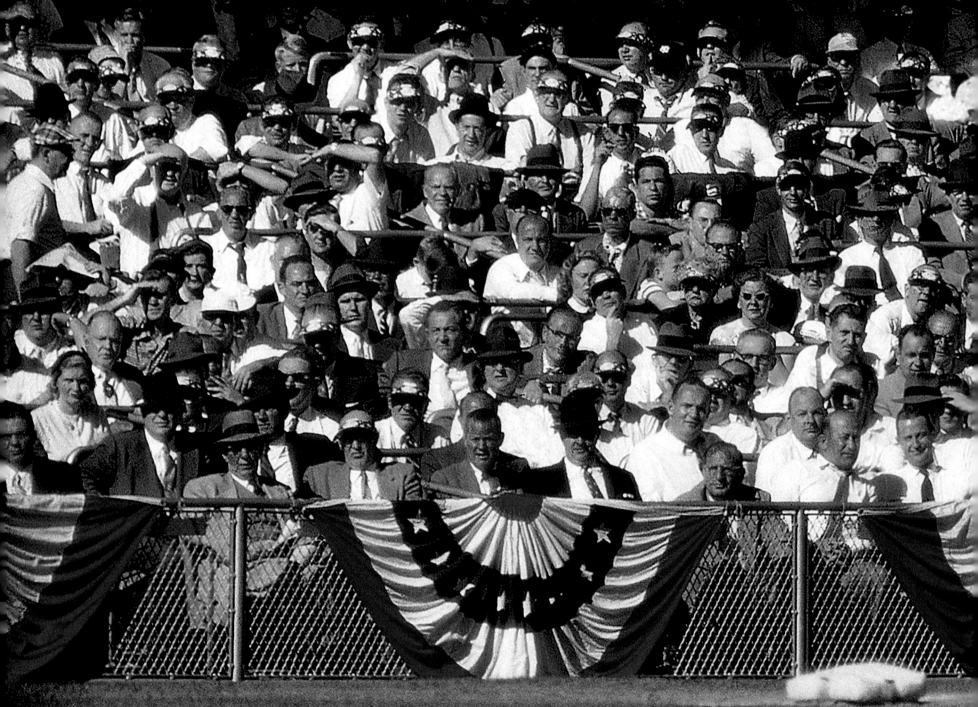

1955 | THE YANKEES forestalled their seven-game World Series defeat, taking a 5–0 first-inning lead in Game 6 and chasing Dodgers starter Karl Spooner, who was replaced by Russ Meyer (above). | *Photograph by* HY PESKIN

Book

A Celebration of the National Pastime

1961 | PRESIDENT KENNEDY turned out for Opening Day in D.C., and Vice President Johnson (far left) joined him. | *Photograph by* NEIL LEIFER

1946 | SPORTSMAN'S PARK in St. Louis was SRO for the World Series opener between the Cardinals and the Red Sox. | *Photograph by* BETTMANN/CORBIS

1903 | BOSTON FANS turned out at the first World Series to see their Pilgrims
(led by Cy Young) beat the Pittsburgh Pirates (led by Honus Wagner). | *Photograph by* BETTMANN/CORBIS

1999 | YANKEES SHORTSTOP Derek Jeter, AL Rookie of the Year in '96, anchored four world champions in his first five years in the league. | *Photograph by* TOM DIPACE

1982 | OZZIE SMITH became a solidly productive bat for St. Louis, but his wizardry at short earned him a ticket to Cooperstown. | *Photograph by* DAN DONOVAN

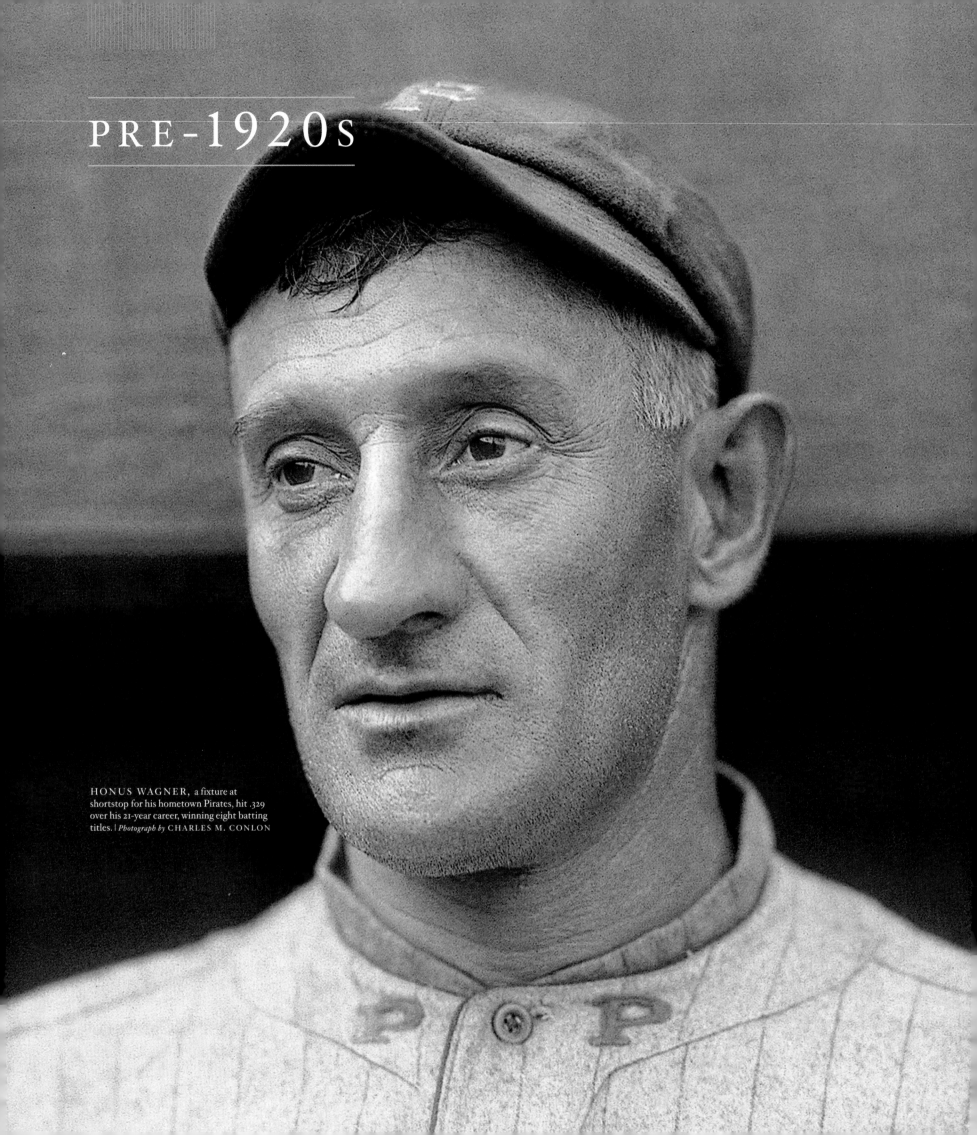

HONUS WAGNER, a fixture at
shortstop for his hometown Pirates, hit .329
over his 21-year career, winning eight batting
titles. | *Photograph by* CHARLES M. CONLON

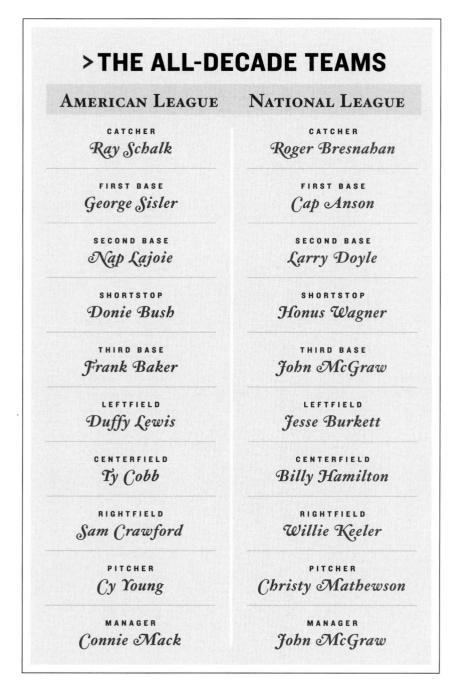

>THE ALL-DECADE TEAMS

AMERICAN LEAGUE	NATIONAL LEAGUE
CATCHER	**CATCHER**
Ray Schalk	*Roger Bresnahan*
FIRST BASE	**FIRST BASE**
George Sisler	*Cap Anson*
SECOND BASE	**SECOND BASE**
Nap Lajoie	*Larry Doyle*
SHORTSTOP	**SHORTSTOP**
Donie Bush	*Honus Wagner*
THIRD BASE	**THIRD BASE**
Frank Baker	*John McGraw*
LEFTFIELD	**LEFTFIELD**
Duffy Lewis	*Jesse Burkett*
CENTERFIELD	**CENTERFIELD**
Ty Cobb	*Billy Hamilton*
RIGHTFIELD	**RIGHTFIELD**
Sam Crawford	*Willie Keeler*
PITCHER	**PITCHER**
Cy Young	*Christy Mathewson*
MANAGER	**MANAGER**
Connie Mack	*John McGraw*

>DEBUT   FINALE<

Year	DEBUT	FINALE
1910	MAX CAREY	WILLIE KEELER
1911	GROVER CLEVELAND ALEXANDER	CY YOUNG
1912	CASEY STENGEL	HARRY WOLVERTON
1913	WALLY PIPP	CY SEYMOUR
1914	BABE RUTH	FRANK CHANCE
1915	ROGERS HORNSBY	ROGER BRESNAHAN
1916	URBAN SHOCKER	CHRISTY MATHEWSON
1917	JOE DUGAN	HONUS WAGNER
1918	WAITE HOYT	HUGHIE JENNINGS
1919	FRANKIE FRISCH	JIM THORPE

>THE LEADERS

HITTING

BATTING AVERAGE* TY COBB	.372
HOME RUNS ROGER CONNOR	138
RBI CAP ANSON	1,879
AT BATS HONUS WAGNER	10,430
HITS HONUS WAGNER	3,415

SINGLES WILLIE KEELER	2,512
DOUBLES NAP LAJOIE	657
TRIPLES SAM CRAWFORD	309
OBP* JOHN McGRAW	465
SLUGGING PCT.* DAN BROUTHERS	519
RUNS HONUS WAGNER	1,736
STOLEN BASES BILLY HAMILTON	912
HIT BY PITCHES HUGHIE JENNINGS	287

WALKS BILLY HAMILTON	1,187
STRIKEOUTS TOM BROWN	708
GAMES HONUS WAGNER	2,792

PITCHING

WINS CY YOUNG	511
LOSSES CY YOUNG	316
WINNING PCT.† DAVE FOUTZ	690
STRIKEOUTS CY YOUNG	2,802

ERA† WALTER JOHNSON	1.65
INNINGS CY YOUNG	7,356
WALKS AMOS RUSIE	1,704
RUNS ALLOWED PUD GALVIN	3,318
HOME RUNS ALLOWED JOHN CLARKSON	160
SAVES MORDECAI BROWN	49
SHUTOUTS WALTER JOHNSON	86
COMPLETE GAMES CY YOUNG	749

INCLUDES PLAYERS FROM 1876 THROUGH 1919 * MINIMUM 2,500 PLATE APPEARANCES †MINIMUM 1,000 INNINGS

>HOT TICKETS 10 Games You Wish You'd Seen

Bennett Park April 25, 1901 Detroit's franchise starts off with a bang as the Tigers, trailing in the seventh by 10 runs, score one in the eighth and then 10 in the bottom of the ninth of their American League debut, to defeat the Milwaukee Brewers 14–13.

Huntington Avenue Grounds Oct. 1, 1903 > The American League champion Boston Pilgrims host the National League champion Pittsburgh Pirates in the first modern World Series game. Boston's Cy Young is outpitched by Pittsburgh's Deacon Phillippe in the 7–3 Pirates win.

Washington Park Sept. 26, 1908 Cubs pitcher Ed Reulbach throws shutouts in both games of a doubleheader, blanking the Brooklyn Superbas 5–0 and then 3–0.

Polo Grounds Oct. 8, 1908 In a special replay of their Sept. 23 game that ended in a tie because of Merkle's Boner (in the bottom of the ninth, Giants base runner Fred Merkle was belatedly called out at second when he failed to touch the base after a teammate crossed the plate with what seemed to be the game-winning run), the Cubs and Giants meet in a contest for the NL pennant. Mordecai Brown beats Christy Mathewson 4–2, and the Cubs win the pennant.

Bennett Park Oct. 14, 1908 The Cubs, appearing in the World Series for the third straight year, win for the second straight time by beating the Tigers in

Boston vs. Pittsburg 3 ADMISSION RAIN CHECK VOID AFTER 5 INNINGS ARE PLAYED

Game 5 in Detroit. The Cubs will not win another world championship in the 20th century.

Polo Grounds Sept. 28, 1919 The shortest game in major league baseball history is played as the Giants beat the Phillies 6–1 in just 51 minutes.

Fenway Park April 20, 1912 Following three straight days of rainouts, the Red Sox finally christen their new home field with a 7–6, 11-inning win over New York.

Fenway Park July 11, 1914 The Red Sox start rookie lefthander George Ruth against the Cleveland Naps. He pitches seven innings, allowing eight hits and three runs. Batting for Ruth in the seventh inning, Duffy Lewis singles and scores the deciding run in Boston's 4–3 win.

Wrigley Field May 2, 1917 Cubs lefty Hippo Vaughn and Reds righty Fred Toney both complete nine innings without giving up a hit. The Reds score a run on their first hit against Vaughn in the top of the 10th, and Toney closes out his no-no by retiring the Cubs in the last half of the inning.

Fenway Park June 23, 1917 Red Sox pitcher Ernie Shore takes the mound in relief of Babe Ruth, who had been ejected after walking the game's leadoff hitter, Ray Morgan, and punching the ump. Morgan is thrown out while trying to steal second base, whereupon Shore retires the next 26 batters in Boston's 4–0 win over Washington.

BEST OF THE PRE-1920S (1901-1919)

TEAM	WINS	LOSSES	WIN PCT.
GIANTS	1,652	1,164	.587
CUBS	1,640	1,185	.581
PIRATES	1,595	1,229	.565
RED SOX	1,548	1,258	.552
WHITE SOX	1,542	1,267	.549

RUBE MARQUARD, GIANTS

WORST OF THE PRE-1920S (1901-1919)

TEAM	WINS	LOSSES	WIN PCT.
CARDINALS	1,167	1,643	.415
BRAVES	1,187	1,620	.423
BROWNS	1,196	1,613	.426
SENATORS	1,235	1,570	.440
DODGERS	1,263	1,542	.450

WALTER JOHNSON, SENATORS

PRE-1920s CULTURE

MUSIC: *You Made Me Love You* (Al Jolson), *Alexander's Ragtime Band* (Irving Berlin), *In the Good Old Summertime* (John Philip Sousa's Band), *It's a Long Way to Tipperary* (John McCormack), *Shine On Harvest Moon* (Miss Walton and Mister MacDonough)

MOVIES: *The Birth of a Nation, The Great Train Robbery, A Tale of Two Cities, Daddy Long-Legs, The Floorwalker*

BOOKS: *The Jungle* by Upton Sinclair; *The Interpretation of Dreams* by Sigmund Freud; *Up from Slavery* by Booker T. Washington; *The Hound of the Baskervilles* by Arthur Conan Doyle; *The Montessori Method* by Marie Montessori

ACHIEVEMENT: On Dec. 17, 1903, brothers Orville and Wilbur Wright take the first powered flight, at Kitty Hawk, N.C.

INVENTIONS: airplane, air conditioning, stainless steel, zipper, electric range

SEX SYMBOLS: Mary Pickford and Douglas Fairbanks.

VILLAIN: Serbian national Gavrilo Princip assassinates Archduke Franz Ferdinand of Austria in 1914, triggering World War I.

PERSONALITY: Theodore Roosevelt

< MARY PICKFORD

>NICKNAMES<

Mordecai [Three Finger] Brown ∧
George [Babe] Ruth
[Shoeless] Joe Jackson
Walter [the Big Train] Johnson
Ty [the Georgia Peach] Cobb
Frank [Ping] Bodie
Denton [Cy] Young
Roger [Doc] Cramer
Frank [Home Run] Baker
Frederick [Mysterious] Walker
Max [Scoops] Carey
Honus [the Flying Dutchman] Wagner
George [Piano Legs] Gore
Eddie [Knuckles] Cicotte
James [Hippo] Vaughn
Charley [Old Hoss] Radbourn
Eugene [Bubbles] Hargrave
Christy [Big Six] Mathewson
[Wahoo] Sam Crawford
Herold [Muddy] Ruel
Adrian [Cap] Anson
John [Happy Jack] Chesbro

BORN		DIED
Jacques Cousteau	1910	< Mark Twain
Ronald Reagan	1911	Joseph Pulitzer
Woody Guthrie	1912	Wilbur Wright
Vince Lombardi	1913	J. Pierpont Morgan
Jack LaLanne	1914	John Muir
Billie Holiday >	1915	Booker T. Washington
Walter Cronkite	1916	Rasputin
Red Auerbach	1917	Buffalo Bill Cody
Sam Walton	1918	Joyce Kilmer
Liberace	1919	Theodore Roosevelt

> NEWS OF THE REAL WORLD

1901: William McKinley is assassinated, Teddy Roosevelt becomes president **1903**: Henry Ford, with $28,000 in cash, starts the Ford Motor Company **1904**: Construction of the Panama Canal begins **1905**: Town of Las Vegas is founded in Nevada **1906**: An 8.3 magnitude earthquake devastates San Francisco **1909**: The Indianapolis Motor Speedway opens **1910**: W.E.B. DuBois founds the NAACP; Heavyweight Jack Johnson knocks out the Great White Hope, James J. Jeffries, setting off race riots across the U.S. **1911**: John D. Rockefeller's Standard Oil declared a monopoly, its breakup ordered by U.S. Supreme Court **1912**: The "unsinkable" *Titanic* hits an iceberg and goes down in the North Atlantic, killing 1,523 **1913**: The 16th Amendment is ratified, paving the way for the federal income tax **1915**: The *RMS Lusitania* is sunk by a German U-boat, killing 1,198 **1919**: 18th Amendment ratified, making the consumption of alcoholic beverages illegal

1965 | DON DRYSDALE, A.K.A. Big D, gave the Dodgers a potent righty-lefty combo in a rotation with Sandy Koufax. | *Photograph by* NEIL LEIFER

2003 | **AFTER HOMERING** In the first inning, the Cubs' Sammy Sosa should have expected something high and tight in his next at bat. | *Photograph by* MIKE LONGO

1940 | **THE CARDINALS'** Bob Bowman (26) had argued with Brooklyn's Joe Medwick, a former teammate, the night before their game, then beaned him. | *Photograph by* DAILY NEWS

A ONE-WAY TICKET
TO OBSCURITY

BY JOHN SCHULIAN

That's what being black in the first half of the 20th century meant for Oscar Charleston, the greatest baseball player you've never heard of. —*from* SI, SEPTEMBER 5, 2005

EVEN WHEN HE WENT into the the Hall of Fame, in 1976, Oscar Charleston was overlooked. How could it have been otherwise when there were big names, white names—Bob Lemon, Robin Roberts—going in with him? Besides, the general public had been conditioned to think only of Satchel Paige and Josh Gibson if it thought of Negro leaguers at all.

Paige and Gibson swept into Cooperstown after its walls of intolerance crumbled five years earlier, and a myth sprang up around them that made it impossible to imagine anyone having paved the way for them. But Oscar Charleston did. He played so long ago that even old-time Negro leaguer Double Duty Radcliffe, who died this year at age 103, said of Charleston, "He was before my time."

Of course, the two of them were actually teammates on the 1932 Pittsburgh Crawfords, but by then Charleston had spent most of two decades as the reigning icon in black baseball. No matter what he did for the Craws—and he played first base, batted third and managed what became the greatest Negro leagues team ever—there was always an old-timer around to say you should have seen him when he was really Oscar Charleston.

Starting in 1915, he turned centerfield into an art gallery on behalf of the Indianapolis ABCs, New York Lincoln Stars, Hilldale Daisies and three kinds of Giants: Chicago American, St. Louis and Harrisburg. His vagabond life was inspired by the disposable nature of the era's contracts and the wisdom of another black baseball pioneer, Pop Lloyd: "Wherever the money was, I was." At every stop, including Cuba in the winter, Charleston hung great catches as if they were paintings. He played shallow, the way Tris Speaker did and Willie Mays would, but when he went back for a ball, legend says he performed acrobatics that have eluded everyone else in the position's history, leaping, spinning, making catches behind his back.

Never, until he moved on to the Homestead Grays in 1930 and declared himself too old and slow for the position, would a team of his put anyone else in center. Fellow centerfielder Cool Papa Bell, mesmerized by the sight of Charleston playing so close that he could almost shake hands with the second baseman, imitated the icon who became his manager on the Crawfords. Gentleman Dave Malarcher, who patrolled the outfield with Charleston for Indianapolis, once said, "People asked me, 'Why are you playing so close to the rightfield foul line?' What they didn't know was that Oscar played all three fields. I just made sure of the balls down the line, and all the foul ones too."

It was a time when every team, black or white, was hunting for its own Babe Ruth, and here was another reformed southpaw pitcher who had the bat and the build: a hair under six feet tall, 190 pounds and getting bigger, with spindly legs and a chest-o'-drawers torso. If, as historian James A. Riley suggests, Charleston never matched the Babe's power, he was easily the black equivalent of Rogers Hornsby, who batted more than .400 three times in one four-year stretch. Of course, he was faster than Hornsby and almost anyone else—the Army clocked him at 23 seconds in the 220-yard dash—and he was capable of dragging a bunt, stealing a base and cutting the glove off your hand if a throw happened to beat him. However you choose to look at Charleston, slugger or slasher, he raised enough hell with his bat to launch a thousand stories.

He hit the triple that gave the ABCs black baseball's unofficial championship in 1916. He won, or tied for, five home run titles. In his best year, 1921, *The Baseball Encyclopedia* says he batted .434 with 14 doubles, 11 triples, 15 homers and 34 stolen bases in 60 league games. That fall he had five homers in five games against a team of major league (i.e., white) barnstormers. Then he roared off to Cuba, where he batted .471. Even when he was calling himself an antique, he rang up a .372 average for the Crawfords in 1933, as if to remind the future Hall of Famers he was managing—Josh and Satch, Cool Papa and Judy Johnson—that he was made of the same stuff.

Teammates and opponents stampeded to proclaim his greatness. One of the few still standing, Buck O'Neil, the eternal flame of the Negro leagues, testifies that, as Double Duty put it, "a better player never drew breath." . . .

DIZZY DEAN, who played against Charleston on barnstorming tours, says pitching to him was a throw-it-and-duck proposition.

1982 | SURE SIGNS of one of Rickey Henderson's career 1,406 steals: the gloves, the wristbands and the cloud of dust on a headfirst slide. | *Photograph by* BRIAN LANKER

1962 | FRANK TORRE proved that it's a game of inches—and feet—on a bang-bang play at first for the Phillies. | *Photograph by* WALTER IOOSS JR.

1993 | THE BRAVES' Jeff Blauser was cut down at the plate in Game 5 of the NLCS, a game and series won by Darren Daulton and the Phillies. | *Photograph by* RONALD C. MODRA

WRIGLEY RAPTURE

BY STEVE RUSHIN

While drinking beer in the sunshine on a Thursday, the author pondered the eternal question: Is there any better place to watch a ballgame than the Friendly Confines? —*from* SI, MAY 28, 2001

THE ELEVATED TRAIN clatters toward Wrigley Field and a female conductor drones "Addison is next" and "Stand clear of the opening doors" and "Parents, hold the hands of your children as you leave the train." Then— from her sealed box, through crackling speakers—she sighs, "It's a beautiful day for a ball game."

Exit the station, blinking against the sunlight. A panhandler says, "Help the beerless?" Chicago cops in checkerboard hatbands tell him to beat it. The sign outside Hi-Tops bar says WELCOME BACK CUB FANS.

An old man in a John Deere feed cap poses, at Sheffield and Addison, before a statue of Harry Caray. His wife tries to take his picture, but she can't find the shutter button. So the old man stands there, stiller than the statue, while his petrified grin becomes a grimace.

It's the last thing you see before you're swept through a turnstile on a tide of humanity and into the Friendly Confines. The stadium smells like concrete and Lysol. An eight-year-old boy in the concourse beneath the grandstand has the blue lips of a choking victim. Then you see, in his right hand, a bale of Smurf-blue cotton candy. He smiles, and his teeth are the color of barbershop-comb disinfectant. And you think, Where on earth would I rather be?

Follow a shaft of sunlight up a tunnel to your seat. The *thwock-thwock-thwock* of batting practice echoes off the bricks. The field is awesome, a brushed baize poker table. Atop the scoreboard a riot of flags flutters in the breeze, like the handlebar tassels on a girl's bike. The beer man arrives unbidden and says, "What'll it be, guys?"

For a couple of brews our change from a 10-dollar bill is one single, soaked in Bud Light. A tractor drags the infield in circles, which looks right because the ballpark organ sounds like the calliope on a merry-go-round. We are drinking beer at noon on Thursday and feeling fully alive, like fugitives from justice, while the rest of the world is at work in a cubicle.

The Cubs were co-owners of baseball's worst record last year and have lost six straight games. Still, 36,014 fans are inside the stadium, and there are filled rooftops beyond the bleachers and, on Waveland Avenue, invisible figures with baseball gloves and radios. So when Houston Astros outfielder Richard Hidalgo hits a home run over the bleachers, the ball is regurgitated onto the leftfield lawn before he can cross home plate, and a cheer goes up for the Unknown Fan responsible.

A cellphone bleats behind first base, and the shirtless man who answers it says, "What? I can't hear you. No, I'm at Wrigley, watching these *&@#%! losers lose." But the complaint sounds insincere, halfhearted. So, too, do those in the men's room: Strangers stand at stainless-steel, trough-style urinals, each man staring a hole in the wall in front of him, while voicing his shock and disappointment in this year's lineup—even though the Cubs, as every one of them knows, haven't won a pennant since 1945.

Shadows travel east across the diamond, from the third base line toward the pitcher's mound, but here, along the rightfield line, the seats are forever in sunshine. Four hours into the afternoon, every hatless head in our section is turning red and painful-looking, like a thousand thumbs struck with hammers. Nobody cares.

Because Sammy Sosa is rabbit-eared and responds in rightfield—with a head nod or a flick of the glove—to each lone voice that hollers his name. "Sam-*my!*" (Nod.) "Sam-*may!*" (Flick.) This happens every time without fail, regardless of what's going on in the game, and children sneak down to the front-row railing to yell "Sam-*may!*" and have a superstar athlete acknowledge their existence.

At the seventh-inning stretch, Chip Caray leans out of the broadcast booth and sings, like his grandfather before him, *Take Me Out to the Ball Game.* We sing along: "Well, we'll root root root for the Cuhhh-bees, if they don't win it's a shame. . . ." They don't win. It's a shame. A glum face stares from a square in the out-of-town scoreboard, on which appear eight letters, stair-stepped down from left to right, across four empty line scores: They spell NITE GAME. (Nite is misspelled, like Sox or sno-cone, in the venerable baseball tradition.)

Just before we exit the ballpark and repair to Murphy's Bleachers bar for "one more," we cast an eye at all those poor be-nited cities on the scoreboard: at New York and Los Angeles, Atlanta and Oakland. And we wonder why, in a free society, everyone doesn't live here. . . .

WRIGLEY HAS its own, more benign, green monster, as Moises Alou, the Cubs leftfielder in 2002–04, would learn.

1928 | YANKEES CENTERFIELDER Earle Combs, a career .325 hitter, was an ideal leadoff man for the powerful New York lineups of the '20s. | *Photograph by* BETTMANN/CORBIS

1987 | DENNIS ECKERSLEY would earn the AL MVP in Oakland in '92 on his way to the Hall of Fame. | *Photograph by* V.J. LOVERO

1956 | THE REDS had sleeveless jerseys made just to accommodate the mighty guns of Ted Kluszewski. | *Photograph by* PAUL SCHUTZER

BASEBALL'S JOHNNY APPLESEED

BY HAROLD PETERSON

In 1845 a New Yorker named Alexander Cartwright Jr.—not Abner Doubleday—invented the game that became America's pastime. Then he headed West, taking with him a ball and a missionary's zeal. —*from* SI, APRIL 14, 1969

O**N A PLEASANT AND** sunny morning in the spring of 1845, six years after Abner Doubleday did not invent baseball in Elihu Phinney's Cooperstown cow pasture (or anywhere else), a black-whiskered 25-year-old New Yorker named Alexander Joy Cartwright Jr., walked off the pleasantly shaded sidewalks of Fourth Avenue into a meadow on Murray Hill between Third Avenue and the railroad cut. There he joined a group of young men lightheartedly playing a game of ball remembered from their childhood—a game, like most children's games, whose antecedents were mysterious and whose rules were subject to constant change and much dispute.

This particular day Cartwright had a carefully drafted diagram in his hand. He beckoned his fellows to gather around and described his plan, which was a distillation of many vague ideas that had been proposed in the previous several years. The plan was simple. Instead of the casual arrangement of bases that had prevailed in the past, the ballplayers would be stationed at first, second and third base around a perfect square, with 90 feet between the bases. Instead of an indefinite number of players in the outfield, there would be only three, at leftfield, centerfield and rightfield. Because most balls were hit between second and third, Cartwright put one player at an entirely new place he called shortstop. There were to be flat bases instead of random posts or rocks that happened to be found where the game was played. There could be only nine men on a side. They would bat in a regular order, announced before the game started. To determine when the hitting and fielding sides would exchange places, Cartwright proposed a rule that he called "three hands out, all out." In cricket, popular in New York in those days, a side continued to bat until the whole team was out.

The game that Cartwright and his friends tried out on Murray Hill was phenomenally successful from the start. The standardized shape and dimensions of the playing field meant that ball clubs could meet each other on equal terms wherever they played. Throwing to bases to make outs—instead of throwing the ball and trying to hit a wildly dodging base runner—tightened and rationalized the game remarkably; it immediately ceased to be a mere children's amusement. The rapid succession of innings rescued the game from the dawdling pace of cricket, a game that, being of English origin, was losing its appeal among Americans, who had indicated they would fight the English rather than give up their claim to all territory south of the 54th parallel in the Northwest. But the best evidence of Cartwright's inventive genius was his placing the men at their positions on the diamond (which have remained almost exactly the same ever since) and his setting the distance between bases at 90 feet. He was exactly, uncannily right. The result was a succession of close plays at first base.

Cartwright's innovation meant the beginning of lightning-fast team play, the development of the art of the shortstop and first basemen and the stricter policing of games by umpires. The latter became suddenly important because of the closeness of plays, but their effect was to bring order into the contests in all respects.

There had been many other games involving bases and balls before 1845 (some of them were even called baseball). A crudely defined game that was known as town ball, derived from the ancient English sport of rounders, had attained some popularity in New York and New England. (The New England version, with bases arranged in a U pattern and the batter's position entirely separate, was called the Massachusetts game.) But all of these primitive exercises were static and aimless, and impossible to codify. Only after Cartwright's revolutionary innovations did the game ignite general excitement. Alexander Cartwright had *invented* baseball—in the same sense that the Wright brothers (and not Leonardo da Vinci) had invented the airplane, and Thomas A. Edison (and not Benjamin Franklin) had invented the electric light. . . .

BY 1896, a game spread far and wide by amateurs had long since turned pro, with teams like the Giants, who played in New York City.

> **Artifacts**

Spheres of Influence

The evolution of the baseball had a major impact on the development of the game

1855 | "Lemon-peel" cover

1858 | Regulation ball

1868 | Two figure-eights ball

1890 | Seamless-cover ball

1916 | Dead-ball era

1923 | World Series, Game 4, box score inscribed

1957 | Last ball thrown in Ebbets Field

1973 | Hank Aaron's 708th home run ball

1988 | Cork-cushioned ball

SEP. 2ᵒ 54
KNICK.
14-13
B. B. C.

1854 | The Knickerbockers ball, the first known baseball

1978 | THE DODGERS' Davey Lopes beat the tag of the Yankees' Thurman Munson in Game 5 of the World Series. | *Photograph by* JOHN IACONO

2006 | THE BREWERS' Prince Fielder scored by barreling over Giants catcher Todd Greene, but Corey Koskie was nailed by pitcher Brad Hennessey. | *Photograph by* JOHN BIEVER

THE 1920s

TRIS SPEAKER, Cleveland's player-manager, led the Indians to their first World Series win, over the Brooklyn Robins, in 1920.
Photograph by CHARLES M. CONLON

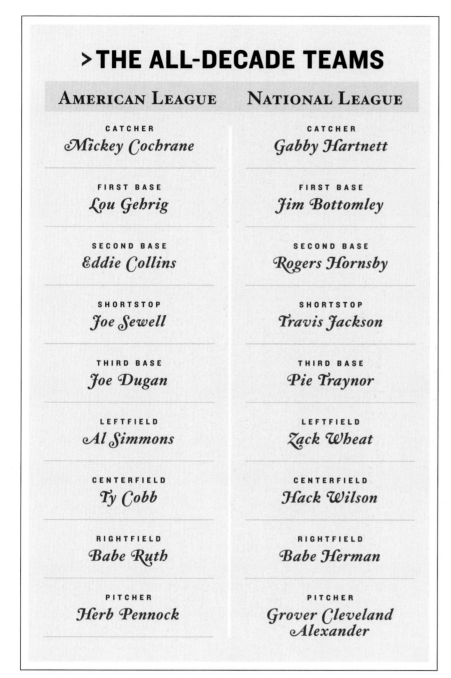

>THE ALL-DECADE TEAMS

AMERICAN LEAGUE	NATIONAL LEAGUE
CATCHER	CATCHER
Mickey Cochrane	*Gabby Hartnett*
FIRST BASE	FIRST BASE
Lou Gehrig	*Jim Bottomley*
SECOND BASE	SECOND BASE
Eddie Collins	*Rogers Hornsby*
SHORTSTOP	SHORTSTOP
Joe Sewell	*Travis Jackson*
THIRD BASE	THIRD BASE
Joe Dugan	*Pie Traynor*
LEFTFIELD	LEFTFIELD
Al Simmons	*Zack Wheat*
CENTERFIELD	CENTERFIELD
Ty Cobb	*Hack Wilson*
RIGHTFIELD	RIGHTFIELD
Babe Ruth	*Babe Herman*
PITCHER	PITCHER
Herb Pennock	*Grover Cleveland Alexander*

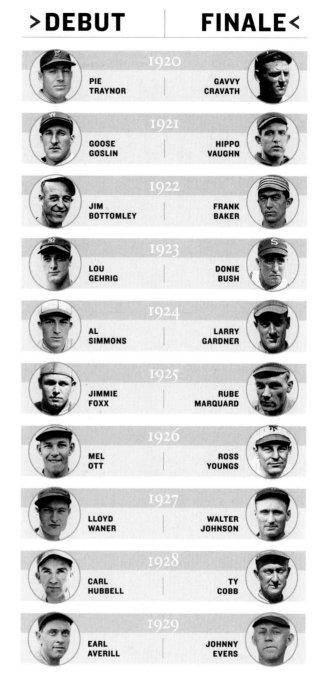

>DEBUT | FINALE<

DEBUT		FINALE
PIE TRAYNOR	1920	GAVVY CRAVATH
GOOSE GOSLIN	1921	HIPPO VAUGHN
JIM BOTTOMLEY	1922	FRANK BAKER
LOU GEHRIG	1923	DONIE BUSH
AL SIMMONS	1924	LARRY GARDNER
JIMMIE FOXX	1925	RUBE MARQUARD
MEL OTT	1926	ROSS YOUNGS
LLOYD WANER	1927	WALTER JOHNSON
CARL HUBBELL	1928	TY COBB
EARL AVERILL	1929	JOHNNY EVERS

>THE LEADERS

HITTING

BATTING AVERAGE* ROGERS HORNSBY	.382
HOME RUNS BABE RUTH	467
RBI BABE RUTH	1,328
AT BATS SAM RICE	6,184
HITS ROGERS HORNSBY	2,085

SINGLES SAM RICE	1,506
DOUBLES ROGERS HORNSBY	405
TRIPLES SAM RICE	133
OBP* BABE RUTH	488
SLUGGING PCT.* BABE RUTH	740
RUNS BABE RUTH	1,365
STOLEN BASES MAX CAREY	346
HIT BY PITCHES BUCKY HARRIS	98

WALKS BABE RUTH	1,240
STRIKEOUTS BABE RUTH	795
GAMES SAM RICE	1,496

PITCHING

WINS BURLEIGH GRIMES	190
LOSSES DOLF LUQUE	146
WINNING PCT.† RAY KREMER	660
STRIKEOUTS DAZZY VANCE	1,464

ERA† GROVER CLEVELAND ALEXANDER	3.04
INNINGS BURLEIGH GRIMES	2,799
WALKS BURLEIGH GRIMES	842
RUNS ALLOWED BURLEIGH GRIMES	1,352
HOME RUNS ALLOWED JESSE HAINES	122
SAVES FIRPO MARBERRY	75
SHUTOUTS WALTER JOHNSON	24
COMPLETE GAMES BURLEIGH GRIMES	234

* MINIMUM 2,500 PLATE APPEARANCES †MINIMUM 1,000 INNINGS

>HOT TICKETS 10 Games You Wish You'd Seen

Yankee Stadium April 18, 1923 The Yankees open their new ballpark, which stands across the Harlem River from their old home, the Polo Grounds. Babe Ruth hits a three-run home run in the third inning against Boston's Howard Ehmke in New York's 4–1 win and the stadium is quickly dubbed The House that Ruth Built by Fred Lieb of New York's *Evening Telegram*.

Yankee Stadium Sept. 30, 1927 Babe Ruth does his old record one better by becoming the first player in baseball history to hit 60 home runs in a season. His two-run blast off Washington's Tom Zachary in the eighth inning breaks a 2–2 tie and gives the Yankees a 4–2 win.

Yankee Stadium Oct. 10, 1926 With two out in the ninth inning of Game 7—Cardinals leading the Yankees 3–2—St. Louis second baseman Rogers Hornsby applies the tag on an attempted steal of second base by Babe Ruth, the final out of the World Series.

Griffith Stadium Oct. 10, 1924 Earl > McNeely's bad hop double over Giants third baseman Fred Lindstrom's head in the 12th inning scores Muddy Ruel with the winning run as the Senators beat New York 4–3 in Game 7 of the World Series. Walter Johnson pitched four scoreless innings in relief for the win.

Sportsman's Park Oct. 9, 1928 Babe Ruth hits three home runs in the

Good only at 7th Street Entrance

16 I 16

ROW   SEC.   SEAT

Lower Grand Stand
$5.50

Clark Griffith Stadium 1924
World's CHAMPIONSHIP Games

AMERICAN LEAGUE vs. NATIONAL LEAGUE

GAME RAIN CHECK

7 Retain This Check
If legal game is not played the attached coupon will be good whenever
this game is played.

Clark C. Griffith
President

The Simplex Ticket Co. Inc. New York, N.Y. 169

decisive Game 4 of the World Series against the Cardinals in St. Louis. The third shot comes off of fellow Hall of Famer Grover Cleveland Alexander; Ruth finishes the Series with a .625 average.

Shibe Park June 15, 1925 The Athletics are losing 15–4 to the Indians in the bottom of the eighth inning when they erupt for nine hits, four walks and 13 runs for a 17–15 victory.

Sportsman's Park April 13, 1926 Walter Johnson, making his 14th Opening Day start for the Senators, shuts down the Athletics for 15 innings in a 1–0 win. Washington's player-manager, Bucky Harris, scores the lone run on a single by Joe Harris.

Wrigley Field Aug. 25, 1922 With the wind blowing out, the Cubs top the Phillies 26–23 in Chicago in the highest scoring game in baseball history.

Sportsman's Park May 5, 1925 Thirty-eight year-old Ty Cobb has six hits, including three home runs, in the Tigers' 14–8 win over the Browns. Cobb set the modern record for total bases with 16. The following day, Cobb, who finished with only 117 career home runs, blasts two more out.

Forbes Field Oct. 2, 1920 The Pirates host baseball's last tripleheader. Pittsburgh loses the first two games to the Reds but avoids the sweep by winning the nightcap 6–0.

BEST OF THE 1920s

TEAM	WINS	LOSSES	WIN PCT.
YANKEES	933	602	608
GIANTS	890	639	582
PIRATES	877	656	572
CARDINALS	822	712	536
CUBS	807	728	526

BILL DICKEY, YANKEES

WORST OF THE 1920s

TEAM	WINS	LOSSES	WIN PCT.
PHILLIES	566	962	370
RED SOX	595	938	388
BRAVES	603	928	394
WHITE SOX	731	804	476
DODGERS	765	768	499

RED RUFFING, RED SOX

1920s CULTURE

MUSIC: *I'm Just Wild about Harry* (Eubie Blake), *Yes! We Have No Bananas* (by Frank Silver and Irving Cohn), *Rhapsody in Blue* (by George Gershwin), *Second-Hand Rose* (Fanny Brice), *Swanee* (Al Jolson)

MOVIES: *The Big Parade, The Jazz Singer, The Gold Rush, The Ten Commandments*

BOOKS: *The Great Gatsby* by F. Scott Fitzgerald; *Babbitt* by Sinclair Lewis; *The Age of Innocence* by Edith Wharton; *The Outline of History* by H.G. Wells; *The Sun Also Rises* by Ernest Hemingway; *Ulysses* by James Joyce

ACHIEVEMENT: Charles Lindbergh makes the first solo nonstop flight across the Atlantic, taking off from Long Island in his *Spirit of St. Louis* and touching down outside of Paris 33½ hours later.

INVENTIONS: Band-Aids, Kleenex, the pop-up toaster, the recliner

SEX SYMBOLS: Greta Garbo and Rudolph Valentino

VILLAIN: Al Capone (a.k.a. Scarface), the Chicago mob boss dubbed Public Enemy No. 1, was responsible for murders, extortion and numerous other crimes, but was imprisoned only for filing false tax returns.

PERSONALITY OF THE DECADE: Babe Ruth

< GRETA GARBO

>NICKNAMES<

Charles [Chief] Bender ∧
[Wahoo] Sam Crawford
Robert [Lefty] Grove
Paul [Big Poison] Waner
Lloyd [Little Poison] Waner
Lewis [Hack] Wilson
Rogers [Rajah] Hornsby
Harold [Pie] Traynor
[Poosh 'em Up] Tony Lazzeri
Hazen [Kiki] Cuyler
Aloysius [Bucketfoot Al] Simmons
George [High Pockets] Kelly
Mickey [Black Mike] Cochrane
Leo [the Lip] Durocher
Leon [Goose] Goslin
Waite [Schoolboy] Hoyt
Charles [Red] Ruffing
Frederick [Firpo] Marberry
William [Judy] Johnson
Norman [Turkey] Stearnes
Lou [Iron Horse] Gehrig
Grover Cleveland [Old Pete] Alexander

	BORN		DIED	
MARIO PUZO		1920		KARL FABERGÉ
CHARLES BRONSON		1921		ENRICO CARUSO
KURT VONNEGUT		1922		ALEXANDER GRAHAM BELL
ALAN SHEPARD		1923		PANCHO VILLA
JIMMY CARTER		1924		SAMUEL GOMPERS
MALCOLM X		1925		WILLIAM JENNINGS BRYAN
PETE ROZELLE		1926		< HARRY HOUDINI
NEIL SIMON		1927		ISADORA DUNCAN
MAYA ANGELOU		1928		ROALD AMUNDSEN
ARNOLD PALMER >		1929		WYATT EARP

> NEWS OF THE REAL WORLD

1920: 19th Amendment ratified, giving American women the right to vote. **1921:** The Avus Autobahn, the world's first highway, opens in Germany **1922:** Josef Stalin becomes secretary general of the Communist Party in the Soviet Union; insulin is used for the first time in the successful treatment of diabetes, in a 14-year-old boy **1923:** President Warren G. Harding dies in office, succeeded by Calvin Coolidge **1924:** Chamonix, France, hosts the first Winter Olympics **1925:** Astronomer Edwin Hubble finds galaxies outside of our own **1926:** John Baird produces television images of moving objects; French team uncovers Sphinx from sand in Egyptian desert **1927:** The Academy of Motion Picture Arts and Sciences is founded **1928:** Penicillin is discovered by Scottish biologist Alexander Fleming **1929:** Black Tuesday—U.S. stock market crashes, nation enters Great Depression

2004 | BASEBALL'S HOTTEST rivalry boiled over when Red Sox catcher Jason Varitek confronted the Yankees' Alex Rodriguez at Fenway. | *Photograph by* DAMIAN STROHMEYER

1949

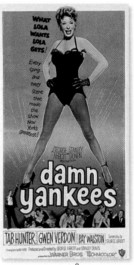

1958

1973

1953

1953

> Marquee Matchups

Hitting into the Screen

The first baseball movie, The Ball Game, *was documentary footage shot in 1898 shot by the Edison Co., followed by the fictional* Casey at the Bat, *a year later. Since then Hollywood has racked up a few hits—and plenty of errors*

1942

1935

1950

1957

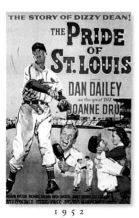

1952

1988

1966 | THE DUST was all that Orioles slugger Boog Powell could hit after a brushback pitch in Tiger Stadium. | *Photograph by* WALTER IOOSS JR.

'EVERYONE IS HELPLESS AND IN AWE'

BY ROY BLOUNT JR.

That, said Reggie Jackson, was the reaction after his majestic drives, and it became commonplace as the Oakland slugger rose to a higher stardom, unfettered in life as he was at the plate.

—*from* SI, JUNE 17, 1974

THE NEARLY EMPTY clubhouse of the world championship Oakland A's looks like the men's room of an old, disreputable movie theater, except that Reginald Martinez Jackson, a superstar advancing toward super-duperstar status, is naked in it, taking his naturally beautiful lefthanded stance and swinging a 35-inch, 37-ounce flame-treated bat, intensely, reflectively. *Whupp. Whupp.* Even though he is cutting through thin air he seems to be making good contact. Last year, after seven big league seasons of ups, downs, moping and controversy, he was the American League's home run leader, RBI leader and Most Valuable Player. This year he might win the Triple Crown.

Whupp. "My strongest point is my strength," he says. "Shoulders to fingertips." Indeed, he has 17-inch biceps, as Sonny Liston had, and he is one of the top raw-power men in the league, along with Chicago's Dick Allen and Detroit's Willie Horton (who once broke a bat in two by abruptly checking his swing). But mighty isn't all he is.

By birth Afro-Latin-American, by faith an Arizona Methodist, Jackson is a man who grew up in a Jewish neighborhood outside Philadelphia, roomed in the majors with a WASP named Chuck, currently pals around with two Portuguese motor sportsmen— one weighing 250 pounds, the other 305—wears around his neck a string of wampum beads and a gold crucifix he bought from a Cuban pitcher and is built like a Greek god. On paper he is a millionaire in land development.

Whupp. Facially, thanks in part to his mustache, beard and fullish Afro, he resembles the charismatic civil-rights leader Jesse Jackson, with overtones of sprightly pop-off Pirates pitcher Dock Ellis. He has the eagerly concerned, unsettled, open-eyed look of a man who will never be cynical, boring or fully aware (or unaware) of how he affects people. He is a half inch over six feet tall and weights 207 pounds, and aside from an arthritic spine, nearsightedness and astigmatism, there is only one thing wrong with him.

"Feel that," Jackson says, indicating the back of his right thigh, which is as big around as a good-sized woman's waist. Though unflexed, it feels like an only slightly deflated football. "Hard, isn't it?" he says. His thighs are overdeveloped. That is why he is prone to pull a hamstring when he turns on his 9.6-in-the-100 speed. This day in Oakland he is out of the lineup and nearly alone in the dressing room because of such a pull, rashly incurred. But he is keeping in touch with his stroke. *Whupp. Whupp.*

"Richie Allen told me once, 'Don't speak with this [he points to his mouth], speak with this.'" With a flowing gesture he indicates his body, and the bat. "'Through this [he holds the bat up like a torch] you can speak to the *world*.'"

But even though Jackson may be on his way to one of the best years anybody ever had with a bat, it was orally that he faded the man who recently passed Babe Ruth. A reporter asked Jackson, who is 28, what he thought of his chances of breaking Aaron's lifetime home-run record. Jackson replied, "No way. They couldn't afford to pay me to play that long."

Now that was a partly humorous remark. Please do not consider it overproud, because Reggie is loath to come on as a braggart. He even feels dubious about all the bare-chested pictures of himself that have been appearing lately. "My peers may not like it," he says. "And I am one of my peers."

To be sure, White Sox pitcher Stan Bahnsen says of Jackson, "he's a helluva ballplayer, but I'm not one of his fans. I don't like him. I think he's a prima donna. That whole team seems to think they're spokesmen for the game." And the aforementioned Allen, whose own thighs are lean and flowing, says, "I look in the record book and I see Reggie has never hit .300. And I wonder how he can do all that talking." But other players commend him roundly. He is established. Whatever his flaws and rough edges, Jackson has put together a package of power, speed, science, flash, funk, outspoken quotability, popularity, fun-lovingness, social and economic independence, responsibility, diversification and winningness that is unique among ballplayers. And Reggie knows and loves it. *Whupp. . . .*

JACKSON HAD a flare for the dramatic and a huge, powerful swing that could take your breath away—even when he whiffed.

2002 | SCOTT PODSEDNIK took some bad hops when he went into the leftfield stands in Anaheim for a foul ball. | *Photograph by* ROBERT LABERGE

1959 | AL SMITH got a shower while Chicago fans vied for a World Series homer hit by the Dodgers' Charlie Neal. | *Photograph by* CHARLES E. KNOBLOCK

THE TRANSISTOR KID

BY ROBERT CREAMER

When Vin Scully came to Los Angeles with the transplanted Brooklyn Dodgers, he was a stranger in alien corn. But in the years that followed, his voice became as much a part of Southern California as the freeways.
—*from* SI, MAY 4, 1964

G IVE A TEST OF WORD associations to a baseball fan from Omaha or Memphis or Philadelphia and suddenly throw in the phrase "Los Angeles Dodgers" and almost certainly the answer will be "Sandy Koufax" or "Maury Wills" or "Don Drysdale." Give the same test to a fan from Los Angeles, and the odds are good that the answer will be "Vin Scully."

Scully is the tall, slim, red-haired native of New York City who has been broadcasting Dodgers games ever since there has been a team called the Los Angeles Dodgers and who, for eight seasons before that, did the play-by-play of their games back in Brooklyn. This year, at 36, he is in his 15th season of broadcasting major league games, a statistic that is bound to startle anyone who ever heard Red Barber turn the mike over to Scully in the old Ebbets Field days with a cheery, "O.K., young fella. It's all yours."

In the six years that he has been in California, Scully has become as much a part of the Los Angeles scene as the freeways and the smog. "Everybody" probably is not a mathematically precise description of Scully's audience, but it is close enough. When a game is on the air the physical presence of his voice is overwhelming. His pleasantly nasal baritone comes out of radios on the back counters of orange juice stands, from transistors held by people sitting under trees, in barber shops and bars, and from cars everywhere—parked cars, cars waiting for red lights to turn green, cars passing you at 65 on the freeways, cars edging along next to you in rush-hour traffic jams.

Vin Scully's voice is better known to most Los Angelenos than their next-door neighbor's is. He has become a celebrity. He is stared at in the street. Kids hound him for autographs. Out-of-town visitors at Dodgers games have Scully pointed out to them—as though he were the Empire State Building—as he sits in his broadcasting booth describing a game, his left hand lightly touching his temple in a pose that's become his trademark.

Baseball broadcasts are popular in all major league cities, but in Los Angeles they are as vital as orange juice. For one thing, the Dodgers have been an eminently successful and colorful club in their six seasons in L.A. (two pennants and a tie for a third, two world championships, a Maury Wills stealing 104 bases, a Sandy Koufax winning 25 games). For a second, the Los Angeles metropolitan area is huge (in the 1960 census, the biggest in the country after New York), and practically everybody drives to and from work and, for that matter, to and from everywhere, and in almost every car there is a radio, and every radio is always on. When a home-rushing driver bogs down in a traffic jam, he finds that nothing else is as soothing as Vin Scully's voice describing the opening innings of a Dodger night game just getting under way a few thousand miles and three time zones to the east. This time difference has been a key factor in the growth of Scully's audience. A man who drives home from work listening to an exciting game is not about to abandon it when he reaches his house. As a result, millions of Southern Californians have Vin Scully with their supper.

But it is not just the happy timing of road games that endears Scully to his audience. He appeals to them when the Dodgers are home too. In fact he holds his listeners when they come to the ballpark to see games with their own eyes. When the Dodgers are playing at home, it seems sometimes as though every member of the crowd is carrying a transistor radio and is listening to Scully tell him about the game he is watching. Taking radios to ballparks to listen to the game as you watch it is a fairly common practice, but nowhere is it so pronounced a characteristic as it is in Los Angeles, and has been since 1958, the year the Dodgers left Ebbets Field and moved west. Los Angeles was hungry for major league ball, and though the Dodgers had a dreadful season that first year, the crowds jammed into Memorial Coliseum, where the team played until Dodger Stadium opened in 1962. Perhaps their unfamiliarity with major leaguers prompted so many fans to bring transistors along at first in order to establish instant identification of the players. But a large percentage brought radios not just to identify players but to learn what they were doing. Scully was talking to an audience that had not been watching baseball. L.A.'s old minor league teams in the Pacific Coast League seldom drew more than a few hundred thousand spectators in their best years. Now a million and a half, two million, two and a half million were pouring into the ball parks. Through Vin Scully they learned the fine points, the subtleties, the language of the game. . . .

EVEN THE fans in Dodgers Stadium brought their radios so that they could enjoy the voice and insights of Scully.

2006 | WHITE SOX second baseman Tadahito Iguchi made a true sidearm throw to nail a runner at first in Chicago. | *Photograph by* DAVID DUROCHIK

1914 | B U T C H   S C H M I D T scored for the Boston's "Miracle" Braves against the Athletics in Game 1 of the World Series, played at Philadelphia's Shibe Park. | *Photograph by* B E T T M A N N / C O R B I S

1985 | ROD CAREW, who won seven batting titles, got his 3,000th hit against the Twins in Anaheim, then sent his batting gloves to the Hall. | *Photograph by* V.J. LOVERO

THE 1930s

HANK GREENBERG was the AL MVP in '35, when he drove in 170 runs for the Tigers; two years later, he had 183 RBI.
Photograph by AP IMAGES

> THE ALL-DECADE TEAMS

AMERICAN LEAGUE	NATIONAL LEAGUE
CATCHER	CATCHER
Bill Dickey	*Gabby Hartnett*
FIRST BASE	FIRST BASE
Lou Gehrig	*Bill Terry*
SECOND BASE	SECOND BASE
Charlie Gehringer	*Billy Herman*
SHORTSTOP	SHORTSTOP
Joe Cronin	*Arky Vaughan*
THIRD BASE	THIRD BASE
Harlond Clift	*Pie Traynor*
LEFTFIELD	LEFTFIELD
Al Simmons	*Joe Medwick*
CENTERFIELD	CENTERFIELD
Joe DiMaggio	*Lloyd Waner*
RIGHTFIELD	RIGHTFIELD
Babe Ruth	*Mel Ott*
PITCHER	PITCHER
Lefty Grove	*Carl Hubbell*

> DEBUT   FINALE <

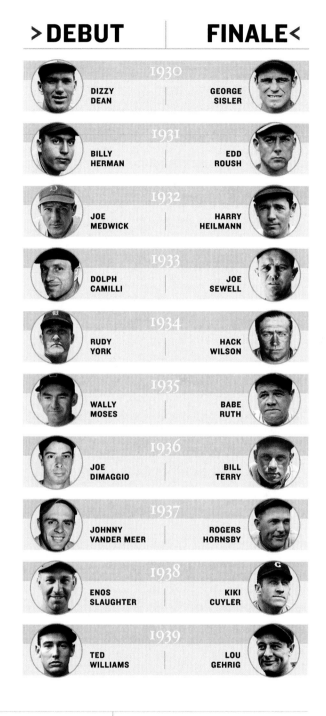

	DEBUT	FINALE
1930	DIZZY DEAN	GEORGE SISLER
1931	BILLY HERMAN	EDD ROUSH
1932	JOE MEDWICK	HARRY HEILMANN
1933	DOLPH CAMILLI	JOE SEWELL
1934	RUDY YORK	HACK WILSON
1935	WALLY MOSES	BABE RUTH
1936	JOE DIMAGGIO	BILL TERRY
1937	JOHNNY VANDER MEER	ROGERS HORNSBY
1938	ENOS SLAUGHTER	KIKI CUYLER
1939	TED WILLIAMS	LOU GEHRIG

> THE LEADERS

HITTING

BATTING AVERAGE*	BILL TERRY	352
HOME RUNS	JIMMIE FOXX	415
RBI	JIMMIE FOXX	1,403
AT BATS	PAUL WANER	5,834
HITS	PAUL WANER	1,959
SINGLES	PAUL WANER	1,405
DOUBLES	CHARLIE GEHRINGER	400
TRIPLES	GUS SUHR, EARL AVERILL	114
OBP*	BABE RUTH	472
SLUGGING PCT.*	JIMMIE FOXX	652
RUNS	LOU GEHRIG	1,257
STOLEN BASES	BEN CHAPMAN	269
HIT BY PITCHES	FRANK CROSETTI	88
WALKS	LOU GEHRIG	1,028
STRIKEOUTS	JIMMIE FOXX	876
GAMES	MEL OTT	1,473

PITCHING

WINS	LEFTY GROVE	199
LOSSES	PAUL DERRINGER	137
WINNING PCT.†	LEFTY GROVE	724
STRIKEOUTS	LEFTY GOMEZ	1,337
ERA†	CARL HUBBELL	2.71
INNINGS	CARL HUBBELL	2,598
WALKS	BUMP HADLEY	1,061
RUNS ALLOWED	WES FERRELL	1,251
HOME RUNS ALLOWED	RED RUFFING	150
SAVES	JOHNNY MURPHY	54
SHUTOUTS	LARRY FRENCH	32
COMPLETE GAMES	WES FERRELL	207

* MINIMUM 2,500 PLATE APPEARANCES † MINIMUM 1,000 INNINGS

>HOT TICKETS 10 Games You Wish You'd Seen

Shibe Park June 3, 1932 Yankees first baseman Lou Gehrig hits four home runs in Philadelphia, becoming the first player of the 20th century to hit four round-trippers in a contest. Gehrig missed getting number 5 when his ninth-inning drive was caught at the wall by A's leftfielder Al Simmons.

League Park May 4, 1937 The Senators and Indians are tied 5–5 in the top of the 11th when Washington's Ben Chapman rambles home at the front end of a triple steal. The Senators go on to score seven runs and win, 12–5.

Forbes Field May 25, 1935 Braves outfielder Babe Ruth homers against the Pirates three times. The last shot, which clears the rightfield roof at Forbes Field, is the 714th of his career. It is also the Babe's last; he retires eight days later.

Ebbets Field Sept. 21, 1934 Cardinals pitcher Dizzy Dean throws a three-hit shutout for a 3–0 win in the first game of a doubleheader against the Dodgers. In the nightcap, Dizzy's brother, Paul Dean, throws a no-hitter.

Crosley Field May 24, 1935 President Franklin Delano Roosevelt presses a button at the White House and the lights go on in Cincinnati for the major league's first night game. The Reds defeat the Phillies 2–1.

Polo Grounds July 10, 1934 Facing a lineup loaded with Hall of Famers in his home park, Giants lefty Carl Hubbell strikes out Babe Ruth,

Lou Gehrig, Jimmie Foxx, Al Simmons and Joe Cronin in succession in the 1934 All-Star Game.

< Wrigley Field Oct. 1, 1932 Babe Ruth comes to the plate in the fifth inning of Game 3 of the World Series and, after some serious bench-jockeying by the Cubs, points toward pitcher Charlie Root—or perhaps the outfield wall. On the next pitch Ruth hits one into the centerfield bleachers for his "called shot." The next batter, Lou Gehrig, also homers.

Yankee Stadium July 4, 1939 Between games of a doubleheader in the Bronx, the Yankees honor their ailing captain, Lou Gehrig, who had received a diagnosis of amyotrophic lateral sclerosis in June. In thanking the crowd, Gehrig says, "Today I consider myself the luckiest man on the face of the Earth."

Ebbets Field June 15, 1938 In the first major league night game played somewhere other than Cincinnati, Reds pitcher Johnny Vander Meer tosses his second consecutive no-hitter, a 6–0 blanking of the Dodgers despite eight walks. Four days earlier Vander Meer had shut down the Boston Bees 3–0.

Wrigley Field Sept. 28, 1938 Chicago player-manager Gabby Hartnett hits "the homer in the gloaming" to give the Cubs a 6–5 win and a half-game lead over the Pirates for the NL pennant with only four days remaining in the season. They will win the flag by two games.

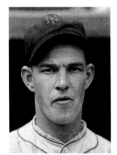

BEST OF THE 1930s

TEAM	WINS	LOSSES	WIN PCT.
YANKEES	970	554	.636
CUBS	889	646	.579
GIANTS	869	657	.569
CARDINALS	869	665	.566
INDIANS	824	708	.539

MEL OTT, GIANTS

WORST OF THE 1930s

TEAM	WINS	LOSSES	WIN PCT.
BROWNS	580	951	.370
ORIOLES	578	951	.378
PHILLIES	581	943	.381
REDS	664	866	.434
WHITE SOX	678	841	.446

CHUCK KLEIN, PHILLIES

1930s CULTURE

MUSIC: *It Don't Mean a Thing If It Ain't Got That Swing* (Duke Ellington), *Brother, Can You Spare a Dime?* (Rudy Vallee), *Somewhere over the Rainbow* (Judy Garland), *Begin the Beguine* (Artie Shaw), *Sing, Sing, Sing* (Benny Goodman)

MOVIES: *Gone with the Wind, The Wizard of Oz, King Kong, Duck Soup, Mr. Smith Goes to Washington*

BOOKS: *The Grapes of Wrath* by John Steinbeck; *How to Win Friends and Influence People* by Dale Carnegie; *Gone with the Wind* by Margaret Mitchell; *The Good Earth* by Pearl Buck; *The Maltese Falcon* by Dashiell Hammett

ACHIEVEMENT: The age of construction, when such landmarks as the Golden Gate Bridge, Hoover Dam and Empire State Building were built.

INVENTIONS: pinball, Spam, sliced bread, scotch tape, photocopier, ballpoint pen

SEX SYMBOLS: Jean Harlow & Clark Gable

VILLAIN: Austrian-born ex-convict Adolf Hitler rises to power in Germany with his Nazi party and by mid-decade declares himself führer; his regime's ruthless expansionism and brutal racial policies lead to World War II.

PERSONALITY OF THE DECADE: Franklin Delano Roosevelt

< JEAN HARLOW

>NICKNAMES<

Joe [Ducky] Medwick ∧
James [Cool Papa] Bell
Joe [Flash] Gordon
Vernon [Lefty] Gomez
Johnny [Pepper] Martin
Jay [Dizzy] Dean
Paul [Daffy] Dean
Jimmie [Double X] Foxx
Frankie [the Fordham Flash] Frisch
Henry [Heinie] Manush
Johnny [the Big Cat] Mize
Clarence [Dazzy] Vance
Joseph [Arky] Vaughan
Harry [Cookie] Lavagetto
Ted [Double Duty] Radcliffe
LeRoy [Satchel] Paige
George [Birdie] Tebbetts
Ray [Hooks] Dandridge
George [Twinkletoes] Selkirk
Charley [Chinski] Root
John [Jocko] Conlan
Howard Earl [Rock] Averill

BORN		DIED
SANDRA DAY O'CONNOR	1930	D.H. LAWRENCE
RUPERT MURDOCH	1931	THOMAS EDISON
ELIZABETH TAYLOR	1932	WILLIAM MORRIS
QUINCY JONES	1933	RING LARDNER
DICK SCHAAP	1934	MARIE CURIE
ELVIS PRESLEY >	1935	WILL ROGERS
JIM BROWN	1936	RUDYARD KIPLING
RICHARD PETTY	1937	GEORGE GERSHWIN
TED TURNER	1938	BENJAMIN CARDOZO
FRANCIS FORD COPPOLA	1939	< SIGMUND FREUD

> NEWS OF THE REAL WORLD

1930: Uruguay tops Argentina 4–2, wins first World Cup **1931:** The *Star-Spangled Banner* becomes official U.S. national anthem **1932:** Son of aviator Charles Lindbergh kidnapped, murdered; Abdal-Aziz Ibn Saud renames his kingdom Saudi Arabia; FDR uses expression "New Deal" in speech accepting Democratic presidential nomination **1933:** Prohibition repealed; Adolf Hitler appointed German chancellor **1934:** John Dillinger, the FBI's Public Enemy No. I, is gunned down by FBI agents outside a theater in Chicago **1935:** FDR's Social Security program passed by congress; Huey Long assassinated in Louisiana capitol building **1936:** Jesse Owens wins four gold medals at Nazi Olympics in Berlin **1937:** Oh, the humanity! *Hindenburg* explodes while landing in Lakehurst, N.J. **1938:** Oil discovered in Saudi Arabia **1939:** Germany invades Poland, triggering World War II

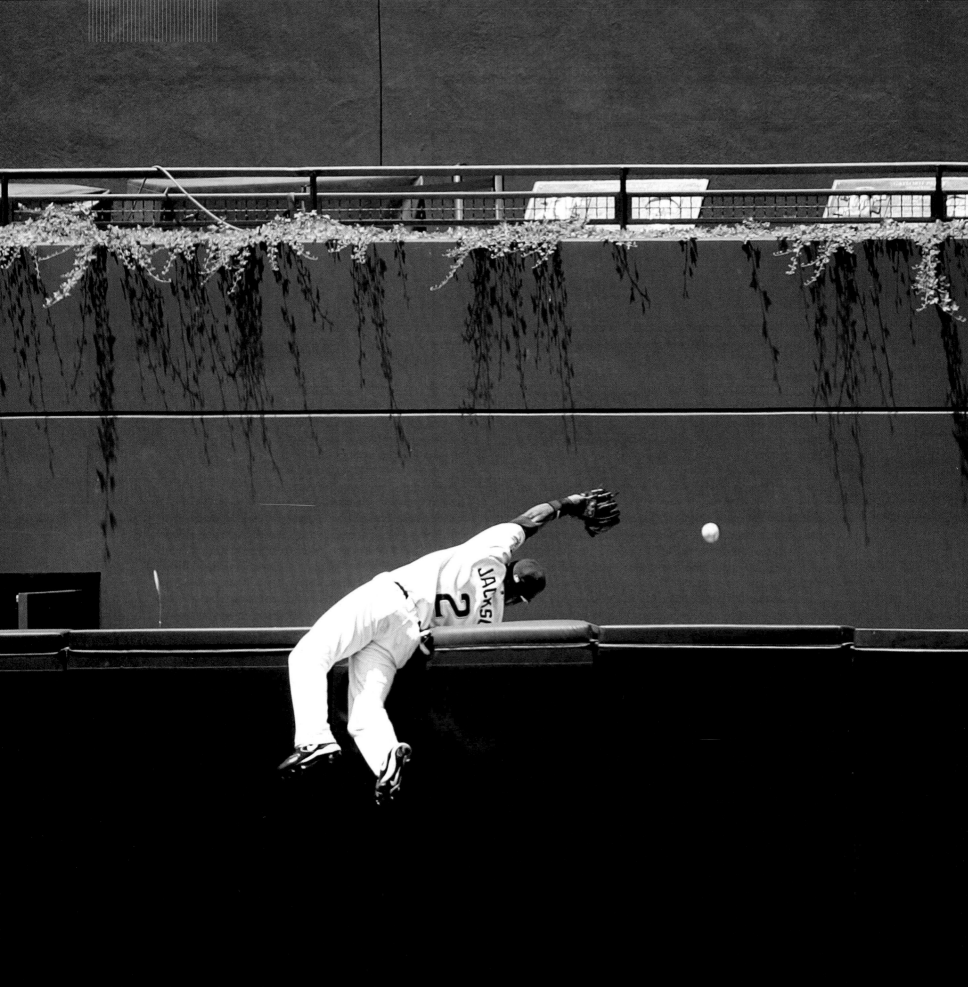

2005 | PADRES CENTERFIELDER Damian Jackson went high and deep, but the Reds' Wily Mo Peña's fly ball went deeper. | *Photograph by* JOHN W. McDONOUGH

1994 | NOT EVEN a shot that cleared the wall was safe from the glove of Blue Jays centerfielder Devon White. | *Photograph by* AL TIELEMANS

> **Artifacts**

Heavy Lumber

A bat is as personal to a hitter as his PIN number (and just as important), made out of hickory, ash or maple, custom-tailored for weight, length, thickness, balance and even a little bit of style

SPALDING
The mushroom knob—c. 1900

WILLIE KEELER
Led NL with 204 hits—1900

TRIS SPEAKER
Hit .322, a subpar year—1915

BABE RUTH
Notches for 28 of his homers c. 1927

MULTIPLE AUTOGRAPHS
Signed by Cobb, DiMaggio, Feller, Foxx, Grove, Ruth—1940s

SATCHEL PAIGE
Batting ninth, but in the Show—1951

CARL YASTRZEMSKI

Won the Triple Crown — 1967

DAVE CONCEPCION

Double-knobbed stick, multiple Gold Gloves — 1982

GEORGE BRETT

The infamous pine-tar bat — 1983

ANDRE DAWSON

Took his timber to the AL — 1993

TONY GWYNN

Knob taped by eight-time batting champ — 1994

ICHIRO SUZUKI

Won batting crown in first season — 2001

BARRY BONDS

Maple bat from World Series — 2002

1949 | DODGERS CATCHER Roy Campanella watched as first baseman Gil Hodges reached vainly for a foul pop at Ebbets Field. | *Photograph by* CHARLES M. CONLON

A SERIES TO SAVOR

BY STEVE RUSHIN

In a World Series of delicious drama, the Minnesota Twins barely beat the Atlanta Braves in what was truly a Fall Classic.
—*from* SI, NOVEMBER 4, 1991

THE TRUTH IS INELASTIC when it comes to the 88th World Series. It is impossible to stretch. It isn't necessary to appraise the nine days just past from some distant horizon of historical perspective. Let us call this Series what it is, now, while its seven games still ring in our ears: the greatest that was ever played.

Both the Minnesota Twins and the Atlanta Braves enlarged the game of baseball, while reducing individual members of both teams to humble participants in a Series with drama too huge to be hyperbolized. There were five one-run duels, four of them won on the game's final play, three extended to extra innings—all categories that apply to the ultimate, unfathomable game played on Sunday night in Minneapolis, in which a 36-year-old man threw 10 innings of shutout baseball in the seventh game of the World Series. Grown men were reduced to tears and professional athletes to ill health in the aftermath of the Twins' winning their second world championship in five seasons.

This was the winners' clubhouse: An hour after Jack Morris beat the Braves 1–0 for the title, Twins pitcher Kevin Tapani broke out in a red rash. "I'm surprised if I don't have ulcers," said infielder Al Newman, slouched lifelessly on a stool. "I think I'll get checked out."

Across the room, Morris lay propped against a television platform, pondering the events of the previous days. "I don't know if it will happen tomorrow or the next day," he said, "but somewhere down the road, they're going to look back on this Series and say. . . . "

Say what, exactly? Morris, like the scribes spread out before him, was overwhelmed by the thought of describing all that had transpired, and he allowed his words to trail off into a champagne bottle. The bubbly had been broken out by clubhouse attendants shortly after 11:00 p.m., when pinch hitter Gene Larkin slapped the first pitch he got from Alejandro Pena to left center, over the head of Brian Hunter, who, like the rest of the Atlanta outfield, was playing only 30 yards in back of the infield in an effort to prevent Minnesota's Dan Gladden from doing pre-

cisely what he did: bound home from third base in the bottom of the 10th, through a cross-current of crazed, dazed teammates, who were leaping from the third base dugout and onto the field.

Even Atlanta second baseman Mark Lemke, whose name had become familiar to the nation earlier in the week, was moved, in defeat, by the momentous nature of the game. "The only thing better," he said, "would have been if we'd stopped after nine innings and cut the trophy in half."

Impossibly, both the Braves and the Twins had loaded the bases with less than two outs in the eighth inning and failed to score. Improbably, both threats had been snuffed with mind-boggling suddenness by double plays. Atlanta was done in by a slick 3-2-3 job courtesy of Minnesota first baseman Kent Hrbek and catcher Brian Harper. The Twins were stymied by a crowd-jolting unassisted DP by Lemke, who grabbed a soft liner off the bat of Hrbek and stepped on second. So by the bottom of the 10th, when Harper, seeing Larkin make contact, threw his batting helmet high into the air in the on-deck circle and Gladden jumped onto home plate with both feet, the switch was thrown on a 30-minute burst of emotion in the Metrodome stands, an energy that, if somehow harnessed, would have lit the Twin Cities through a second consecutive sleepless night.

For it was only 24 hours earlier that Minnesota centerfielder Kirby Puckett had virtually single-handedly forced a seventh game by assembling what has to rank among the most outrageous all-around performances the World Series has ever seen. Puckett punctuated his night by hitting a home run in the bottom of the 11th inning off Atlanta's Charlie Leibrandt. The solo shot gave the Twins a 4–3 win and gave Puckett's teammates the same "chill-bump feeling" Braves manager Bobby Cox confessed to having had in Atlanta, where the Braves had swept Games 3, 4 and 5 earlier in the week to take a three games to two lead into Minneapolis.

Hrbek was reduced to a 10-year-old when the Series was tied last Saturday night; Sunday morning would be Christmas Day. "Guys will be staring at the ceiling tonight," he said following Game 6. "They won't even know if their wives are next to 'em. I know I won't. She won't want to hear that, but. . . . "

Minnesota hitting coach Terry Crowley was reduced to a doddering man in long underwear that same evening, pacing a small circle in the clubhouse, head down and muttering to no one, "It's unbelievable. Unbelievable."

And Twins manager Tom Kelly fairly shed his skin in the af-

termath of that game, wriggling from the hard exterior he has worn throughout his career and revealing himself to be, like the rest of us, both awed and addled by all he had witnessed. "This is storybook," Kelly said. "Who's got the script? Who is writing this? Can you imagine this?"

Understand what Kelly and 55,155 paying customers had just seen Puckett do beneath the dome. In addition to his game-winning home run, he had singled, tripled, driven in a run on a sacrifice fly, stolen a base and scored a run of his own. In the third inning he had leapt high against a Plexiglas panel in centerfield, hanging there momentarily like one of those suction-cup Garfield dolls in a car window, to rob Ron Gant of extra bases and Atlanta of an almost certain run.

After the game had remained tied at three through the 10th inning, Cox brought in lefthander Leibrandt to face the righthanded-hitting Puckett, who was leading off in the bot-

tom of the 11th. But it didn't matter whom he put on the mound to face Puckett. The man was going to hit a home run. That was the only logical conclusion to his Saturday in the park. Puckett did just that, and the tortured Leibrandt walked off the field, his face buried in the crook of his right arm. When the seventh game and the Series had finally been bled from the bodies on both sides, when the two teams had stopped their cartoon brawl, raising ridiculous lumps by alternately slugging each other over the head with a sledgehammer, when all of 60 minutes had passed after the last game, Mike Pagliarulo stood wearily at his locker. "This was the greatest game," he said. "How could the TV guys describe it? They had a chance to win—but they didn't. We had a chance to win—but we didn't. Then we did. This is why baseball is the greatest game there is."

The greatest game there is. The greatest games that ever were. . . .

KIRBY PUCKETT'S homer in the bottom of the 11th off the Braves' Charlie Leibrandt won Game 6 of the '91 Fall Classic for the Twins.

1956 | MILWAUKEE BRAVES ace Warren Spahn, who won 20 or more
games 13 times, was the Cy Young winner in '57. | *Photograph by* MARK KAUFFMAN

1997 | THE 6′ 10″ Randy Johnson had 4,161 strikeouts and five Cy Young Awards before he joined his fifth team, the Yankees, in 2005. | *Photograph by* WALTER IOOSS JR.

THE BENCHING OF A LEGEND

BY ROGER KAHN

The prideful struggle of an aging Stan Musial to prolong his career—a painful experience for everyone involved—was poignantly recounted by one of the game's most astute observers.
—*from* SI, SEPTEMBER 12, 1960

DISTURBING PARADOXES surround an aging baseball player. He is old but not gray; tired but not short of breath; slow but not fat as he drives himself down the first base line. Long after the games, when the old ballplayer thinks seriously, he realizes that he has become obsolete at an age when most men are still moving toward their prime in business and, in politics, are being criticized for their extreme youth. It is a melancholy thing, geriatrics for a 40-year-old.

To Joe DiMaggio, age meant more injuries and deeper silences. To Bob Feller it meant months of forced jokes, with nothing to pitch but batting practice. To more fine ballplayers than anyone has counted age has meant Scotch, bourbon and rye. The athletes seldom bow out gracefully.

Amid the miscellaneous excitements of the current National League pennant race, the most popular ballplayer of his time is trying desperately to overcome this tradition; Stanley Frank Musial of the St. Louis Cardinals, now 39 and slowed, intends to end his career with dignity and with base hits. Neither comes easily to a ballplayer several years past his peak, and so to Musial, a man accustomed to ease and to humility, this has been a summer of agony and pride.

Consider one quiet June evening in Milwaukee when Musial walked toward the batting cage to hit with the scrubs, dragging his average (.235) behind him. He had been riding the bench for two weeks.

"Hey, what a funny-looking ballplayer," called Red Schoendienst of the Braves, who was Musial's roommate on the Cardinals for five years. Musial grinned wide. It was an old joke between old friends, and he stood silently among anonymous second-liners, attempting to act as though he were used to the company. . . . Then he stepped in to hit. He swung three times but never got the ball past the batting practice pitcher. A knot of Milwaukee fans jeered as Musial stepped out of the cage, and the sound, half boos, half yays, was harsh. Musial blushed and began talking very quickly about the old Brooklyn Dodgers.

"Yeah, I could really hit those guys," he said. It was strange and a little sad to see so great a figure tapping bouncers to the pitcher and answering boos with remembrances of past home runs.

Why was he doing it, one wondered. He was long since certain of election to the Baseball Hall of Fame. He was wealthy, independent of the game. He was a man who had always conducted himself sensibly. Now here was sensible old Stan Musial reduced to benchwarmer, as he waged a senseless war with time.

The answer, of course, is pride; more pride than most of us suspected Musial possessed, more pride than Musial ever displayed when he was Stan the Man, consistent .350 hitter, owner and proprietor of most National League pitching staffs.

The issues in the case of Stan Musial versus time have cleared considerably since his May benching and his dramatic July comeback. He was not through in June as many suspected (but, because Musial is well-loved, few put it into words); neither was he the young Musial in July (though many said loudly that he was, and I imagine few really believed it). Both the benching and the comeback represent skirmishes in the continuing battle Musial joins each time he puts on a pair of spikes and heads out toward leftfield, trotting a shade more slowly than he once did.

After a career in which he had never batted lower than .310, Musial hit .255 in 1959. Since he was 38, the wise conclusion was that he was finished, and most baseball men assumed that he would retire. In fact most hoped he would choose retirement instead of the awkward exit that seemed inevitable if he played this season. "No," Musial insisted during the winter. "I want to go out on a good year. I'm not quitting after a lousy year like that." Athletes, like chorus girls, are usually the last to admit that age has affected them, and Musial appeared to be following the familiar unhappy pattern. His timing seemed gone—changeups made him look foolish—and he appeared to be the only man who didn't know it.

In the winter Musial enrolled in a physical education program. The exercises were orthodox—push-ups and such—with an emphasis on tumbling. He came to spring training splendidly conditioned and hit well during exhibition games. For the first three weeks of the regular season he played first base, batted about .300 and fielded poorly. Then his hitting dropped sharply, and over the next three weeks his average drifted toward .200. Finally, on May 21, Solly Hemus, the Cardinal manager, benched Musial. The decision brought pain to Musial and pain to Hemus, too, since what the manager did, after all, was bench a legend. . . .

IN '58 the Musial who'd won seven batting crowns and three MVPs began to show signs of decline.

from THIS OLD HOUSE | BY WILLIAM NACK
SI JUNE 7, 1999

BACK IN 1921, NOT LONG AFTER THE New York Giants' baseball team moved to evict the Yankees from the Polo Grounds in Manhattan—the Giants were sore that Babe Ruth's Yankees were outdrawing them—the Yankees' owners, beer baron Jake Ruppert and Til Huston, announced that they had purchased a 10-acre lot across the river, in the Bronx, and that they planned to build a ballyard of their own. The Giants' manager, John McGraw, scoffed at the scheme. "This is a big mistake," said Little Napoleon. "They are going up to Goatville, and before long they will be lost sight of."

Today, nearly 80 years later, old Goatville is the richest repository of memories in American sports. It was way up there, in the wilds of the Bronx, that the New York Yankees won 33 American League pennants and 24 world championships. Close your eyes, and you can see, on the grainy film of memory, Lou Gehrig listening to the echoes of his farewell speech in 1939 . . . Al Gionfriddo twice looking over his shoulder and then reaching out for Joe DiMaggio's 415-foot drive in the '47 Series . . . Mickey Mantle's thunderous shot denting the copper frieze lining the upper deck in right . . . Reggie Jackson driving a knuckleball into the black tarp covering the seats in center for his third home run in the final game of the '77 Series . . . Yogi Berra leaping into Don Larsen's arms at the end of the Perfect Game . . . the dying Ruth, bracing himself on a bat, waving that last, long goodbye.

For decades the Stadium has been one of New York's most popular tourist attractions, the Bronx's answer to the Empire State Building and the Statue of Liberty; on this sparkling Tuesday morning, tour guide Tony Morante was leading 20 visitors up the walkway into Monument Park when they all seemed to stop at once. There before them, rising like tombstones in the corner of a churchyard, were four marble slabs bearing bronze plaques depicting in bas-relief the visages of Yankees legends Ruth, Mantle, Lou Gehrig and Miller Huggins. Deirdre Weldon had brought nine boys from Yorktown, N.Y., to celebrate the birthday of her son, Terry; as they all gathered reverently around, staring at the faces on the monuments staring back at them, 10-year-old Chris Raiano said aloud what all his friends were wondering: "Are they all buried here?"

"No, they are not," Weldon replied. "Only the memories are." . . .

1949 | YANKEE STADIUM was decked out in bunting for Game 2 of the World Series against the Dodgers. | *Photograph by* BETTMANN/CORBIS

2004 | ANY WAY you look at it, the power stroke of Cardinals slugger Albert Pujols is a swing of beauty. | *Photograph by* JEFFREY PHELPS

1962 | CLETE BOYER didn't need a glove to catch the raindrops that forced postponement of Game 5 of the Series. | *Photograph by* CHARLES M. CONLON

2003 | THE TABLOID headline could've been SNOWPENING DAY for Ellis Burks and the Indians after their lid lifter in Baltimore. | *Photograph by* ROBERTO BOREA

THE QUIET WARRIOR

BY ESMERALDA SANTIAGO

Vladimir Guerrero has been called the most talented player in baseball, but he'd much rather talk about his large family and his mother's home cooking. —*from* SI, AUGUST 30, 2004

VLADIMIR THE GREAT, prince of Kiev (956–1015), was a savage warrior with a sword, a barbarian who converted to Christianity, then gave away his fortune, spread the gospel to his countrymen and was later made a saint. Doña Altagracia Guerrero's Vladimir, born and raised in Don Gregorio, a small town outside Santo Domingo, is both a Guerrero and a guerrero, a warrior with a bat. "They were raised Christian," Doña Altagracia says of her children, "and while they sometimes stray, they still believe, and do the best they can."

The best that Vladimir Guerrero—now, officially, an Angel—has been able to do against major league pitching so far this year is a .323 batting average with 27 home runs, 94 RBIs (including nine in one game) and a slugging percentage of .564. Not that any of that should come as a surprise. "He's the best player in the league," says onetime teammate Rondell White. "He's Superman, and there's not too much kryptonite in the league."

A quiet, thoughtful man, Guerrero's not comfortable talking about who he is or what he does. That discomfort is partly due to his unsteady English, but even when speaking Spanish, he is modest and shy, and he subtly deflects questions he deems too personal. He knows the media loves a rags-to-riches story, and that the trajectory of his life could easily be trivialized into a cliché. "One is grateful for the opportunity to play baseball at the professional level," Guerrero says. "There are many more who don't make it this far."

His ability has awed people in both leagues. "He's just one of those special hitters," says Braves manager Bobby Cox. "I'll bet he's had that same swing since he was six years old." He's an aggressive hitter who frequently lunges at first pitches as if he's not going to get another chance. "If it's coming forward, he's pretty much going to swing at it," says Angels pitcher John Lackey. "Back in June he hit a slider about 800 feet. He came back to the dugout and said, 'I like slider.' I said, 'Yeah, I can tell.'"

As a boy Vladimir wanted to be a singer-dancer. His mother remembers her four boys putting on shows for the family in which they imitated the popular *merengueros* Los Kenton. They concocted costumes that vaguely approximated the spiffy outfits the band wore, and they perfected the acrobatic moves Los Kenton performed in concerts. Vladimir is still fond of merengue music, which he listens to at ear-splitting volume, but it was his ability to play baseball that distinguished him early from other boys. This was not baseball as it is played in Little Leagues across America. Vladimir and his friends sometimes had to play with sticks for bats and lemons wrapped in rags for balls. They played on cobblestoned streets, in cleared pastures and sandy lots. "Whenever the kids got together to play," his mother says, "they always chose him for their team because he could hit."

Vladimir tries to deflect even this compliment. "I didn't run fast, though," he says, "because I was fat."

"My mother," Doña Altagracia adds, "once told me, 'All your boys play baseball well, but this one—Vladimir—someday will be a famous *pelotero*. I won't live to see it, but the ants will come and tell me in my grave.'"

The Guerreros' first home was a sod dwelling with a palm-frond roof built by Don Damián, Vladimir's father, and Doña Altagracia while she was pregnant with Eliezer, her first child. "Little by little, we improved it," she says, "first with wood, then concrete walls with a tin roof. That roof blew away in a hurricane, but we fixed it."

She pulls out pictures of the new dwelling the family is building near their first home. Vladimir watches proudly as his mother describes what is depicted in the photographs. "Over here will be the gym," she says, "and the pool will go right there."

The sprawling house sits in a valley surrounded by mountains. "Everyone has already claimed a room," Vladimir says laughing. "The house is not finished yet, but the rooms are all spoken for."

During the season Guerrero's house, 15 minutes from Angel Stadium, is filled with relatives, whom he flies to California because he likes having them near. "My nieces and nephews are my children," he says. "I love them all as if they were my own and treat them all as if I were their father."

He sits down on a roomy leather sofa in the den of his home, and within seconds there is a child on his lap, and then another is leaning on him as she watches a big-screen TV. "It makes me happy to have my family here," he says, smiling as he looks around the room to take it all in. He is clearly happy with what he has accomplished as a man, as a son, and as a father. . . .

GUERRERO SHIES away from his rags-to-riches story, which includes rags wrapped around lemons because he couldn't afford baseballs.

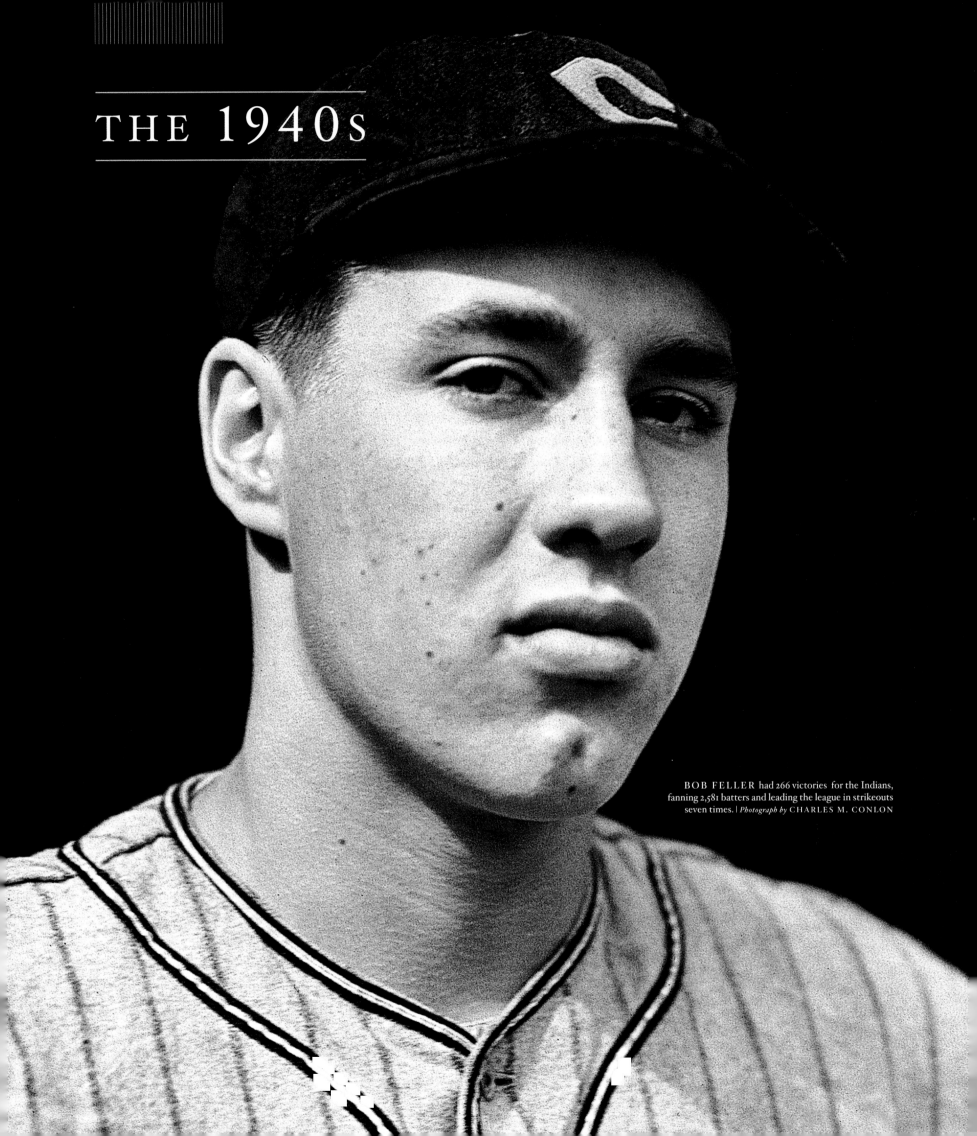

BOB FELLER had 266 victories for the Indians, fanning 2,581 batters and leading the league in strikeouts seven times. | *Photograph by* CHARLES M. CONLON

>THE ALL-DECADE TEAMS

AMERICAN LEAGUE	NATIONAL LEAGUE
CATCHER Yogi Berra	CATCHER Walker Cooper
FIRST BASE Rudy York	FIRST BASE Johnny Mize
SECOND BASE Bobby Doerr	SECOND BASE Jackie Robinson
SHORTSTOP Lou Boudreau	SHORTSTOP Pee Wee Reese
THIRD BASE Ken Keltner	THIRD BASE Bob Elliott
LEFTFIELD Ted Williams	LEFTFIELD Ralph Kiner
CENTERFIELD Joe DiMaggio	CENTERFIELD Pete Reiser
RIGHTFIELD Tommy Henrich	RIGHTFIELD Stan Musial
STARTING PITCHER Hal Newhouser	STARTING PITCHER Mort Cooper
RELIEF PITCHER Joe Page	RELIEF PITCHER Hugh Casey

>DEBUT | FINALE<

DEBUT	Year	FINALE
PEE WEE REESE	1940	WALLY BERGER
STAN MUSIAL	1941	LEFTY GROVE
WARREN SPAHN	1942	CHARLIE GEHRINGER
ANDY PAFKO	1943	LEFTY GOMEZ
JOE NUXHALL	1944	CHUCK KLEIN
RED SCHOENDIENST	1945	JIMMIE FOXX
RALPH KINER	1946	BILL DICKEY
JACKIE ROBINSON	1947	HANK GREENBERG
ROY CAMPANELLA	1948	ARKY VAUGHAN
MINNIE MINOSO	1949	RIP SEWELL

>THE LEADERS

HITTING

BATTING AVERAGE*	TED WILLIAMS	356
HOME RUNS	TED WILLIAMS	234
RBI	BOB ELLIOTT	903
AT BATS	BOB ELLIOTT	5,361
HITS	LOU BOUDREAU	1,578
SINGLES	LOU BOUDREAU	1,118
DOUBLES	LOU BOUDREAU	339
TRIPLES	STAN MUSIAL	108
OBP*	TED WILLIAMS	496
SLUGGING PCT.*	TED WILLIAMS	647
RUNS	TED WILLIAMS	951
STOLEN BASES	GEORGE CASE	285
HIT BY PITCHES	BILL NICHOLSON	48
WALKS	TED WILLIAMS	994
STRIKEOUTS	BILL NICHOLSON	708
GAMES	BOB ELLIOTT	1,455

PITCHING

WINS	HAL NEWHOUSER	170
LOSSES	DUTCH LEONARD	123
WINNING PCT.†	SPUD CHANDLER	714
STRIKEOUTS	HAL NEWHOUSER	1,579
ERA†	SPUD CHANDLER	2.67
INNINGS	HAL NEWHOUSER	2,453
WALKS	HAL NEWHOUSER	1,068
RUNS ALLOWED	HAL NEWHOUSER	927
HOME RUNS ALLOWED	TINY BONHAM	117
SAVES	JOE PAGE	63
SHUTOUTS	HAL NEWHOUSER	31
COMPLETE GAMES	HAL NEWHOUSER	181

* MINIMUM 2,500 PLATE APPEARANCES † MINIMUM 1,000 INNINGS

>HOT TICKETS 10 Games You Wish You'd Seen

Ebbets Field April 15, 1947 Jackie Robinson starts at first base for the Brooklyn Dodgers, breaking baseball's color barrier. Robinson goes hitless in the Dodgers' 5–3 win.

Ebbets Field Oct. 3, 1947 Yankees > pitcher Bill Bevens is working on a no-hitter with two outs in the ninth when Dodgers pinch hitter Cookie Lavagetto drives a two-run double to left in Brooklyn's 3–2 win in Game 4 of the World Series.

Municipal Stadium July 17, 1941 Joe DiMaggio goes 0 for 3 against the Indians, snapping his major league record 56-game hitting streak. The play of the game is a backhanded stop in the seventh inning by third baseman Ken Keltner, who throws out DiMaggio.

Shibe Park Sept. 28, 1941 With one day and two games left in his season, Ted Williams is batting .39955 and has a chance to be the AL's first .400 hitter since '23. He has six hits in the twin bill and ends the year with a .406 average.

Sportsman's Park Oct. 15, 1946 In the eighth inning of Game 7, Cardinals rightfielder Enos Slaughter tries to score from first base on a double to center by Harry Walker. Red Sox shortstop Johnny Pesky hesitates before making his relay throw to the plate, giving Slaughter just enough time to slide in safely with what turns out to be the game-winning run.

Comiskey Park April 16, 1940 Indians starter Bob Feller throws a no-hitter on Opening Day in Chicago against the White Sox.

Fenway Park Oct. 4, 1948 The Indians and Red Sox, who both finished with 96–58 records, meet in Boston for a one-game playoff to decide the AL pennant. Indians player-manager Lou Boudreau hits two home runs in the Tribe's 8–3 win.

Municipal Stadium Sept. 27, 1940 With two days left in the season and the Tigers holding a two-game lead over the Indians, the teams meet to decide the AL championship. Rookie Floyd Giebell outpitches Cleveland ace Bob Feller in a Tigers 2–0 win, to clinch the pennant.

Crosley Field June 10, 1944 Two months shy of his 16th birthday, Reds pitcher Joe Nuxhall makes his major-league debut—kicking off a 16-year career—pitching two-thirds of an inning, allowing five runs in an 18–0 drubbing by the Cardinals.

Ebbets Field Oct. 5, 1941 The Dodgers are leading 4–3 and are one out away from tying the World Series at two games apiece, but Brooklyn catcher Mickey Owen can't hold on to the third strike from Hugh Casey, allowing Yankee Tommy Henrich to reach first base. New York then goes on to score four runs and take the game 7–4.

BEST OF THE 1940s

TEAM	WINS	LOSSES	WIN PCT.
CARDINALS	960	580	.623
YANKEES	929	609	.604
DODGERS	894	646	.581
RED SOX	854	683	.556
TIGERS	834	705	.542

ENOS SLAUGHTER, CARDINALS

WORST OF THE 1940s

TEAM	WINS	LOSSES	WIN PCT.
PHILLIES	584	951	.380
ATHLETICS	638	898	.415
SENATORS	677	858	.441
BROWNS	698	833	.456
WHITE SOX	707	820	.463

LUKE APPLING, WHITE SOX

1940s CULTURE

MUSIC: *White Christmas* (Bing Crosby), *In the Mood* (Glenn Miller), *I've Heard That Song Before* (Harry James), *Rum and Coca-Cola* (Andrews Sisters)

MOVIES: *Bambi, Casablanca, It's a Wonderful Life, The Philadelphia Story, Citizen Kane*

TELEVISION SHOWS: *Texaco Star Theater, The Ed Sullivan Show, Candid Camera, The Lone Ranger, Captain Video*

BOOKS: *1984* by George Orwell; *Dr. Spock's Baby and Child Care* by Benjamin Spock; *All the King's Men* by Robert Penn Warren; *Sexual Behavior in the Human Male* by Alfred Charles Kinsey; *The Naked and the Dead* by Norman Mailer; *For Whom the Bell Tolls* by Ernest Hemingway

ACHIEVEMENT: On Oct. 14, 1947, flying a rocket-powered Bell X-1 airplane at 45,000 feet, World War II ace Chuck Yeager becomes the first man to break the sound barrier.

INVENTIONS: computer; bikini, microwave oven, transistor; Velcro

SEX SYMBOLS: Rita Hayworth & Frank Sinatra

VILLAIN: Adolf Hitler

PERSONALITY OF THE DECADE: Winston Churchill

< RITA HAYWORTH

>NICKNAMES<

Elwin [Preacher] Roe ∧
Ted [the Splendid Splinter] Williams
Edwin [Duke] Snider
Stan [the Man] Musial
Virgil [Fire] Trucks
Bob [Rapid Robert] Feller
Harold [Pee Wee] Reese
Tommy [Old Reliable] Henrich
Mel [Wimpy] Harder
Marty [the Octopus] Marion
Harry [the Cat] Brecheen
Albert [Red] Schoendienst
Enos [Country] Slaughter
Ernest [Tiny] Bonham
Lawrence [Crash] Davis
Walter [Hoot] Evers
Phil [Scooter] Rizzuto
Ewell [the Whip] Blackwell
Sylvester [Blix] Donnelly
Granville [Granny] Hamner
[Steady] Eddie Lopat
Charlie [King Kong] Keller

BORN		DIED
JACK NICKLAUS	1940	WALTER P. CHRYSLER
BOB DYLAN >	1941	JAMES JOYCE
MUHAMMAD ALI	1942	GEORGE M. COHAN
MICK JAGGER	1943	GEORGE WASHINGTON CARVER
AL MICHAELS	1944	GLENN MILLER
BOB MARLEY	1945	FRANKLIN D. ROOSEVELT
BILL CLINTON	1946	W.C. FIELDS
STEPHEN KING	1947	HENRY FORD
RICHARD SIMMONS	1948	< MOHANDAS GANDHI
ANNIE LEIBOVITZ	1949	ROBERT L. RIPLEY

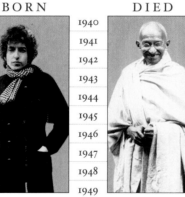

> **NEWS OF THE REAL WORLD** **1940:** Germany occupies France, but invasion of Great Britain is repelled; Howard Florey develops penicillin as a practical antibiotic **1941:** Sneak attack! Japan bombs U.S. fleet at Pearl Harbor, Hawaii; U.S. enters World War II **1942:** Manhattan Project established by FDR to develop the atomic bomb **1943:** Tide turns: Allies take Italy, Soviets beat back Germans at Stalingrad **1944:** D Day: Allied troops land in France at Normandy **1945:** FDR dies, is succeeded by Harry S. Truman; Hitler commits suicide; Allies declare victory in Europe; first atomic bomb detonated by U.S. at test site in New Mexico; Allies declare victory in Pacific **1946:** Baby Boom begins: U.S. birthrate skyrockets as G.I.'s return **1947:** India, led by Gandhi, gains independence from Britain. **1948:** The state of Israel is established in former British territory of Palestine **1949:** The People's Republic of China is founded; Chinese nationalists flee to Taiwan

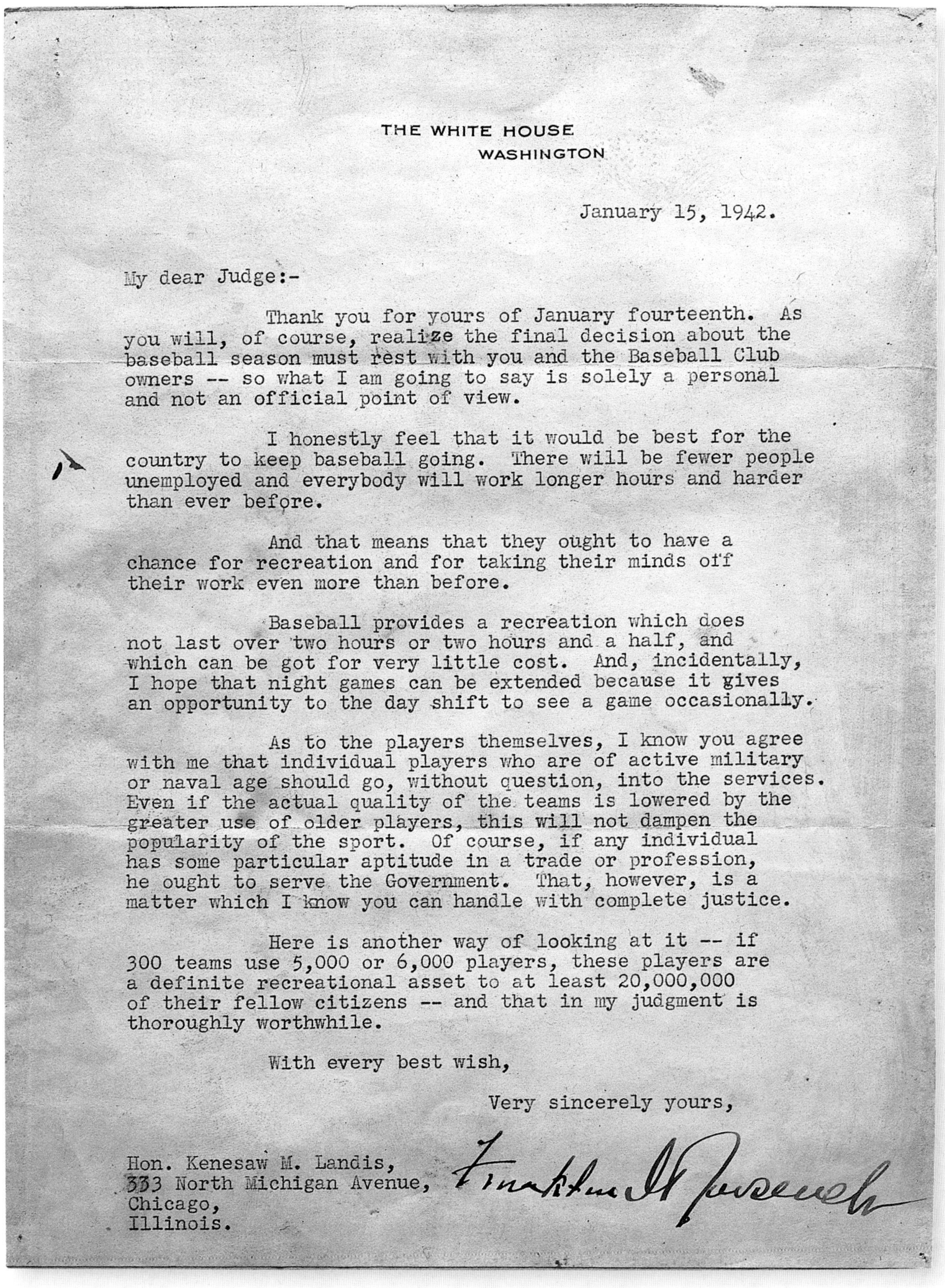

THE WHITE HOUSE
WASHINGTON

January 15, 1942.

My dear Judge:-

Thank you for yours of January fourteenth. As you will, of course, realize the final decision about the baseball season must rest with you and the Baseball Club owners -- so what I am going to say is solely a personal and not an official point of view.

I honestly feel that it would be best for the country to keep baseball going. There will be fewer people unemployed and everybody will work longer hours and harder than ever before.

And that means that they ought to have a chance for recreation and for taking their minds off their work even more than before.

Baseball provides a recreation which does not last over two hours or two hours and a half, and which can be got for very little cost. And, incidentally, I hope that night games can be extended because it gives an opportunity to the day shift to see a game occasionally.

As to the players themselves, I know you agree with me that individual players who are of active military or naval age should go, without question, into the services. Even if the actual quality of the teams is lowered by the greater use of older players, this will not dampen the popularity of the sport. Of course, if any individual has some particular aptitude in a trade or profession, he ought to serve the Government. That, however, is a matter which I know you can handle with complete justice.

Here is another way of looking at it -- if 300 teams use 5,000 or 6,000 players, these players are a definite recreational asset to at least 20,000,000 of their fellow citizens -- and that in my judgment is thoroughly worthwhile.

With every best wish,

Very sincerely yours,

Franklin D. Roosevelt

Hon. Kenesaw M. Landis,
333 North Michigan Avenue,
Chicago,
Illinois.

1941 | PRESIDENT ROOSEVELT, who threw out the first ball in '41, later urged baseball, in the "green light letter," not to shut down because of the war. | *Photograph by* AMERICAN STOCK

2000 | IT LOOKED like a line drive in the box score after the Rockies' Todd Hollandsworth legged out a hit in the twilight of Denver's Coors Field. | *Photograph by* BRETT WILHELM

1990 | HE CUT a slighter figure in only his fifth season, but Barry Bonds always knew how to strike a home run pose. | *Photograph by* BETTMANN/CORBIS

1987 | AS THE AL's Rookie of the Year, Mark McGwire pounded out 49 homers for Oakland. | *Photograph by* RONALD C. MODRA

THE VERY BEST ACT IN TOWN

BY JACK OLSEN

Sandy Koufax was baseball's top pitcher in the early Sixties and one of the game's biggest attractions. He had money, a bronze Oldsmobile, an ear for Mendelssohn and a realization that none of it could last. —*from* SI, JULY 29, 1963

THREE HOURS BEFORE game time, Philadelphians began leaving their cream-cheese assembly plants and scrapple refineries for the sooty, dreary transitional neighborhood around 21st and Lehigh, home of Connie Mack Stadium and the poor but honest Phillies. By four o'clock, long lines of fans surrounded the ancient ballpark, and word went out that the twi-night doubleheader against the Los Angeles Dodgers was SRO. Still the fans remained, sipping from thermos jugs against the humid 90° heat, hoping to be accorded the privilege of leaning against a girder inside for 18 innings. A few thousand extra got in, making the official paid attendance 35,353. Another 15,000 were turned away.

If you had to list 10 reasons for such an extraordinary turnout on such an ordinary day, the first nine would have to be Sandy Koufax. It takes a good act to score in Philadelphia, and Koufax is a very good act. At 27, he holds the National League record for most strikeouts in a season, for most strikeouts per nine innings pitched, for most strikeouts in a single game (18, a feat he has brought off twice). He has two no-hitters. He led the league in earned run average (2.54 in 1962), and until a finger injury wrecked him last year, he was the best pitcher in baseball, with a 14–4 record and a 2.06 ERA. This year he can wiggle his finger just fine, and he is the best pitcher in baseball. Some of the wisest old watchers in the game will go so far as to tell you that at this moment Koufax is the best ever.

On a team that counts among its personnel the man who gave history the definitive lowdown on where nice guys finish, Koufax serves as a constant reminder that no absolute statement—even one by Leo Durocher—is absolutely true. For years reporters and fans who did not know Koufax reckoned that he was aloof and stuffy, when the truth is that he was as painfully shy as a six-year-old boy at his first piano recital. In his ninth season in the majors, he is still frightened of the reporters who rush to his locker after a game. He answers their questions patiently and politely, but it is easy to see that he is not enjoying himself. In some ways he borders on being a Pollyanna. When he does find something to say about other people, it is always good, but actually, as he puts it, "I hate like hell to talk about other people at all." He also hates like hell to be quoted using words like hell. He knows youngsters are influenced by him, and he therefore refuses to be photographed smoking. He would rather not talk about drinking at all. (The fact is that Koufax both smokes and drinks, but in such laughably small quantities that one wonders why he bothers.)

Koufax belongs to none of the several cliques within the Dodgers. His roommate, catcher Doug Camilli, is about as voluble as Harpo Marx, and Koufax and Camilli are likely to spend the long, boring hours on road trips sitting in their hotel room listening to one of the several dozen musical comedy scores Koufax carries with him on tape. He is bemused by reports that he listens only to Beethoven and Mendelssohn and reads only Thomas Wolfe and Aldous Huxley, as though this were proof that he is some kind of intellectual. "I don't know what's so highbrow about Mendelssohn," he says. "I may have read Thomas Wolfe in school, but I don't think I've ever read Aldous Huxley. I'm normal, that's all."

Sanford Koufax is as normal as any other red-blooded American youth with a bronze Oldsmobile, a gorgeous Hollywood-type girlfriend, a neat bachelor home in Studio City, a $40,000-a-year salary, part ownership of a radio station, an interest in a motel, and a fastball that is frequently heard but not always seen by National League batters. He has a college background (University of Cincinnati), an accent absolutely devoid of the tiniest trace of his Brooklyn years, a rich singing and speaking voice, and good looks that once moved a columnist to gush, "I have met Clark Gable, William Holden and Gregory Peck. But since meeting Sandy Koufax, they can all take a backseat. He's all of them rolled into one— only younger!" . . .

KOUFAX CAPPED his 25–5 season in '63 in Game 4 of the World Series, his second complete-game win over the Yanks.

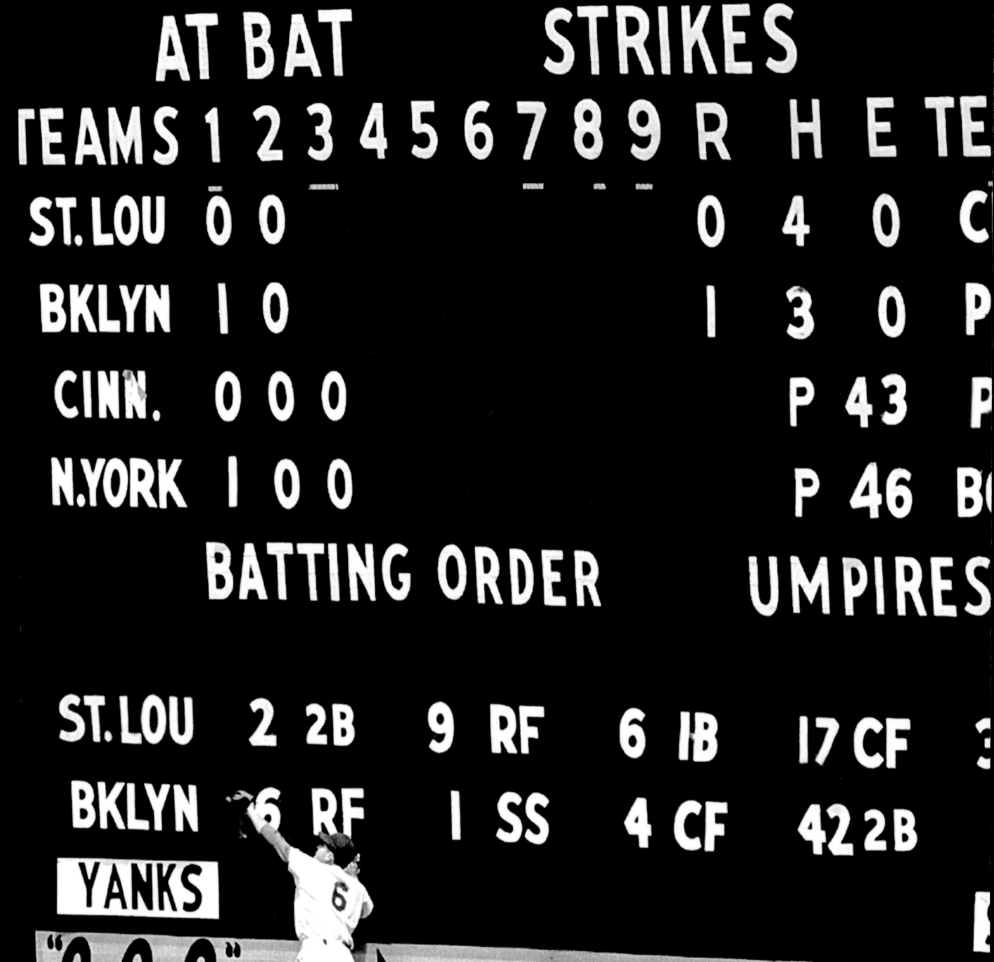

1951 | DODGERS RIGHTFIELDER Carl Furillo, a.k.a. the Reading Rifle, snagged Stan Musial's fly ball at the Ebbets Field wall. | *Photograph by* HARRY HARRIS

1970 | ALLTIME HIT king Pete Rose was intense about every aspect of the game—even the informal portrait. | *Photograph by* OZZIE SWEET

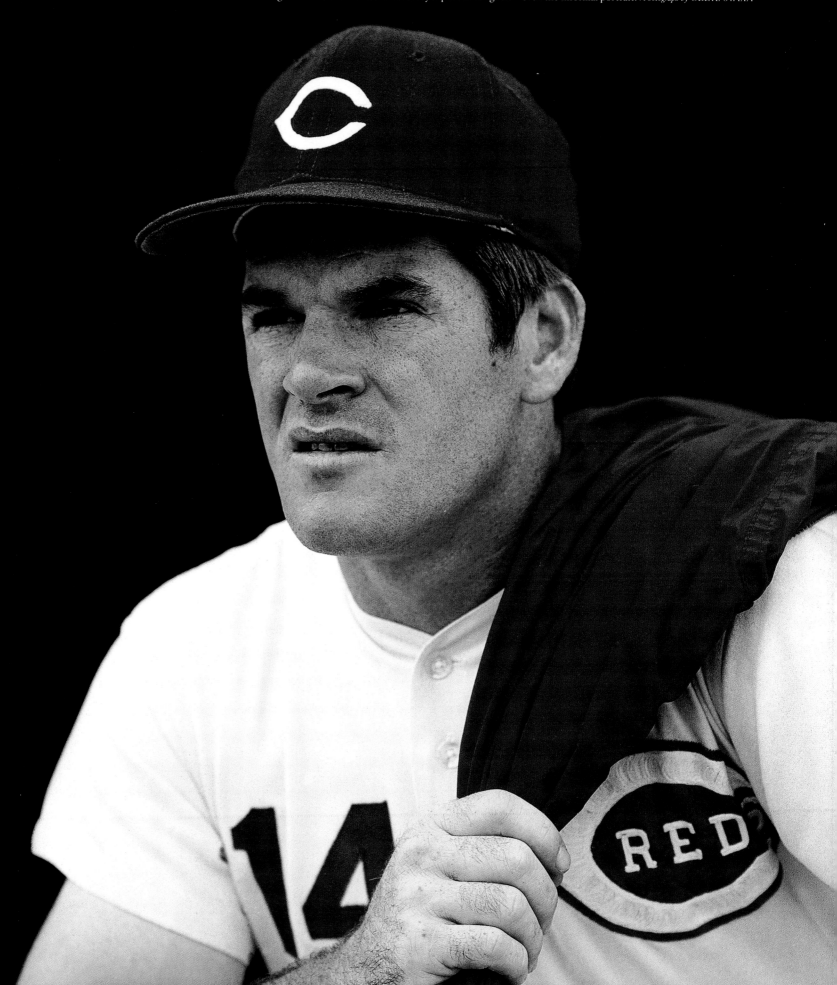

SI's ALLTIME All-Star Team

WHO WOULD YOU RATHER HAVE: Mays or Mantle? Koufax or Spahn? Berra or Bench? Aaron or Williams? This is the classic baseball argument, sublime in its infinite variety. Gehrig or Musial? Robinson or Hornsby? Cobb or DiMaggio? ☙ Any real fan could take either side of such debates and argue persuasively, but every real fan would also have an unshakable conviction about who was the better player. Wagner or A-Rod? Eckersley or Rivera? Young or Mathewson or Clemens? And though it is the nature of the game— indeed, a vital part of its appeal—that the debate will never end, SPORTS ILLUSTRATED polled a panel of current and former baseball writers and editors and distinguished outside experts to select our dream team. Voters received a ballot listing a total of 246 position

players, pitchers and managers (along with a spot for write-in votes) and were asked to rank their preferences at each position to create a 25-man roster, plus a manager and two coaches. The resulting team, brought together for the first time in this portrait created by photo illustrator Aaron Goodman, is a pretty fair bunch of ballplayers. But so is the second team, the guys who didn't quite make the cut: Josh Gibson, Jimmie Foxx, Joe Morgan, Rod Carew, Ernie Banks, Cal Ripken Jr., George Brett, Brooks Robinson, Barry Bonds, Oscar Charleston, Roberto Clemente, Rickey Henderson, Bob Gibson, Grover Cleveland Alexander, Greg Maddux, Tom Seaver, Nolan Ryan, Bob Feller, Satchel Paige, Steve Carlton, Pedro Martinez, Rollie Fingers and Goose Gossage. ☙ So who would you rather have?

— PHOTO ILLUSTRATION BY AARON GOODMAN —
UNIFORMS BY MITCHELL & NESS

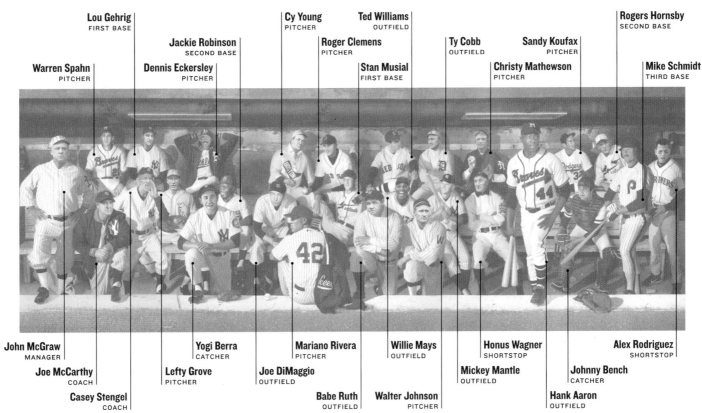

Lou Gehrig FIRST BASE
Cy Young PITCHER
Ted Williams OUTFIELD
Rogers Hornsby SECOND BASE
Jackie Robinson SECOND BASE
Roger Clemens PITCHER
Ty Cobb OUTFIELD
Sandy Koufax PITCHER
Warren Spahn PITCHER
Dennis Eckersley PITCHER
Stan Musial FIRST BASE
Christy Mathewson PITCHER
Mike Schmidt THIRD BASE

John McGraw MANAGER
Yogi Berra CATCHER
Mariano Rivera PITCHER
Willie Mays OUTFIELD
Honus Wagner SHORTSTOP
Alex Rodriguez SHORTSTOP
Joe McCarthy COACH
Lefty Grove PITCHER
Joe DiMaggio OUTFIELD
Mickey Mantle OUTFIELD
Johnny Bench CATCHER
Casey Stengel COACH
Babe Ruth OUTFIELD
Walter Johnson PITCHER
Hank Aaron OUTFIELD

1946 | THE CARDINALS' Stan Musial could run but not hide between second and third in Boston during Game 3 of the World Series. | *Photograph by* BETTMANN/CORBIS

1913 | YANKEES INFIELDER Roy Hartzell got caught in heavy traffic near third against the Washington Senators. | *Photograph by* BETTMANN/CORBIS

FINAL TWIST OF THE DRAMA

BY GEORGE PLIMPTON

At the moment destiny touched Henry Aaron it reached out to immortalize a cast of essential supporting players as well.
— *from* SI, APRIL 22, 1974

I**T WAS A SIMPLE ACT BY AN** unassuming man which touched an enormous circle of people, indeed an entire country. It provided an instant that people would remember for decades—exactly what they were doing at the time of the home run that beat Babe Ruth's great record, whether they were watching it on television, or heard it over the radio while driving on the turnpike, or even whether a neighbor leaned over a fence and told them about it the next morning.

For those who sat in the stadium in Atlanta, their recollections would be more intimate—the sharp cork-popping sound of the bat hitting the ball, startlingly audible in the split second of suspense before the crowd began a roar that lasted for more than 10 minutes. Perhaps that is what they would remember—how people stood and sucked in air and bellowed it out in a sustained tribute that few athletes have ever received. Or perhaps they would remember their wonder at how easy and inevitable it seemed—that having opened the season in Cincinnati by hitting the tying home run, No. 714, with his first swing of the year, it was obviously appropriate that the man who has been called Supe by his teammates (for Superman) was going to duplicate the feat in Atlanta with his first swing of *that* game. That was why 53,775 had come. Or perhaps they would remember the odd way the stadium emptied after the excitement of the fourth inning, as if the crowd felt that what they had seen would be diluted by sitting through any more baseball that night.

And then finally there were those few in the core of that immense circle—the participants themselves—who would be the ones most keenly touched: the pitcher, in this case a pleasant, gap-toothed veteran named Al Downing who happened to be the one who threw a fastball at a certain moment that did not tail away properly; the hitter, Henry Aaron himself, for whom the event, despite his grace in dealing with it,

had become so traumatic that little in the instant was relished except the relief that it had been done; the Braves announcer, Milo Hamilton, whose imagination for months had been working up words to describe the event to the outside world; and a young bullpen pitcher named Tom House, who would reach up in the air and establish contact with a ball whose value as baseball's greatest talisman had been monetarily pegged at $25,000 and whose sentimental value was incalculable.

A more eloquent testimonial than anything the Braves management can probably think up is already in place just across the expressway from the stadium—a life-size statue of Aaron in the cluttered front yard of a 70-year-old black gravestone cutter named E.M. Bailey. Bailey works only in concrete (marble is far too expensive for his customers), and each of his headstones, with the name and date chiseled on it, sells for $10. In his off time he works on pieces of sculpture—massive-winged birds with thin, curved necks, a pair of girls bent like mangrove roots in a wild dance, a memorial to John F. Kennedy with *Air Force One* flying above the White House—all his constructions made of Portland cement.

He began working on the Aaron sculpture last spring and had it finished and brightly painted just in time to move it, with the assistance of three helpers, into his small front yard on the night of the opener. The statue weighs more than 2,000 pounds. It shows Aaron at the completion of the swing of a massive bat, his eyes, somewhat slanted, watching the ball sail off. When it was in place, the children came down the street, leaning up against a chicken-wire fence to look up briefly at the statue on their way home to watch the game on TV.

Bailey, somewhat exhausted by his afternoon's labors with the statue, relaxed in his springback chair for the game. His wife sat across the room. When Aaron hit No. 715 the two could hear the shouts rising along the street from the neighbors' houses. "Just then," Bailey says, "I kind of thought back, and when I realized how far he had come and what the hardships were and what it means when one of us makes good." . . .

HAMMERIN' HANK had plenty of company at home in Atlanta after he surpassed Babe Ruth to become the home run king.

1968 | JOHNNY BENCH, considered by many the best catcher in history, was NL Rookie of the Year for the Reds. | *Photograph by* ERIC SCHWEIKARDT

1928 | THE CARDINALS, even at home in St. Louis, were a study in futility against the Yankees, who swept them in the '28 Series. | *Photograph by* BETTMANN/CORBIS

> ## Basebrawls

Throwing Down

Every angry batter, agitated pitcher or aggrieved base runner knows that there's more than one way to get your last licks

Robin Ventura quickly learned that Nolan Ryan can throw a high, hard one with his fists too.

After Darren Dreifort hit him with a pitch, Atlanta's Andres Galarraga (helmet) hit the hurler.

White Sox pitcher Jim Parque had an angry Tiger (Bobby Higginson) on his hands after a bean ball.

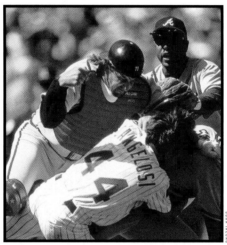

The Braves' Charlie O'Brien nailed the Mets' John Cangelosi, who'd already been hit by two pitches.

Tino Martinez retaliated for his beaning by Miguel Batista after being forced out at second.

Paul O'Neill didn't much care for a brushback pitch or for John Marzano's mitt in his face.

Michael Barrett didn't have to wait for the umpire to punch out A.J. Pierzynski.

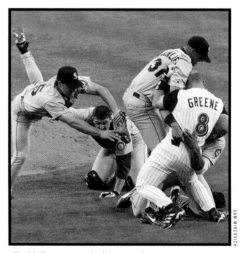

Todd Greene got held up on his way to repaying Brett Hinchliffe for his beaning.

1973 | THE FUR—and fists—flew in the NLCS between the Mets and Reds when Bud Harrelson took exception to Pete Rose's hard slide on a double play. | *Photograph by* JOHN IACONO

1967 | CARDINALS LEFTFIELDER Lou Brock was the big leagues' steal magnate
until Rickey Henderson ran him down. | *Photograph by* WALTER IOOSS JR.

1995 | THE ROYALS' Pat Borders will never forget the time he bumped into Tigers DH Kirk Gibson at home in Detroit. | *Photograph by* CHUCK SOLOMON

2004 | THE BREWERS' Scott Podsednik easily beat the throw to the Astros' Adam Everett for one of his NL–best 70 steals. | *Photograph by* DARREN HAUCK

THE 1950s

NELLIE FOX, a 12-time All-Star second-baseman, was the AL MVP in '59, when he led the White Sox to their first World Series in 40 years. | *Photograph by* RICHARD MEEK

>THE ALL-DECADE TEAMS

AMERICAN LEAGUE	NATIONAL LEAGUE
CATCHER *Yogi Berra*	CATCHER *Roy Campanella*
FIRST BASE *Bill Skowron*	FIRST BASE *Gil Hodges*
SECOND BASE *Nellie Fox*	SECOND BASE *Jackie Robinson*
SHORTSTOP *Harvey Kuenn*	SHORTSTOP *Ernie Banks*
THIRD BASE *Al Rosen*	THIRD BASE *Eddie Mathews*
LEFTFIELD *Ted Williams*	LEFTFIELD *Stan Musial*
CENTERFIELD *Mickey Mantle*	CENTERFIELD *Willie Mays*
RIGHTFIELD *Jackie Jensen*	RIGHTFIELD *Hank Aaron*
STARTING PITCHER *Whitey Ford*	STARTING PITCHER *Warren Spahn*
RELIEF PITCHER *Ellis Kinder*	RELIEF PITCHER *Clem Labine*

>DEBUT   FINALE<

DEBUT		FINALE
WHITEY FORD	1950	LUKE APPLING
WILLIE MAYS	1951	JOE DIMAGGIO
EDDIE MATHEWS	1952	LOU BOUDREAU
AL KALINE	1953	JOHNNY MIZE
HANK AARON	1954	ALLIE REYNOLDS
ROBERTO CLEMENTE	1955	RALPH KINER
FRANK ROBINSON	1956	JACKIE ROBINSON
ROGER MARIS	1957	GEORGE KELL
FELIPE ALOU	1958	PEE WEE REESE
BOB GIBSON	1959	LARRY DOBY

>THE LEADERS

HITTING

BATTING AVERAGE* TED WILLIAMS	.336
HOME RUNS DUKE SNIDER	326
RBI DUKE SNIDER	1,031
AT BATS NELLIE FOX	6,115
HITS RICHIE ASHBURN	1,875
SINGLES RICHIE ASHBURN	1,522
DOUBLES STAN MUSIAL	356
TRIPLES RICHIE ASHBURN, NELLIE FOX	82
OBP* TED WILLIAMS	.476
SLUGGING PCT.* TED WILLIAMS	.622
RUNS MICKEY MANTLE	994
STOLEN BASES WILLIE MAYS	179
HIT BY PITCHES MINNIE MINOSO	149
WALKS EDDIE YOST	1,185
STRIKEOUTS MICKEY MANTLE	899
GAMES RICHIE ASHBURN	1,523

PITCHING

WINS WARREN SPAHN	202
LOSSES ROBIN ROBERTS	149
WINNING PCT.† WHITEY FORD	.708
STRIKEOUTS EARLY WYNN	1,544
ERA† WHITEY FORD	2.66
INNINGS ROBIN ROBERTS	3,012
WALKS EARLY WYNN	1,028
RUNS ALLOWED ROBIN ROBERTS	1,229
HOME RUNS ALLOWED ROBIN ROBERTS	327
SAVES ELLIS KINDER	96
SHUTOUTS BILLY PIERCE, SPAHN, WYNN	33
COMPLETE GAMES ROBIN ROBERTS	237

* MINIMUM 2,500 PLATE APPEARANCES † MINIMUM 1,000 INNINGS

>HOT TICKETS 10 Games You Wish You'd Seen

Yankee Stadium Oct. 8, 1956 Yankees righthander Don Larsen retires all 27 Dodgers hitters in Game 5 of the World Series, a 2–0 New York win, completing the only perfect game (or even no-hitter) in postseason history.

Polo Grounds Oct. 3, 1951 The Giants' Bobby Thomson hits "the shot heard 'round the world," a pennant-winning home run off Brooklyn's Ralph Branca in the bottom of the ninth in the deciding game of a three-game playoff for the National League pennant.

Polo Grounds Sept. 29, 1954 Giants > centerfielder Willie Mays makes a spectacular over the shoulder catch of a 430-foot drive by Cleveland's Vic Wertz with two runners on in the eighth inning of a 2–2 tie in Game 1 of the World Series. The Giants win on a pinch-hit three-run home run by Dusty Rhodes in the 10th.

Seals Stadium Apr. 15, 1958 Only 23,448 fans turn out in San Francisco as a bitter rivalry relocates to the West Coast. The Giants blank the Dodgers 8–0 in the first West Coast game in major league history.

Yankee Stadium October 4, 1955 Years of futility are washed away as "dem Bums," the Brooklyn Dodgers, beat the Yankees 2–0 in Game 7 behind a five-hitter by Johnny Podres—the first World Series title in franchise history.

Forbes Field May 26, 1959 Pirates pitcher Harvey Haddix throws 12 perfect innings but loses to the Braves in the 13th on an apparent home run by Joe Adcock. However Adcock passes teammate Hank Aaron on the base paths and is credited with only a game-winning double.

Sportsman's Park Aug. 19, 1951 The St. Louis Browns send 3' 7" Eddie Gaedel to the plate wearing uniform number ⅛. Gaedel walks on four pitches and is promptly pulled for a pinch runner.

Sportsman's Park April 23, 1952 Indians ace Bob Feller throws a one-hitter but loses 1–0 to St. Louis starter Bob Cain, who also tosses a one-hitter.

Sportsman's Park Aug. 24, 1951 Browns owner Bill Veeck has placards handed out to 1,115 fans who "manage" the home team by voting YES or NO on strategy questions during the game. The Browns defeat the Athletics 5–3 with their manager, Zach Taylor, watching from a box seat.

Fenway Park June 8, 1950 Three Red Sox batters hit multiple home runs—Ted Williams and Walt Dropo (two each) and Bobby Doerr (three)—in Boston's 29–4 win over St. Louis. The Red Sox set records for extra base hits (17) and for total bases (60).

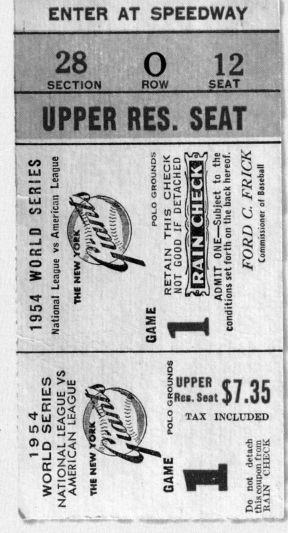

BEST OF THE 1950s

TEAM	WINS	LOSSES	WIN PCT.
YANKEES	955	582	.621
DODGERS	913	630	.592
INDIANS	904	634	.588
BRAVES	854	687	.554
WHITE SOX	847	693	.550

PEE WEE REESE, DODGERS

WORST OF THE 1950s

TEAM	WINS	LOSSES	WIN PCT.
PIRATES	616	923	.400
ATHLETICS	624	915	.405
BROWNS/ORIOLES	632	905	.411
SENATORS	640	898	.416
CUBS	672	866	.436

ELROY FACE, PIRATES

1950S CULTURE

MUSIC: *Elvis' Christmas Album* (Elvis Presley), *Kind of Blue* (Miles Davis), *Tutti-Frutti* (Little Richard); *Mona Lisa* (Nat King Cole)

MOVIES: *Lady and the Tramp, Rebel Without a Cause, Singin' in the Rain, On the Waterfront, Sunset Boulevard*

TELEVISION SHOWS: *I Love Lucy, The Ed Sullivan Show, The Honeymooners, Dragnet, What's My Line?*

BOOKS: *The Catcher in the Rye* by J. D. Salinger; *From Here to Eternity* by James Jones; *The Power of Positive Thinking* by Norman Vincent Peale; *Lolita* by Vladimir Nabokov; *Atlas Shrugged* by Ayn Rand

ACHIEVEMENT: In 1956, President Eisenhower approves funding for interstate highway system, spurring commerce and the population shift to the suburbs.

INVENTIONS: pacemaker, cordless TV remote control, bar codes, microchip.

SEX SYMBOLS: Marilyn Monroe & James Dean

VILLAIN: Sen. Joseph McCarthy (R-Wis.) held congressional hearings that became a witch hunt for communists in government, the military and the entertainment industry.

PERSONALITY OF THE DECADE: Elvis Presley

< MARILYN MONROE

>NICKNAMES<

Bill [Moose] Skowron ∧
Willie [the Say Hey Kid] Mays
Lawrence [Yogi] Berra
Henry [Hammerin' Hank] Aaron
Edward [Whitey] Ford
Billy [the Kid] Martin
Orestes [Minnie] Minoso
Ernie [Mr. Cub] Banks
Don [Popeye] Zimmer
Wilmer [Vinegar Bend] Mizell
[Puddin' Head] Willie Jones
James [Dusty] Rhodes
Luis [Yo-Yo] Arroyo
Sal [the Barber] Maglie
Frank [Taters] Lary
Harvey [the Kitten] Haddix
Roy [Squirrel] Sievers
Joe [Goofy] Adcock
Felix [the Cat] Mantilla
Frank [Pig] House
Norm [Smiley] Siebern
Mickey [the Commerce Comet] Mantle

BORN		DIED
LANCE ITO	1950	GEORGE BERNARD SHAW
STING	1951	WILLIAM RANDOLPH HEARST
BOB COSTAS	1952	EVITA PERON
HULK HOGAN	1953	JOSEF STALIN
OPRAH WINFREY >	1954	ENRICO FERMI
BILL GATES	1955	ALBERT EINSTEIN
LARRY BIRD	1956	JACKSON POLLOCK
SPIKE LEE	1957	< HUMPHREY BOGART
MICHAEL JACKSON	1958	TYRONE POWER
SARAH FERGUSON	1959	FRANK LLOYD WRIGHT

> NEWS OF THE REAL WORLD

1950: The Brink's bank job in Boston nets 11 thieves more than $2.7 million in 17 minutes **1951**: The 22nd Amendment to the U.S. Constitution, limiting Presidents to two terms, is ratified **1952**: They like Ike: Gen. Dwight Eisenhower elected president; he travels to Korea seeking end to conflict there **1953**: Francis Crick and James Watson discover the double-helix structure of DNA **1954**: British runner Roger Bannister runs the mile in 3:59.4 **1955**: Rosa Parks arrested in Montgomery, Ala., after refusing to give up her seat on a bus to a white man **1956**: Fidel Castro and Ché Guevara mount the insurgency in Cuba that will eventually overthrow regime of Fulgencio Batista **1957**: The U.S.S.R. launches *Sputnik I* and *II*, the first man-made satellites **1958**: U.S. aircraft accidentally drops atom bomb on Mars Bluff, S.C.—but it's a dud **1959**: Alaska and Hawaii become 49th and 50th states.

1959 | FRAMED BY the legs of his first base coach, the White Sox' Luis Aparicio beat the tag at first against the Indians. | *Photograph by* FRANCIS MILLER

1970 | JIM PALMER reared back and let it fly during a win against the Reds in Game 1 of the World Series. | *Photograph by* TONY TRIOLO

1964 | THE CARDINALS' potent battery of Bob Gibson and Tim McCarver made their jubilant exit after
Gibby's complete-game victory over the Yankees in Game 7 of the World Series. | *Photograph by* MARVIN E. NEWMAN

WILLIAMS DOES IT!

BY RICHARD HOFFER

*The author imagines a return to 1941 in order to recall one
of the great feats in baseball history—Ted Williams's run at .400.*
—*from* SI, JULY 19, 1993

PHILADELPHIA, SEPT. 28, 1941—
You can say this about the Kid: He does
some damage. He hit a shot here today in
Shibe Park that punched a hole in one of
Connie Mack's loudspeaker horns way out
there in right center. You add that bit of destruction to all the lights he took out in Fen-
way last year while he was taking target practice with a .22 on
the 400-foot sign, and you've got to admit that Ted Williams is
a player who brings a lot of overhead to the ballpark. If the Kid
continues to dismantle American League stadiums piece by
piece, well, the boys in the press box will have to come up with
another nickname for him—maybe the Splendid Splinter or
some such. (Hey, you heard it here first.)

Of course, if the Kid turns in a couple more .400 seasons like
this one for Boston, Mr. Tom Yawkey will gladly pay Mr. Mack for
the horn, even on top of the $18,000 salary he pays Williams.
It's well known that Mr. Yawkey thinks the world of the Kid—
just last year the two spent a couple afternoons shooting pigeons
inside Fenway with 20-gauge shotguns. But on Sunday against the
Athletics in Philadelphia, in a season-ending doubleheader,
Williams worked alone and used no firepower other than his
Louisville Slugger. Including that bolt off the speaker in right-
center (after the game, Williams said it was the hardest he'd ever
hit a ball), he was 6 for 8 in the twin bill and—*whew!*—finished
with a .406 average. Keep in mind, it's been 11 years since anyone
topped that magic mark; the last was Bill Terry, who batted .401
back in 1930 for the New York Giants. Williams was hitting as
high as .438 in June and .414 in mid-August, and people were
wondering if he'd break Hugh Duffy's record of .440, set before
the turn of the century.

But the Kid cooled with the weather, and in a recent 10-day
stretch he dropped nearly a point a day. With only the final
three games in Philadelphia left to play, he stood at .401. That
meant he'd need to go 5 for 12 to finish at .400. Even Joe Cronin,
the Red Sox manager, approached the Kid on Friday and of-
fered to sit him out, to protect that .401. But Williams told him
to pass the word that he wouldn't take any mollycoddling.

Down the stretch, most people have been rooting for the
Kid. In Yankee Stadium three weeks ago, the fans booed Lefty
Gomez when he walked Williams with the bases loaded. In
Detroit, Harry Heilmann (who hit .403 for the Tigers in 1923)
came down on the field from the Tiger radio booth, took
Williams aside and said, "Now, forget about that short fence.
Just hit the ball where you want it." In Philadelphia there was
at least one guy rooting against Williams: A's coach Al Simmons. Simmons hit .390 one year with the A's, and that ap-
parently was as high as he felt anyone should bat. "How much
do you want to bet you don't hit .400?" he groused to Williams
before Saturday's game.

Sure enough, the Kid got only one hit Saturday, and his average fell—we were back to doing high-level math—to .39955. A lot
of people might be inclined to round that off to .400, and maybe
with any other average you would. But the papers had it right
Sunday morning: WILLIAMS DROPS BELOW .400.

Saturday night Williams walked the streets of Philly with
the clubhouse boy, Johnny Orlando. His best friends are po-
licemen, theater managers and, of course, Johnny. According
to Johnny, the two of them walked about 10 miles; every now
and then Johnny would slip into a tavern for a quick Scotch
while the Kid would stop in a malt shop for a milk shake. You
knew something was up because Ted didn't get back to the
hotel until 10:30. He's usually in bed by 10.

So it all came down to the last day. Never mind the Kid's terrific year; never mind his game-winning homer in the All-Star
Game or even the 374-pound tuna he caught on an off-day. If he
missed .400, it was going to feel like a failed season.

His first time up, Williams rifled a drive in the hole between
first and second for a single. Almost before we could calculate
his average, the Kid homered and then singled two more times.
In the ninth inning he reached first on an error. It was a wild
game, with the Red Sox winning 12–11, but the only numbers
anyone paid attention to were 4 for 5. Williams was up to .404.
He'd have to go hitless in his next five at bats to drop below
.400. In the Kid's first at bat in the second game, he singled to
right. And then, in the fourth inning, he locked on that loudspeaker at the top of the wall and had to settle for a double,
while Mr. Mack tallied the damage in his notebook. Williams finally popped up in the seventh inning, the first time all day he
made an out, just before the game was called on account of
darkness. Final: Athletics 7, Red Sox 1, Williams .4057. . . .

ON THE last day of the season, playing a doubleheader and chasing .400, Williams had four singles, a double and a homer.

1981 | SCREWBALL SAVANT Fernando Valenzuela became the winner of Rookie of the Year and Cy Young honors in the same season. | *Photograph by* ANDY HAYT

1998 | IVAN RODRIGUEZ, a perennial Gold Glover, was the AL MVP in '99 with the Texas Rangers. | *Photograph by* PAUL BUCK

1948 | SATCHEL PAIGE had logged many miles on his cleats (above) and was already in his 40s by the time he made it to the major leagues. | *Photograph by* GEORGE SILK

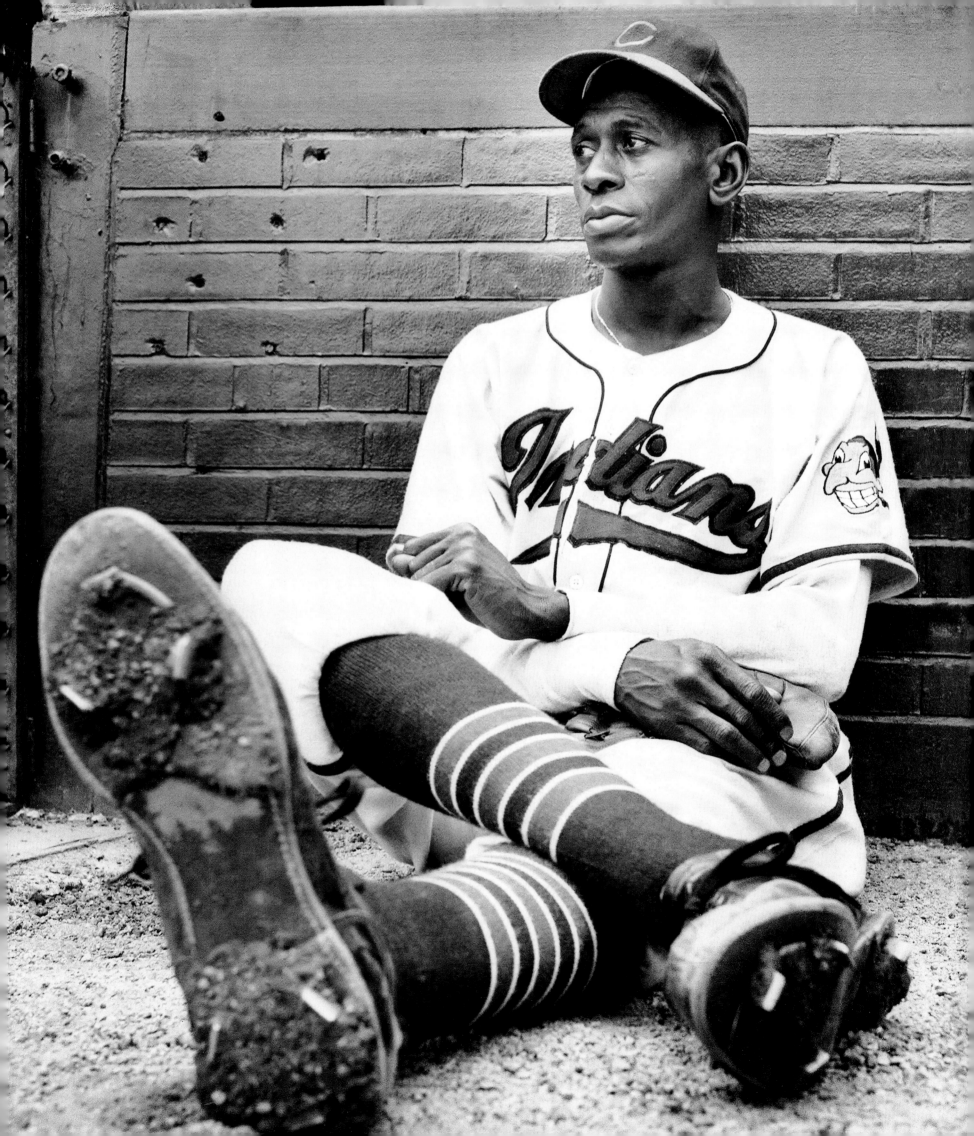

A WORKINGMAN'S HERO

BY RICHARD HOFFER

By showing up every day, Cal Ripken restored the faith of baseball fans and showed that while he's not the greatest player of his generation, he is one of the game's greatest sportsmen.

—*from* SI, DECEMBER 18, 1995

THERE'S A MAN, CLOSE-cropped gray hair, looks older than 35 in the partial glow of stadium lights, standing along the railing of an empty field, signing autographs hours after a game. He doesn't really have any place to go, his family is asleep, so it's no big deal. He signs away, not to rekindle a country's love affair with its national pastime (that kind of calculation is beyond him) but because somebody wants something and it's easy to give. A teammate offers him a big leaguer's diagnosis: "You're sick."

The man shrugs. He has played in more games consecutively than any other man, dead or alive. Punched in, punched out. It's not so much a record, not a reward for greatness, as it is a by-product of sustained adolescence and, of course, unusual good health. A milestone is all it is. He knows it too. The man shrugs, signing away beneath the stadium lights. "If you could play baseball every day," he says, "wouldn't you?"

Cal Ripken Jr., though he'll surely go into the Hall of Fame, is not the greatest baseball player ever, or even of his day. But he's dedicated to his craft, respectful of his game and this year, he almost single-handedly restored the once loyal fan's faith in baseball, single-handedly turned attention to a pioneer work ethic. His "assault" on Lou Gehrig's record of 2,130 consecutive games played was surely the least dramatic record run of all time. We knew for years that, barring an injury to Ripken, Gehrig's record was going to fall. There was nothing conditional about this record except Ripken's attendance. He didn't have to hit in his 57th straight game, pitch a seventh no-hitter, clout his 62nd home run. And assuming a fan could read a baseball schedule, he knew months in advance exactly when (Sept. 6) and where (Camden Yards) it would occur. No record, before or since, has been set with less pressure. All Ripken had to do to set it was be there.

Yet it turned out to be one of the great feel-good events in sports—ever—and if there wasn't a lump in your throat when Ripken circled the field in a reluctant victory lap, you weren't paying attention. In a sport accustomed to celebrating freaks of different and unique abilities, Ripken was instead a freak of disposition. He just liked to play baseball. You can't play 14 seasons through and through if you don't like it. Why Ripken liked baseball this much is anyone's guess, though there surely is a genetic component to it.

For him family life was the residue of baseball; it was whatever was left over from the game. Cal Sr. was a longtime manager and coach in the Orioles organization, making stops in places like Elmira and Rochester, dragging the family along. And Cal Jr. took to the game, understanding his childhood to be privileged—taking infield practice with future major leaguers or just listening to his father detail the Orioles cutoff play. As a 12-year-old he was developing resource material.

Still, heredity doesn't account for the sense of obligation and appreciation he has for baseball. Nor does his entry into pro ball, when scouts placed him on the slow track, to the extent they put him on any track at all. Remember that Ripken was not encouraged to believe he had any special talents back in 1978, when eight shortstops were picked ahead of him in the baseball draft.

Sixteen years later he has outlasted those eight and plenty more. His endurance has become the new standard of sport, and his run for the record couldn't have been more timely. In an era of slouching gods, this devotion to duty was a curative. Here was Ripken, looking somewhat old in his gray-stubble buzz cut, coming to the park every day. It helped that he didn't bounce around, didn't exaggerate his love of the game, didn't act like some caricatured goof from a Norman Rockwell painting. He just kept coming to work because . . . why *wouldn't* you? "Look," he says, wholly ignorant of the heavenly glow he might attach to his myth with this statement, "the season's long, 162 games, and a pennant could be decided in any one of them. You never know which one. But do you want to take a chance? Is that the game you'd want to sit out?"

A devotion to principle, whether that principle makes much sense to the rest of us, is usually something to marvel at. And Ripken's devotion to his principle, to play well and at every opportunity, knows no season. . . . Of course no country, not even one as unabashedly sentimental as ours, would reward an athlete with affection based on attendance. Ripken did more than just show up every day; he was and is a good player: Maybe his offensive numbers don't stack up

with Gehrig's, but they'll do for a shortstop of any generation. Just in case you thought the Streak was the product
of some Baltimore hype, remember that he was chosen by
fans across the nation to start in 13 straight All-Star Games
and that in 1991—when he hit .323 with 34 home runs and
114 RBIs in one of the best years ever by a shortstop—he
was the American League MVP.

It is no doubt infuriating to today's athletes that our expec-
tations of them are contradictory. We want them to behave as
adults, even though we want them to play with the enthusi-
asm of children. We want them to act modestly, even though we
shower them with attention. We want them to treat their job

like work, even though we consider it a game. Not many athletes of any generation can deal gracefully with our antitheti-
cal yearnings; Ripken is one of the few. . . .

How long has it been since the fan has had to acknowledge
the athlete's give instead of his take? Since he was forced to
recognize an athlete's diligence, stability, effort? It feels as if
it has been ages, doesn't it, since sports was something other
than a playful preamble to an advertising career? But at least
the fan had this year to arrest his growing cynicism. Maybe the
fan just needs to know where to look: down the first base line,
where in the half glow of stadium lights a gray-haired guy signs
autographs into the wee hours. . . .

RIPKEN REACHED out to fans in Baltimore after he surpassed Gehrig's consecutive-games streak.

2005 | MARLINS CATCHER Matt Treanor went flat-out in the home stretch to nail Padres rightfielder Brian Giles. | *Photograph by* ROBERT BECK

1933 | YANKEES OUTFIELDER Ben Chapman beat the tag of Senators catcher Luke Sewell in Washington. | *Photograph by* BETTMANN/CORBIS

1938 | THE DODGERS' Pete Coscarart was dwarfed by Reds' catcher Ernie Lombardi at Ebbets Field's first night game. | *Photograph by* BETTMANN/CORBIS

1961 | ROGER MARIS could steal home runs from Yankee Stadium's short rightfield porch as well as hitting them there. | *Photograph by* BETTMANN/CORBIS

YOU HAD TO SEE IT TO BELIEVE IT

BY RICK REILLY

In his pursuit of Roger Maris and the mystical home run record, Mark McGwire briefly took baseball—and America—on a fantasy ride back to a simpler time. —from SI, SEPTEMBER 14, 1998

TO MY GRANDDAUGHTER: I write this now, 40 years after the fact, because I want you to know how it really was, not through some yellowed video you play on your contact lenses. I've seen a few things. I saw a 46-year-old Jack Nicklaus win a Masters with tears in his eyes. I saw North Carolina State win an NCAA basketball title with eight nobodies. I saw a heavyweight title fight turn into a human buffet. But I've never seen anything like Mark McGwire chasing Roger Maris's home run record.

People stood on seats through every one of his at bats. Fans held up MARK, HIT IT HERE signs at football games. So many flashes would go off as he swung, Busch Stadium looked like a giant bowl of blinking Christmas lights.

That was such an odd time in this country. Washington seemed to be filled with liars, cheats and scumbags, yet our games were as pure and shiny as I'd ever seen them. I still think that year in sports, 1998, was the best of my lifetime. A bow-legged magician named John Elway finally won a Super Bowl. Michael Jordan became the first person in history to steal an NBA title in 42 seconds. Pete Sampras's serve was only a rumor.

But the best of all was this simple, joyful home run chase that didn't involve salary caps or parole boards or even Don King. Around laptops logged on to the Internet, nightly TV highlight shows and morning sports sections, the whole nation was brought together by a giant playing a kid's game. One day as McGwire was coming up on 60, an older couple was making their way through the airport in St. Louis, he limping along, she holding his hand. Suddenly from every cocktail lounge came this huge roar. It could only mean one thing. The couple turned and hugged. Their son had hit another.

You're the 14-year-old MVP of your Mark McGwire League and you always have your chocolatey McGwire after the game and all your buddies' parents are named McGwire This and McGwire That, but back then we knew him as a person.

I can still see his face. He had this withering glare at the plate, like a bouncer with bunions, but he was as quick to laugh as any man I've known. He would sign for all the kids, but he could spot a collector at a hundred rows. He would pick a piece of spinach out of his teeth and it would make the 11 o'clock news, yet he stayed decent and next-door through it all.

And then the strangest thing started happening. People started acting decent and next-door too. Nearly every time he'd hit a home run, fans would give the ball back to him, walking straight past collectors offering tens of thousands of dollars. Opposing pitchers talked about how "cool" it would be to give up number 62. The home run race was as American as a Corvette. The day McGwire tied Babe Ruth at 60, for instance, began with the St. Louis Cardinals unveiling a statue of Stan (the Man) Musial, who then went out and stood at home plate and played *Take Me Out to the Ball Game* on his harmonica in a red sport coat and red shoes at high noon on Labor Day weekend in the middle of the nation.

Sometimes you were sure the whole thing was a DreamWorks production. When McGwire hit his 61st, he hit it in front of his father, John, who turned 61 that day. He hit it in front of his 10-year-old Cardinals batboy son, Matt, whom he scooped up and hugged. He hit it in front of the sons of Maris, the man who had been so tortured by the number, and now, thanks to McGwire, redeemed by it. McGwire saluted them, touched his heart and threw a kiss to the sky in Maris's memory. And in the chaos John said quietly to himself, "What a wonderful gift."

Earlier, after another cloudscraper, McGwire sat down in a cavern under the stands and started answering questions from 600 reporters in his own square-as-fudge way. Two seconds after each answer, he'd hear this great cheer coming from the field. He couldn't figure it out until somebody explained that the press conference was being piped outside to the thousands of fans who had waited, in the wilting Missouri heat, an hour after the game to hear him.

Well, that was just too much for McGwire. He took his big waffle-sized hands and pulled his hat over his head and leaned back in his chair and giggled. "They're still here?" he said.

Some of us never left. . . .

LONG BEFORE BALCO entered the baseball vocabulary, Mark McGwire thrilled the nation with his 70th home run, against the Expos.

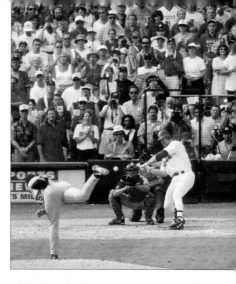

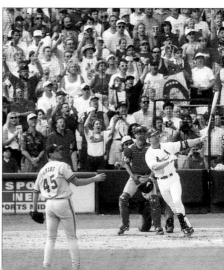

4 8 31 TOR 4 20 CWS 0 2 43 BALT 61 CLE 45 SEA
12 61 BOS 4 6 52 NYY 0 2 30 T.B. 41 K.C. 55 OAK

2004 | THE MILWAUKEE light was prettier than the bat-work by the Brewers' rightfielder Ben Grieve,
who bounced harmlessly to Astros first baseman Jeff Bagwell. | *Photograph by* JONATHAN DANIEL

THE MICK ALWAYS SWUNG FROM THE HEELS

BY RICHARD HOFFER

Upon Mickey Mantle's passing in 1995, SI considered the legacy of the greatest player on the last great team.

—*from* SI, AUGUST 21, 1995

MICKEY MANTLE, with his death Sunday at 63, passes from these pages forever and becomes the property of anthropologists, people who can more properly put the calipers to celebrity, who can more accurately track the force of personality. We can't do it anymore, couldn't really do it to begin with. He batted this, hit that. You can look it up. But there's nothing in our library, in all those numbers, that explains how Mantle moved so smoothly from baseball history into national legend, a country's touchstone, the lopsided grin on our society.

He wasn't the greatest player who ever lived, not even of his time perhaps. He was a centerfielder of surprising swiftness, a switch-hitter of heart-stopping power, and he was given to spectacle: huge home runs (the Yankees invented the tape-measure home run for him); huge seasons (.353, 52 HRs, 130 RBIs to win the Triple Crown in 1956); one World Series after another (12 in his first 14 seasons). Yet, for one reason or another, he never became Babe Ruth or Joe DiMaggio—or, arguably, even Willie Mays, his exact contemporary.

But for generations of men, he's the guy, has been the guy, will always be the guy. And what does that mean exactly? A woman beseeches Mantle, who survived beyond his baseball

MANTLE HAD awesome power from both sides of the plate.

career as a kind of corporate greeter, to make an appearance, to surprise her husband. Mantle materializes at some cocktail party, introductions are made, and the husband weeps in the presence of such fantasy made flesh. It means that, exactly.

IT'S EASY TO ACCOUNT, AT least partly, for the durability and depth of his fame: He played on baseball's most famous team during the game's final dominant era. From Mantle's rookie season in 1951—the lead miner's son signed out of Commerce, Okla., for $1,100—to his injury-racked final year in 1968, baseball was still the pre-eminent game in the country. Year in, year out, men and boys in every corner of the country were given to understand during this autumnal rite that there really was only one baseball team and that there really was only one player: No. 7, talked with a twang, knocked the ball a country mile. But it was more than circumstance that fixed Mantle in the national psyche; he did hit 18 World Series home runs, a record, over the course of 65 of the most watched games of our lives.

Even knowing that, acknowledging the pin-striped pedigree, the fascination still doesn't add up. If he was a pure talent, he was not, as we found out, a pure spirit. But to look upon his youthful mug today, three decades after he played, is to realize how uncluttered our memories of him are. Yes, he was a confessed drunk; yes, he shorted his potential—he himself said so. And still, looking at the slightly uplifted square jaw, all we see is America's romance with boldness, its celebration of muscle, a continent's comfort in power during a time when might did make right. Mantle was the last great player on the last great team in the last great country, a postwar civilization that was booming and confident, not a trouble in the world.

Of course, even had he not reflected the times, Mantle would have been walking Americana. His career was storybook stuff, hewing more to our ideas of myth than any player's since Ruth. Spotted playing shortstop on the Baxter Springs Whiz Kids, he was delivered from a rural obscurity into America's distilled essence of glamour. One year Mantle is dropping 400 feet into the earth, very deep into Oklahoma, to mine lead on his father's crew, another he's spilling drinks with Whitey Ford and Billy Martin at the Copa.

A lesson reaffirmed: Anything can happen to anybody in this country, so long as they're daring in their defeats and outsized in victory. Failure is forgiven of the big swingers, in whom even foolishness is flamboyant. Do you remember Mantle in Pittsburgh in the 1960 Series, twice whiffing in Game 1 and then, the next day, crushing two? Generations of men still do. The world will always belong to those who swing from the heels.

Still, Mantle's grace was mostly between the lines; he developed no particular bonds beyond his teammates, and he established no popularity outside of baseball. As he was dying from liver cancer, none of the pre-tributes remarked much on his charm. And, as he was dying from a disease that many have presumed was drinking-related, there was a revisionist cast to the remembrances. Maybe he wasn't so much fun after all.

But back then, he most certainly was. Drunkenness had a kind of high-life cachet in the '50s. Down the road, as Mantle would later confess from the other side of rehabilitation, it was merely stupid. But palling around with Billy and Whitey—just boys, really, they all had little boys' names—it amounted to low-grade mischief. Whatever harm was being done to families and friends, it was a small price to pay for the excitement conferred upon a workaday nation.

In any event, we don't mind our heroes flawed, or even doomed. Actually, our interest in Mantle was probably piqued by his obvious destiny, the ruin he often foretold. As a Yankee he was never a whole person, having torn up his knee for the first time in his first World Series in '51. Thereafter, increasingly, he played in gauze and pain, his prodigal blasts heroically backlit by chronic injury. But more: At the hospital after that '51 incident, Mantle learned that his father, Mutt, admitted to the same hospital that same day, was dying of Hodgkin's disease. It was a genetic devastation that had claimed every Mantle male before the age of 40. The black knowledge of this looming end informed everything Mickey did; there was little time, and every event had to be performed on a grand scale, damn the consequences. Everything was excused.

As we all know, it didn't end with that kind of drama. It was Billy, the third of Mantle's four sons, who came down with Hodgkin's, and who later died of a heart attack at 36. Mickey lived much longer, prospering in an era of nostalgia, directionless in golf and drinking, coasting on a fame that confounded him.

Then Mantle, who might forever have been embedded in a certain culture, square-jawed and unchanged, did a strange thing. Having failed to die in a way that might have satisfied the mythmakers, he awoke with a start and checked himself into the Betty Ford Center. This was only a year and a half ago, and, of course, it was way too late almost any way you figure it. Still, his remorse seemed genuine. The waste seemed to gall him, and his anger shook the rest of us.

The generations of men who watched him play baseball, flipped for his cards or examined every box score must now puzzle out the attraction he held. Let's just say you were of this generation: that you once had been a kid growing up in the '50s, on some baseball team in Indiana, and you remember stitching a No. 7 on the back of your KIRCHNER'S PHARMACY T-shirt, using red thread and having no way of finishing off a stitch, meaning your hero's number would unravel indefinitely and you would have to do it over and over, stupid and unreformed in your idolatry. And today here's this distant demigod, in his death, taking human shape. What would you think now? . . .

MANTLE WAS widely regarded as the fastest man in baseball when he broke in, but he was hobbled by injuries, and had four knee surgeries.

1999 | ASTROS FIRST baseman Jeff Bagwell bagged a hot smash off a Braves bat during the NL divisional playoffs in Atlanta. | *Photograph by* AL TIELEMANS

1987 | METS OUTFIELDER Kevin McReynolds tried but failed to keep Ozzie Smith from turning a double play at Shea. | *Photograph by* BETTMANN/CORBIS

SANDY KOUFAX won 25 games three times for the Dodgers, claimed five straight ERA titles and threw four no-hitters, including a perfect game in 1965. | *Photograph by* JOHN G. ZIMMERMAN

>THE ALL-DECADE TEAMS

AMERICAN LEAGUE	NATIONAL LEAGUE
CATCHER	CATCHER
Elston Howard	Joe Torre
FIRST BASE	FIRST BASE
Harmon Killebrew	Orlando Cepeda
SECOND BASE	SECOND BASE
Bobby Richardson	Bill Mazeroski
SHORTSTOP	SHORTSTOP
Luis Aparicio	Maury Wills
THIRD BASE	THIRD BASE
Brooks Robinson	Ron Santo
LEFTFIELD	LEFTFIELD
Carl Yastrzemski	Billy Williams
CENTERFIELD	CENTERFIELD
Mickey Mantle	Willie Mays
RIGHTFIELD	RIGHTFIELD
Frank Robinson	Hank Aaron
STARTING PITCHER	STARTING PITCHER
Jim Bunning	Sandy Koufax
RELIEF PITCHER	RELIEF PITCHER
Hoyt Wilhelm	Elroy Face

>DEBUT   FINALE<

DEBUT	Year	FINALE
RON SANTO	1960	TED WILLIAMS
CARL YASTRZEMSKI	1961	TED KLUSZEWSKI
GAYLORD PERRY	1962	RICHIE ASHBURN
PETE ROSE	1963	STAN MUSIAL
TONY PEREZ	1964	DUKE SNIDER
JIM PALMER	1965	YOGI BERRA
NOLAN RYAN	1966	SANDY KOUFAX
TOM SEAVER	1967	DON LARSEN
BOBBY BONDS	1968	MICKEY MANTLE
CARLTON FISK	1969	DON DRYSDALE

>THE LEADERS

HITTING

BATTING AVERAGE* ROBERTO CLEMENTE	...328
HOME RUNS HARMON KILLEBREW	.393
RBI HANK AARON	1,107
AT BATS BROOKS ROBINSON	6,093
HITS ROBERTO CLEMENTE	1,877

SINGLES MAURY WILLS	1,529
DOUBLES CARL YASTRZEMSKI	318
TRIPLES ROBERTO CLEMENTE	99
OBP* MICKEY MANTLE	415
SLUGGING PCT.* HANK AARON	565
RUNS HANK AARON	1,091
STOLEN BASES MAURY WILLS	535
HIT BY PITCHES FRANK ROBINSON	113

WALKS HARMON KILLEBREW	970
STRIKEOUTS FRANK HOWARD	1,103
GAMES BROOKS ROBINSON	1,578

PITCHING

WINS JUAN MARICHAL	191
LOSSES JACK FISHER	133
WINNING PCT.† SANDY KOUFAX	695
STRIKEOUTS BOB GIBSON	2,071

ERA† HOYT WILHELM	2.16
INNINGS DON DRYSDALE	2,629
WALKS STEVE BARBER	834
RUNS ALLOWED DICK ELLSWORTH	993
HOME RUNS ALLOWED JIM BUNNING	230
SAVES HOYT WILHELM	152
SHUTOUTS JUAN MARICHAL	45
COMPLETE GAMES JUAN MARICHAL	197

* MINIMUM 2,500 PLATE APPEARANCES † MINIMUM 1,000 INNINGS

>HOT TICKETS 10 Games You Wish You'd Seen

EXHIBITION GAME NO. 1
HOUSTON vs.
NEW YORK YANKEES

THE ASTRODOME

WELDON, WILLIAMS & LICK, FT. SMITH, ARK.

Forbes Field Oct. 13, 1960 Pirates second baseman Bill Mazeroski hits the first walk-off World Series–ending home run, in Game 7 against the Yankees.

Candlestick Park Oct. 16, 1962 Yankees second baseman Bobby Richardson catches Willie McCovey's line drive with two on and two out in the bottom of the ninth inning of Game 7 to lock up a 1–0 win and a World Series title for New York.

Yankee Stadium Oct. 1, 1961 In the fourth inning of New York's final game, reigning AL MVP Roger Maris hits his 61st home run of the season into the rightfield stands off Tracy Stallard of the Red Sox to break Babe Ruth's 34-year-old single-season record.

Fenway Park Sept. 28, 1960 In the final at bat of his Hall of Fame career, Ted Williams hits his 521st career home run against the Orioles' Jack Fisher in the eighth inning of a 5–4 Boston win.

Busch Stadium Oct. 2, 1968 St. Louis righthander Bob Gibson fans a World Series–record 17 Tigers and allows just five hits in the Cardinals' 4–0 Game 1 win.

∧ **The Astrodome** April 9, 1965 Baseball's first indoor stadium opens with an exhibition game between the newly renamed Astros (formerly the Colt .45s) and the Yankees. Mickey Mantle hits the first indoor home run, but the Astros win 2–1 in 12 innings.

Wrigley Field Aug. 19, 1965 The Reds' Jim Maloney no-hits the Cubs for 10 innings and wins 1–0. Two months earlier Maloney pitched 10 hitless innings against the Mets only to lose the no-hitter and the game on an 11th-inning home run.

Crosley Field June 8, 1961 Eddie Mathews, Hank Aaron, Joe Adcock and Frank Thomas of the Braves hit consecutive home runs in the seventh inning against the Reds, but Cincinnati wins 10–8.

Candlestick Park July 3, 1966 Braves pitcher Tony Cloninger drives in nine runs with two grand slams and an RBI single in a 17–3 win over the Giants.

Municipal Stadium Sept. 25, 1965 Negro leagues great Satchel Paige, at age 59 years, 2 months and 18 days, makes his final major league appearance, hurling three scoreless innings for the A's against the Red Sox. He's still the oldest player to suit up in a big league game.

BEST OF THE 1960s

TEAM	WINS	LOSSES	WIN PCT.
ORIOLES	911	698	.566
GIANTS	902	704	.562
YANKEES	887	720	.551
CARDINALS	884	718	.551
TIGERS	882	729	.547

WILLIE McCOVEY, GIANTS

WORST OF THE 1960s

TEAM	WINS	LOSSES	WIN PCT.
EXPOS	52	110	.321
PADRES	52	110	.321
METS	494	799	.382
PILOTS	64	98	.395
SENATORS ('61–69)	607	844	.418

NOLAN RYAN, METS

1960s CULTURE

MUSIC OF THE DECADE: *Sgt. Pepper's Lonely Hearts Club Band* (The Beatles), *Blonde on Blonde* (Bob Dylan), *Live at the Apollo* (James Brown), *Pet Sounds* (Beach Boys)

MOVIES OF THE DECADE: *The Sound of Music, The Graduate, Psycho, 2001: A Space Odyssey, Butch Cassidy and the Sundance Kid*

TELEVISION SHOWS OF THE DECADE: *Bonanza, The Ed Sullivan Show, The Dick Van Dyke Show, Star Trek, The Price Is Right*

BOOKS OF THE DECADE: *Catch-22* by Joseph Heller; *Human Sexual Response* by William Masters and Virginia Johnson; *In Cold Blood* by Truman Capote; *Portnoy's Complaint* by Philip Roth; *Understanding Media* by Marshall McLuhan

ACHIEVEMENT: President Kennedy challenged the U.S. space program to put a man on the moon by the decade's end, and on July 20, 1969 NASA did just that.

INVENTIONS: audio cassette; AstroTurf; Kevlar; computer mouse

SEX SYMBOLS: Raquel Welch & Steve McQueen

VILLAINS: Assassins Lee Harvey Oswald (John F. Kennedy, Dallas, November '63), James Earl Ray (Martin Luther King Jr., Memphis, April '68) and Sirhan Sirhan (Robert F. Kennedy, L.A., June '68)

PERSONALITIES OF THE DECADE: The Beatles

< RAQUEL WELCH

>NICKNAMES<

[Sudden] Sam McDowell ∧
Ken [Hawk] Harrelson
Johnny [Blue Moon] Odom
Octavio [Cookie] Rojas
Jimmy [the Toy Cannon] Wynn
Willie [Stretch] McCovey
Gene [Stick] Michael
Derrel [Bud] Harrelson
Jim [Mudcat] Grant
Tom [Terrific] Seaver
Clarence [Choo Choo] Coleman
Pete [Charlie Hustle] Rose
Jim [Kitty] Kaat
Bob [Buck] Rodgers
Orlando [Baby Bull] Cepeda
Clay [Dimples] Dalrymple
Bob [Beetle] Bailey
John [Boog] Powell
Albert [Sparky] Lyle
Dick [the Monster] Radatz
Elijah [Pumpsie] Green
Juan [the Dominican Dandy] Marichal

BORN		DIED
Bono	1960	Clark Gable
Barack Obama	1961	Ernest Hemingway
Tom Cruise >	1962	Marilyn Monroe
Michael Jordan	1963	John F. Kennedy
Russell Crowe	1964	Harpo Marx
J.K. Rowling	1965	Winston Churchill
Mike Tyson	1966	< Walt Disney
Pamela Anderson	1967	Carl Sandburg
LL Cool J	1968	Martin Luther King Jr.
Brett Favre	1969	Dwight D. Eisenhower

> NEWS OF THE REAL WORLD

1960: Soviets shoot down U2 spy plane near Yekaterinburg, Russia—U.S. pilot Gary Powers captured; FDA approves birth control pill **1961:** John F. Kennedy becomes first Catholic—and youngest man—elected U.S. President **1962:** Missiles spotted in Cuba trigger nuclear standoff between U.S. and U.S.S.R. **1963:** The Zone Improvement Plan is instituted by Postal Service, giving birth to ZIP codes **1964:** Three civil rights workers murdered in Mississippi, helping prompt passage of U.S. Civil Rights Act **1965:** Martin Luther King Jr., leads four-day voting rights march from Selma to Montgomery, Ala. **1966:** Supreme Court rules in *Miranda* vs. *Arizona*, establishing rights for criminal suspects when arrested **1967:** Packers beat Chiefs 35–10 in first AFL-NFL title game, dubbed "Super Bowl" **1968:** Antiwar protesters battle Chicago police near Democratic convention **1969:** Followers of Charles Manson kill seven, including actress Sharon Tate, in Beverly Hills

2001 | LARRY WALKER (center) made a catch in short rightfield despite an assist from Rockies infielders Todd Helton and Todd Walker. | *Photograph by* ROBERT BECK

1995 | BRAVES SHORTSTOP Jeff Blauser took the high road to field the throw when the Dodgers' Delino DeShields stole second. | *Photograph by* V.J. LOVERO

1968 | THE ONLY pennant-winning Cardinals not identifiable by their jerseys were Roger Maris (far left) and manager Red Schoendienst (right). | *Photograph by* NEIL LEIFER

1993 | CARDINALS MASCOT Fredbird took some time to smooth his feathers and smother his appetite in St. Louis. | *Photograph by* RONALD C. MODRA

ACHES AND PAINS AND THREE BATTING TITLES

BY MYRON COPE

How good was Roberto Clemente? Though the Pirates outfielder suffered countless real and imagined ailments, Sandy Koufax said that the only way to pitch him was to roll the ball up to the plate. —*from* SI, MARCH 7, 1966

THE BATTING CHAMPION of the major leagues lowered himself to the pea-green carpet of his 48-foot living room and sprawled on his right side, flinging his left leg over his right leg. He wore gold Oriental pajama tops, tan slacks, battered bedroom slippers and— for purposes of the demonstration he was conducting—a tortured grimace. "Like dis!" he cried, and then dug his fingers into his flesh, just above his upraised left hip. Roberto Clemente, the Pittsburgh Pirates' marvelous rightfielder and their steadiest customer of the medical profession, was showing how he must greet each new day in his life. He has a disk in his back that insists on wandering, so when he awakens he must cross those legs, dig at the flesh and listen for the sound of the disk popping back where it belongs.

Around the room necks were craned and ears alerted for the successful conclusion of the demonstration. Clemente's wife—the tall, beautiful Vera—sat solemnly in a gold wing chair a few feet away. Way out in the rightfield seats, ensconced on a $1,000 velvet sofa in what may be called the Italian Provincial division of Clemente's vast living room, were his 18-year-old nephew, Pablo, and Pablo's buddy, Wilson. They sat fascinated, or at least they seemed fascinated, for it may have been that Wilson, who says his hobby is girls, was wishing that minute that Roberto would lend them his Cadillac.

"No, you cannot hear the disk now," shouted Roberto. "It is in place now. But every morning you can hear it from here to there, in the whole room. *Boop!*"

Boop? Certainly, boop. Not only one boop but two, for there is another disk running around up in the vicinity of Roberto's neck. For that one he must have someone manipulate his neck muscles until the boop is heard.

All this herding of disks, mind you, is but a nub on the staggering list of medical attentions that Clemente has undergone during his 11 years as a Pirate. Relatively small at 5' 10" and 180 pounds when able to take nourishment, the chronic invalid has smooth skin, glistening muscles and perfect facial contours that suggest the sturdy mahogany sculpture peddled in the souvenir shops of his native Puerto Rico. His countrymen regard him as the most superb all-round big-leaguer to emerge from this island, while many Pittsburghers have concluded that the only thing that can keep Clemente from making them forget Paul Waner is a sudden attack of good health.

Now 31, Clemente over the past five pain-filled years has won three National League batting championships (to say nothing of leading both leagues for the past two years) and has averaged .330, a level of consistency that no other big-leaguer has equaled during this half decade. In strength and accuracy his throwing arm has surpassed that of the old Brooklyn cannon, Carl Furillo, and if Roberto's genes are any indication, his arm is not about to weaken. "My mother is 75," he says. "Last year she threw out the first pitch of the season. She put something on it, too." Because Roberto smolders with an intense belief in himself, some ballplayers argue that his only real malady is a serious puffing of the head, but the clicking of the X-ray machines, the scraping of scalpels, the trickle of intravenous feeding and the scratching of pens upon prescription pads have mounted to such a fortissimo that Roberto would seem to be a fit subject for graduate research. The moment when Roberto first set eyes on his wife is the story of his life: He spied her in a drugstore, where he had gone to buy medication for an ailing leg.

"I played only two innings in the winter league this year," sighed Roberto, having picked himself off the carpet and dumped himself into a chair. "I was having headaches, headaches, headaches, so I had to quit. . . . My head still hurts. The pain splits my head. The doctors say it's tension. They say I worry too much. I've tried tranquilizers, but they don't work. My foot is killing me. I got this tendon in my left heel that rubs against the bone, and I cannot run on it at all. I'm weary, I tell you. All the time it's go here, speak there, do dis,

do dat. Always, always, always. When I go to spring training, that's when I take my rest." . . .

Surely the Lord cannot be punishing Roberto. A generous man and the devoted father of an infant son, he has been the sole support—since age 17—of his parents, a niece and nephew Pablo, to whom he recently gave an 18-foot cruiser. Before that he built a house for his parents. When pitcher Diomedes Olivo joined the Pirates at age 41, too late to make a pile, Roberto gave him half of all his banquet fees.

"I always try to lead the clean life," says Roberto. He does not smoke and rarely drinks, indulging himself only in his original milkshake recipes. Sighing and limping through his clean life, Roberto has acquired a reputation as baseball's champion hypochondriac, but his personal physician, Dr. Roberto Busó of San Juan, says, "I wouldn't call him a true

hypochondriac, because he doesn't go to the extreme of just sitting down and brooding." Far from it. Roberto gallops across the outfield making acrobatic catches; with a bat in his hands he is all over the batter's box, spinning like a top when he swings.

"I'm convinced of his weakness," says Dodger vice president Fresco Thompson. "Throw the best ball you've got right down the middle. If you pitch him high and outside, he'll rap a shot into rightfield. If you pitch him high and outside, he'll rap a shot into rightfield. If you throw one to him on one hop, he'll bounce it back through the mound and it'll probably take your pitcher and second baseman with it."

In the past few years, alas, Roberto has become relatively orthodox. "If I have to jump three feet over my head to hit the ball, now I don't do it," he points out, deadly serious. . . .

CLEMENTE WAS an incomparable outfielder, with a cannon for an arm, and he was fearsome with a bat in his hands.

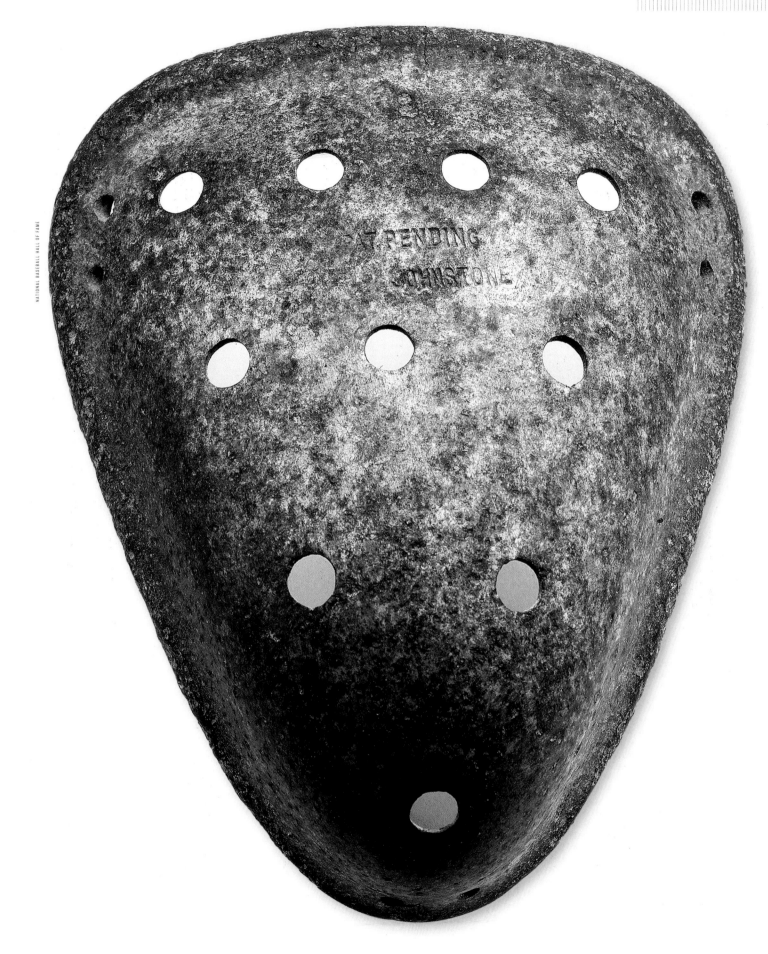

PAT. PENDING
JOHNSTONE

1915 | THE FIRST known protective cup was worn by Claude Berry when he was catching for the Pittsburgh Rebels. | *Photograph by* BRET WILLS

1930 | AL LOPEZ broke into the bigs with the Dodgers in '28 and played 19 years before a Hall of Fame managing career. | *Photograph by* TSN ARCHIVE

1908 | JOHNNY EVERS kicked up a cloud of dust trying to slide past the Tigers' Boss Schmidt in the last World Series won by the Cubs. | *Photograph by* DAVID R. PHILLIPS COLLECTION

2001 | CHRIS STYNES of the Red Sox thought he could score from first on a double against the Devil Rays; he was wrong. | *Photograph by* STEVE JACOBSON

STANDING TALL AT SHORT

BY STEVE WULF

The great abundance of hungry young players in the Dominican Republic made the tiny, impoverished country the world's leading exporter of shortstops. —*from* SI, FEBRUARY 9, 1987

THE SMELLS FROM THE sugarcane factory and the garbage dump are playing one another in the Barrio Blanco of San Pedro de Macorís, and for now, at least, the sugar is winning. So is the pickup team that has Carlos Ramirez at shortstop. Kids, both children and goats, look on as Carlos takes his position to start the fourth inning. He carries himself like Tony Fernandez, the great Cabeza—the way he stands, daring the batter to hit the ball to him, the way he wears his hat, tilted down over his head. The batter sends a grounder deep into the hole between short and third, and Carlos ranges far to his right to get his glove on it. His throw to first arrives on a bounce, too late to get the runner, and he kicks the dirt in frustration. But there is plenty of time for him to get other runners, for he is only 12 years old.

On farmland north of Santo Domingo, Epy Guerrero, the scout who signed Cabeza and so many others, runs a baseball farm, Complejo Deportivo Epy, for the Toronto Blue Jays. On this winter day, Guerrero is hitting grounders to infielders he will soon be sending to Toronto's minor league teams. Each ball stretches them to the limits of their range. *"Tú eres el hombre de La Mancha,"* Guerrero shouts as he hits one just past the glove of a shortstop named Batista del Rosario, *"¡Cazas el sueño!"* You are Don Quixote, chasing the dream.

Exact figures aren't available, but at least 71 shortstops from the Dominican Republic were under contract to major league teams last season. Every team had at least one in its system; the Blue Jays had no fewer than eight, including Santiago Garcia, from the Barrio Blanco. And even as you read these words, more shortstops are being signed. *"Nosotros somos la Tierra de Mediocampistas,"* says Felix Acosta Nuñez, the sports editor of Santo Domingo's *Listín Diario*. "We are the Land of Shortstops."

The Land of Shorlys might be a more appropriate motto; the word shortstop comes out "shorly" when Dominican children gather for a pickup game. "Shorly! Shorly!" they'll shout to claim the position. Hundreds of games are under way at any one time in San Pedro de Macorís, the heart of Dominican baseball. San Pedro is a port city of 78,562 people, but it is also a region encompassing 150,000, with several small sugarcane communities. Thirteen Macorístas played in the majors last year, seven of them shortstops.

The players who have made it in the big leagues generously buy gear for the kids, but there is never enough to go around. Too often the youngsters must make do with a glove fashioned from a milk carton, a ball that is a sewed-up sock and a bat made from a guava tree limb. (Ironically, a baseball made in Haiti, the western tenant of the island of Hispaniola, costs $7 in the Dominican Republic and $5 in New York City.)

In the Dominican Republic, where the average family income is $1,200 a year, poverty is not an isolated problem; it's the way of life. Also, the quality of education is very low, lower than in the Caribbean's other pools of baseball talent, Puerto Rico and Venezuela. So the kids don't stay in school, not when they can be out on the streets or in the fields playing baseball. "It's very much like the United States in the '30s, during the Depression," says Art Stewart, director of scouting for the Kansas City Royals. "Those were sad times, but they produced great ballplayers because baseball was one of the only avenues of escape."

Hungry players are in endless supply in the Dominican Republic, but there's more to it than that. Rivaling the hunger is the passion for baseball. When Gollo Olivarez, who oversees games in the Barrio Blanco garbage dump, was asked why his country produces so many ballplayers, he simply pointed to his heart. Cervantes put the words, "Sing away sorrow, cast away care," in the mouth of Don Quixote, and Dominicans seem to live by that creed. There seems no better place to cast away care than on the baseball diamond.

There are other reasons for the abundance of talent. People can play ball the year-round, of course. If they work in the fields, their bodies are lean and muscled, and their arms are strong from cutting the cane. And they're accustomed to hard work. Epy Guerrero, for instance, subjects his players to much more demanding workouts than they would have in the States, and they never stop hustling and never start complaining.

The flip side of this land of baseball opportunity is that for every player driving a Mercedes, there are countless others who never make it. They're Don Quixotes chasing a dream, and most of them are tilting at windmills. . . .

PICKUP GAMES in San Pedro de Macorís often involve any implement kids can pick up to serve as a bat or ball.

2002 | JASON GIAMBI was the AL MVP for the A's in 2000, then brought his power stroke and great eye to the Yankees. | *Photograph by* HOWARD SCHATZ

1995 | TONY GWYNN carried a big stick—eight of them, in fact; one for each of the batting titles he would win with the Padres. | *Photograph by* TIM MANTOANI

1959 | LUIS APARICIO, a sure-handed shortstop for the White Sox, couldn't come up with an errant throw in Game 4 of the World Series, allowing Dodgers outfielder Don Demeter to advance to second. | *Photograph by* PHIL BATH

GIANTS AMONG MEN

BY FRANK DEFORD

Exactly 100 years ago, Christy Mathewson and John McGraw rescued the woeful New York Giants and helped make baseball the true national pastime. —*from* SI, AUGUST 25, 2003

I T WAS IN 1903, A CENTURY ago, that John McGraw and Christy Mathewson were on the Giants for their first full season together. In many ways, that was the start of baseball as we would come to know it. ❧ Among other things, Nineteen-Aught-Three was also the year that New York City got a franchise in the brash young American League. Until then the Giants of the mature National League had been Gotham's only team. Well, Brooklyn had become a borough of New York City and had its Superbas, but let's not get into those geopolitics. In America's national pastime, in America's grandest city, the Giants were the team. Only they were dreadful—"the rankest apology for a first-class team ever imposed on a major league city," according to a contemporary newspaperman.

In 1902 the Giants had posted the worst record in the majors. Fewer and fewer Gotham cranks (as fans were known then) would leave work early and take the Eighth Avenue El up to the 155th Street stop and the Polo Grounds to watch the "Harlemites" play. Why, few cranks would so much as bother to stand up on Coogan's Bluff and watch the games for free.

Who would have imagined that in just another few years a rookie named "Laughing" Larry Doyle would utter these words that would become the baseball leitmotif of its time: "It's great to be young and a Giant!" But, you see, it all turned around very quickly in that summer 100 years ago, when two uncommon men, who were so unlike each other, came together as friends and force. Never was there such an odd couple in sport. Nevertheless, it was because of their association that the Giants ascended and baseball bloomed as a signal part of Americana in the bully new century.

The most promising Giant at the start of the 1903 season was Mathewson, a 22-year-old righthander. He was wholesome and handsome, broad-shouldered at a towering 6' 2", with a clean-shaven face, bright blue eyes and wavy brown hair that he parted in the middle. At a time when only 6% of Americans had finished so much as high school, Matty was a college man, from Bucknell. One admirer, the writer Homer Croy, summed him up: "He talks like a Harvard graduate, looks like an actor, acts like a businessman and impresses you as an all-around gentleman." Christy Mathewson was a whiz-bang, sports' original all-American boy.

The Giants' manager, by contrast, was stumpy, only 5' 6½"; not for nothing would he come to be known, redundantly, as Little Napoleon. McGraw was pasty-faced, which set off his black eyes and black hair all the more. He wore his hair swirled fashionably on the sides (known as the fish-hook effect) and tried hard to be stylish, favoring Cuban shirts with the blue serge suits that every gentleman then wore, all year round.

McGraw and Mathewson came together in New York at one of those rare moments when everything sure and reliable seemed to be in play. The Flatiron Building, then one of the world's tallest skyscrapers, had just gone up on 23rd Street, the gaslights were going out, and somewhere beneath them more than nine miles of subway were being tunneled. For not much longer would there be the need at the Polo Grounds to park horse-drawn carriages behind centerfield.

America, however, remained mostly rural (there were still 1,800 farms within the New York City limits), and by far the most famous athlete in the U.S. was a horse. God in heaven, Dan Patch paced a mile in 1:56¼! But that was in 1903, just as the Giants began to win. Soon baseball would replace horse racing in the prime space of the sports pages. Crowds of more than 25,000 began to spill over at the Polo Grounds, and invariably they could count on seeing Matty or "Iron Man" Joe McGinnity twirl. In 1903 the Iron Man went 31–20, winning three doubleheaders in August. Matty was 30–13.

Likewise, it is unlikely that any American athlete has ever been so great the hero, even till now. As baseball became more popular, it needed an appropriate idol. Matty's primacy was heightened by the fact that the few national sports stars who had preceded him had been not only outside the Anglo-Protestant mainstream but also, more important, of dubious ethical grounding. (McGraw himself, for openers.) Well, yes, everybody liked the Pittsburgh Pirates' Honus Wagner, but he fell between two stools. Germans were the largest immigrant group in the U.S., but Wagner was homely and beer-bellied, so he could never be the first German-American crossover figure. (That distinction would be earned a generation later by one George Herman Ruth.) As Mathewson's biographer Ray Robinson has written, "In the public thirst for a saint among ballplayers, Mathewson became something entirely apart." . . .

THEY WERE opposites in almost every way imaginable, but Mathewson (far left) and McGraw were an unbeatable pair on the diamond.

2005 | THERE ARE very few chinks visible in the modern armor of Washington Nationals catcher Brian Schneider. | *Photograph by* TOM DIPACE

> **Artifacts**

Masking Agents

Adapted from fencing in 1877 and initially ridiculed as a rat-trap, the catcher's mask now protects and adorns

1878

1885

1889

1901

1930

1941

1970

1988

2006

JOE MORGAN won five Gold Gloves
as the Reds' second baseman and was the
National League MVP in '75 and '76.
Photograph by CO RENTMEESTER

>THE ALL-DECADE TEAMS

AMERICAN LEAGUE	NATIONAL LEAGUE
CATCHER	CATCHER
Thurman Munson	Johnny Bench
FIRST BASE	FIRST BASE
George Scott	Willie Stargell
SECOND BASE	SECOND BASE
Rod Carew	Joe Morgan
SHORTSTOP	SHORTSTOP
Bert Campaneris	Dave Concepcion
THIRD BASE	THIRD BASE
Graig Nettles	Mike Schmidt
LEFTFIELD	LEFTFIELD
Jim Rice	Lou Brock
CENTERFIELD	CENTERFIELD
Amos Otis	Cesar Cedeño
RIGHTFIELD	RIGHTFIELD
Reggie Jackson	Pete Rose
DESIGNATED HITTER	PINCH HITTER
Hal McRae	Manny Mota
STARTING PITCHER	STARTING PITCHER
Jim Palmer	Tom Seaver
RELIEF PITCHER	RELIEF PITCHER
Rollie Fingers	Tug McGraw

>DEBUT   FINALE<

	DEBUT		FINALE
1970	DON BAYLOR		BOB ALLISON
1971	J.R. RICHARD		ERNIE BANKS
1972	MIKE SCHMIDT		ROBERTO CLEMENTE
1973	GEORGE BRETT		WILLIE MAYS
1974	ROBIN YOUNT		AL KALINE
1975	DENNIS ECKERSLEY		BOB GIBSON
1976	ANDRE DAWSON		HANK AARON
1977	EDDIE MURRAY		BROOKS ROBINSON
1978	OZZIE SMITH		SANDY ALOMAR
1979	RICKEY HENDERSON		LOU BROCK

>THE LEADERS

HITTING

BATTING AVERAGE* ROD CAREW	.343
HOME RUNS WILLIE STARGELL	296
RBI JOHNNY BENCH	1,031
AT BATS PETE ROSE	6,523
HITS PETE ROSE	2,045

SINGLES PETE ROSE	1,508
DOUBLES PETE ROSE	394
TRIPLES ROD CAREW	80
OBP* ROD CAREW	.408
SLUGGING PCT.* WILLIE STARGELL	.555
RUNS PETE ROSE	1,068
STOLEN BASES LOU BROCK	551
HIT BY PITCHES RON HUNT	142

WALKS JOE MORGAN	1,071
STRIKEOUTS BOBBY BONDS	1,368
GAMES PETE ROSE	1,604

PITCHING

WINS JIM PALMER	186
LOSSES PHIL NIEKRO	151
WINNING PCT.† DON GULLETT	.686
STRIKEOUTS NOLAN RYAN	2,678

ERA† JIM PALMER	2.58
INNINGS GAYLORD PERRY	2,905
WALKS NOLAN RYAN	1,515
RUNS ALLOWED PHIL NIEKRO	1,228
HOME RUNS ALLOWED FERGUSON JENKINS	301
SAVES ROLLIE FINGERS	209
SHUTOUTS JIM PALMER	44
COMPLETE GAMES GAYLORD PERRY	197

* MINIMUM 2,500 PLATE APPEARANCES † MINIMUM 1,000 INNINGS

>HOT TICKETS 10 Games You Wish You'd Seen

Fenway Park Oct. 21, 1975 In one of the > greatest World Series games ever played, the Reds and Red Sox go toe-to-toe for 12 innings, until Boston catcher Carlton Fisk ends it with a walk-off home run that hits the leftfield foul pole.

Fenway Park Oct. 2, 1978 The Yankees and Red Sox meet in a one-game playoff to determine the winner of the AL East. With the Yankees trailing 2–0 with two out in the seventh inning, light-hitting Bucky Dent connects for a three-run homer, and the Yankees go on to win 5–4.

Yankee Stadium Oct. 18, 1977 New York rightfielder Reggie Jackson earns the nickname Mr. October by hitting home runs on three consecutive at bats against Dodgers pitchers Burt Hooton, Elias Sosa and Charlie Hough in Game 6 of the World Series.

Memorial Stadium Oct. 17, 1971 Steve Blass pitches a four-hitter for the Pirates in a Game 7 World Series victory over the Orioles. Series MVP Roberto Clemente hits his second homer of the Series and Jose Pagan drives in Willie Stargell with the winning run on an eighth-inning double.

Shea Stadium April 22, 1970 Mets pitcher Tom Seaver ties the major league record with 19 strikeouts, retiring the game's final 16 batters—the last 10 on K's—in a 2–1 win over the Padres.

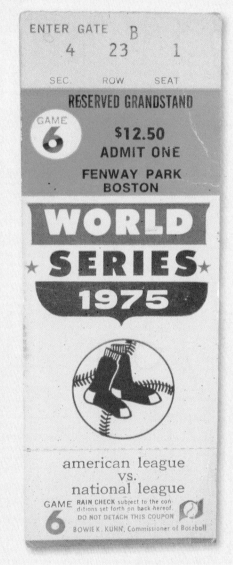

ENTER GATE B
4 23 1
SEC. ROW SEAT
RESERVED GRANDSTAND
GAME 6 $12.50 ADMIT ONE
FENWAY PARK BOSTON
WORLD SERIES 1975
american league vs. national league
GAME 6 RAIN CHECK subject to the conditions set forth on back hereof. DO NOT DETACH THIS COUPON
BOWIE K. KUHN, Commissioner of Baseball

Atlanta-Fulton County Stadium April 8, 1974 Hank Aaron hits the 715th homer of his career, off Dodgers pitcher Al Downing, to replace Babe Ruth as the Home Run King.

Wrigley Field May 17, 1979 The Cubs and Phillies combine for 45 runs, 11 home runs and 50 hits in the Phillies' 23–22 win in windswept Chicago. Philadelphia leads the game 21–9 after the top of the fifth, but the Cubs rally to tie on an eighth-inning single by Barry Foote. Mike Schmidt's two-out homer in the 10th gives the Phillies the win.

Wrigley Field April 17, 1976 The Phillies trail the Cubs 13–2 before Mike Schmidt blasts home runs in four consecutive trips to the plate, including a two-run 10th-inning shot that caps Philadelphia's 18–16 comeback win.

Wrigley Field Sept. 16, 1975 Pirates second baseman Rennie Stennett sets the modern major league record with seven hits in a nine-inning game (four singles, two doubles and a triple) in a 22-0 rout of the Cubs.

Fenway Park April 6, 1973 For the first time in baseball history, a pitcher is not in the batting order as the American League unveils the designated hitter. The first DH to come to the plate is Ron Blomberg of the Yankees, who walks with the bases loaded off Boston's Luis Tiant.

BEST OF THE 1970s

TEAM	WINS	LOSSES	WIN PCT.
REDS	953	657	.591
ORIOLES	944	656	.590
PIRATES	916	695	.567
DODGERS	910	701	.565
RED SOX	895	714	.556

GEORGE FOSTER, REDS

WORST OF THE 1970s

TEAM	WINS	LOSSES	WIN PCT.
BLUE JAYS	166	318	.343
MARINERS	187	297	.386
PADRES	667	942	.415
BRAVES	725	883	.451
INDIANS	737	866	.460

DAVE WINFIELD, PADRES

1970S CULTURE

MUSIC: *The Wall* (Pink Floyd), *Rumours* (Fleetwood Mac), *What's Going On* (Marvin Gaye), *Born to Run* (Bruce Springsteen), *Led Zeppelin IV* (Led Zeppelin)

MOVIES: *Star Wars, The Godfather, Rocky, The Exorcist, Saturday Night Fever*

TELEVISION SHOWS: *Saturday Night Live, All in the Family, Happy Days, The Waltons, Charlie's Angels*

BOOKS: *Fear and Loathing in Las Vegas* by Hunter S. Thompson; *The Right Stuff* by Tom Wolfe; *Roots* by Alex Haley; *All the President's Men* by Bob Woodward and Carl Bernstein; *The Joy of Sex* by Alex Comfort; *The Complete Book of Running* by James F. Fixx

ACHIEVEMENT: On Sept. 17, 1978 Israel's Menachem Begin and Egypt's Anwar al-Sadat reach agreement at Camp David, Md., that will lead, a year later, to a formal peace treaty.

INVENTIONS: Microprocessor, GPS, video games (Pong), cellular phone, Sony Walkman

SEX SYMBOLS: Farrah Fawcett & John Travolta

VILLAIN: Pol Pot, leader of the Khmer Rouge regime from 1975 to '79, killed more than one million Cambodians, including intellectuals, religious leaders, minorities and the disabled.

PERSONALITY OF THE DECADE: Richard Nixon

< FARRAH FAWCETT

>NICKNAMES<

Mark [the Bird] Fidrych ∧
Reggie [Mr. October] Jackson
Al [the Mad Hungarian] Hrabosky
Willie [Pops] Stargell
Dave [Cobra] Parker
Bill [Spaceman] Lee
Carlton [Pudge] Fisk
Mike [the Human Rain Delay] Hargrove
John [the Count] Montefusco
Fred [Chicken] Stanley
Phil [Scrap Iron] Garner
Bill [Mad Dog] Madlock
Rich [Goose] Gossage
Albert [Sparky] Lyle
Ron [the Penguin] Cey
Rick [Rooster] Burleson
Dick [Dirt] Tidrow
Dave [Kong] Kingman
Jim [Catfish] Hunter
Greg [the Bull] Luzinski
Russell [Bucky] Dent
Rusty [Le Grand Orange] Staub

BORN			DIED
SECRETARIAT		1970	< JIMI HENDRIX
RICKY MARTIN		1971	JIM MORRISON
CAMERON DIAZ		1972	HARRY S. TRUMAN
TYRA BANKS		1973	PABLO PICASSO
DALE EARNHARDT JR. >		1974	DUKE ELLINGTON
TIGER WOODS		1975	HAILE SELASSIE
REESE WITHERSPOON		1976	J. PAUL GETTY
TOM BRADY		1977	ELVIS PRESLEY
KATIE HOLMES		1978	NORMAN ROCKWELL
TRACY MCGRADY		1979	JOHN WAYNE

> NEWS OF THE REAL WORLD

1970: Four Kent State students killed, nine wounded by National Guardsmen during antiwar protest **1971:** 26th Amendment ratified—U.S. voting age reduced from 21 to 18 **1972:** President Nixon travels to China and U.S.S.R. **1973:** OPEC oil embargo against countries that support Israel; long lines at gas pumps in Europe, U.S. **1974:** Nixon resigns presidency in wake of Watergate scandal; pardoned by President Gerald Ford **1975:** 18 years of U.S. war in Vietnam ends with fall of Saigon **1976:** College dropouts Steve Wozniak and Steve Jobs start Apple Computer in Jobs's garage **1977:** The King is dead: Elvis Presley succumbs to apparent heart attack at Graceland, his mansion in Memphis. **1978:** 900 cult members commit suicide by drinking poisoned Kool-Aid at settlement at Jonestown, Guyana **1979:** Jimmy Carter mediates historic peace treaty between Israel and Egypt at Camp David, Md.

1956 | YOGI BERRA stood only 5' 8", but like the 6' 3" Ted Williams, he was a giant of the game. | *Photograph by* MARK KAUFFMAN

1954 | THE INDIANS' Early Wynn had to sweat out a World Series at bat by the NL's top hitter, Willie Mays, at the Polo Grounds. | *Photograph by* MARK KAUFFMAN

2001 | THE CARDINALS' Edgar Renteria got his ash in a fling when his bat shattered against the Diamondbacks in Phoenix. | *Photograph by* PETER READ MILLER

2001 | THE BALL and bat seemed frozen for an instant on this bunt by the Indians' Omar Vizquel in a loss to the Reds in Cincinnati. | *Photograph by* CHUCK SOLOMON

LOST IN HISTORY

BY WILLIAM NACK

From 1929 to 1931, the Philadelphia A's were the best team in baseball, with four future Hall of Famers and a lineup that dominated Babe Ruth's legendary Yankees. So why hasn't anyone heard of them? —from SI, AUGUST 19, 1996

I N HIS BOX FESTOONED with bunting along the third base line, President Herbert Hoover had just quietly flashed the sign that the fifth game of the 1929 World Series was over. The President had buttoned up his overcoat. At his side his wife, Lou, had taken the cue and pulled on her brown suede gloves. Around them Secret Service men were arranging a hasty Presidential exit from Philadelphia's Shibe Park. Yogi Berra had not yet illuminated the world with his brilliant epiphany—"It ain't over till it's over"—so how on earth were the Hoovers to know?

It was nearing 3:15 p.m. on Monday, Oct. 14, and the Chicago Cubs were beating the Philadelphia Athletics 2–0 behind the elegant two-hit pitching of starter Pat Malone. For eight innings, bunching a potpourri of off-speed pitches around a snapping fastball, Malone had benumbed one of the most feared batting orders in the history of baseball. At its heart were Al Simmons, who batted .334 and hit 307 home runs over his major league career; Jimmie Foxx, who once hit a home run with such force that it shattered a wooden seat three rows from the top of the upper deck at Yankee Stadium; and Mickey Cochrane, who batted .331 in the '29 regular season and is widely regarded as one of the finest hitting catchers ever to play the game.

Now it was the last of the ninth in a game Chicago had to win to stay alive in the Series. The Cubs were down three games to one, and all they needed to return the Series to Chicago was one more painless inning from Malone. Out at shortstop, scuffing the dirt, a 22-year-old Ohio country boy named Woody English had been watching Malone cut down the A's one by one. Only Simmons and Bing Miller, Philadelphia's rightfielder, had been able to rap out hits, a measly pair of singles.

THE 1929 ATHLETICS *(from left)* Eddie Collins, Kid Gleason, Walter French, Jimmy Dykes, Carroll Yerkes, Homer Summa, Max Bishop, Jim Cronin, DeWitt LeBourveau, Mickey Cochrane, Cy Perkins, William Breckinridge, Jimmie Foxx, bat boy (unidentified), Connie Mack, Bing Miller, Al Simmons, Eddie Rommel, Rube Walberg, Lefty Grove, Howard Ehmke, George Earnshaw, Jack Quinn, Mule Haas.

Of the 50 players who suited up that day, only English survives, and the 89-year-old former All-Star remembers savoring the prospect of returning to Wrigley Field for Game 6. "Malone could throw real hard, and he was throwing very well," English recalls. "All we needed was three more outs and we were back in Chicago for the last two games. It looked like we had it salted away."

As things would turn out, only the peanuts were salted. For this was the '29 Series, which had already been one of the wildest, most twisting, most dramatic Fall Classics of all time. By the bottom of the ninth inning of Game 5, 24 Series records had been either broken or tied. The Cubs had struck out 50 times, and their surpassing second baseman, Rogers Hornsby, had fanned eight times.

This was the Series in which A's manager and part owner Connie Mack had stunned everyone in baseball by reaching around his pitching rotation—the strongest of its era, anchored by the sensational southpaw Robert (Lefty) Grove—and handing the ball in the opener to an aging, sore-armed righthander named Howard Ehmke. This was the Series in which Philadelphia, losing 8–0 in the seventh inning of Game 4, had come back swinging in what is still the most prolific inning of scoring in more than 90 years of Series history. Finally, this was the Classic that crowned a regular season in which the A's had won 104 American League games and finished 18 ahead of the second-place New York Yankees, the vaunted pin-

stripes of Babe Ruth, Lou Gehrig, Tony Lazzeri and Bill Dickey.

The 1927 Yankees, who won 110 games and finished 19 ahead of second-place Philadelphia, are venerated as the finest team ever assembled. In fact, according to most old-timers who played in that era, the 1927 and '28 Yankees and the 1929 and '30 Athletics were nearly equal, with the A's given the nod in fielding and pitching, and the Yankees in hitting.

"I pitched against both of them, and you could flip a coin," recalls Willis Hudlin, 90, who won 157 games for the Cleveland Indians between 1926 and '40. "They both had power and pitching. A game would be decided on who was pitching and what kind of a day he had. You could throw a dart between 'em."

In truth the chief difference between the two teams had less to do with how they played in any given game than with where they played their home games. Many veteran baseball observers believe that the Yankees' far more exalted status in history is due largely to the fact that they played in New York, in media heaven, where the manufacture of myth and hype is a light industry. "Those A's never got the credit they deserved," says Shirley Povich, 91, the retired sports editor of *The Washington Post*, who covered both teams. "The A's were victims of the Yankee mystique. Perhaps the 1927 Yankees were the greatest team of all time. But if there was a close second, perhaps an equal, it was those A's. They are the most overlooked team in baseball." . . .

1991 | GREG OLSON held on to the ball after putting the tag on Dan Gladden in Game 1 of the Twins–Braves World Series. | *Photograph by* RICHARD MACKSON

1986 | METS CLOSER Jesse Orosco was much relieved after saving Game 7 of the Series against the Red Sox. | *Photograph by* CHUCK SOLOMON

1962 | DODGERS SHORTSTOP Maury Wills got the lead runner, but was late with the throw to first against the Reds. | *Photograph by* HY PESKIN

FABRIC OF THE GAME

BY SARAH BALLARD

The baseball uniform has a history as colorful as the players who have worn it —*from* SI, APRIL 5, 1989

BASKETBALL PLAYERS don't gripe about the color of their shorts. A football player doesn't get agitated over the stripe on his helmet. The Edmonton Oilers won't be found having heated discussions in the locker room about what makes a classic hockey uniform. But scratch a major league baseball player and you uncover a fashion analyst.

Maybe it's all those hours spent sitting in the dugout with nothing to do but spit that makes aesthetes out of these athletes. Or maybe it's the nature of the baseball uniform itself. A football or hockey player needs the armor of a tank just to survive, but he gives up his flexibility, his freedom of movement. A basketball player needs plenty of skin exposed to the air to keep his body temperature down, so he sacrifices protection. But a baseball player, with fewer practical demands upon his attire, has a uniform that, functionally speaking, covers all the bases, leaving him free to devote himself to the finer points of style.

Bud Black, an Indians pitcher who has a reputation as something of a fashion trendsetter, has studied the American League in depth from the vantage point of the bullpen. "I like the Tigers' home uniforms," he says. "I like the number of belt loops in the back. I like the Old English 'D.' I like the small pinstripe down the sides. They also have two hats, a road hat with an orange D, a home hat with a white D. I like that they have orange stripes on their shoes on the road and white stripes at home."

Now and then a player feigns indifference, but don't be taken in. He cares. "The Yankee uniform's not bad," says Yankee outfielder Rickey Henderson. "Not bad at all. But they're all the same. There's no uniform I really hate." What about the 1976 White Sox with those weird collars? "Now *that* was a bad uniform," says Henderson. "I wouldn't play in that uniform."

Some care more than others. Ken Landreaux achieved a sort of fashion martyrdom in 1980 when, as a Twins outfielder, he refused to go along with a front office edict that his blue stirrup socks be worn low enough that the team's logo on the sock show at the calf. But Landreaux liked to pull his stirrups high over his white sanitary socks and pull his pant legs low, so that only a band of colored stirrup ran up either side of his ankles, the way many players wear their socks today.

"Landreaux had a good year, a 31-game hitting streak," says Twins media relations director Tom Mee, "but he pouted all summer and refused to wear his socks low, and it caused problems." The next season he was playing in L.A.

Mets pitcher Ron Darling sees a uniform as a philosophical statement. "The more conservative the look, the better," he says. "That's why I wear my socks so low. I believe in the hardworking, nothing-fancy work ethic. I like to think of myself as a puritan, or maybe a Calvinist in a baseball uniform."

The celebrated architect Mies van der Rohe liked to say, "God is in the details." If he was right, then baseball must be on close terms with the Almighty. Although the characteristic elements of the uniform—short-legged pants and long socks—were set in 1867 and have not changed, the rest, the details, have been in a state of constant flux. The uniform has been added to, subtracted from, embellished and streamlined with such frequency and imagination that the only constant in its long history is change. A few of the changes have survived; most have sunk under their own weight, victims of fickle fashion, public ridicule or plain absurdity. In 1876, Albert G. Spalding, a defector from the Boston Red Stockings, became pitcher-manager of the Chicago White Stockings. Being an ambitious young man, Spalding, on the side, founded a sporting goods business that supplied the Chicago team with uniforms and eventually grew into a commercial empire. That was Spalding's good idea. Another, less laudable, idea of his was to assign a cap of a different color to each field position, which someone said made the White Stockings look like "a Dutch bed of tulips." At present, baseball is caught up in a wave of nostalgic fervor, a postmodernist period, designers might say. Teams are reaching into their pasts for a button here, a belt there, adding pinstripes, abandoning color, rehabilitating long-neglected symbols.

Andy Van Slyke, the Pittsburgh outfielder, has been observing the march of fashion from dugout level for six years, and has reached the conclusion that it's the man who makes the uniform. "Tommy Lasorda," he says, "wouldn't look good in *any* uniform. But Jose Canseco, you could put a softball uniform on him and he'd look like a major leaguer. Then there's [Pirates pitcher] Bob Walk. He goes out there with sunflower seeds and spit on his uniform, old gum, pine tar and resin, coffee stains on his pants, burns from cigarettes, and he hasn't shaved, but somehow he looks good, even if he's getting his butt beat.". . .

THERE HAVE been Braves in the National League since 1912, first with Boston (where this jacket came from), then Milwaukee and Atlanta.

1969 | MR. CUB, Hall of Famer Ernie Banks, had power and a sweet glove at short, then at first during his 19 years in Chicago. | *Photograph by* NEIL LEIFER

2002 | NOMAR GARCIAPARRA won batting titles in 1999 and 2000 while playing short for the Red Sox. | *Photograph by* CHUCK SOLOMON

HIGH-WIRE ACT

BY TOM VERDUCCI

There's no safety net for major league closers, who put it all on the line each time they work, saving the day . . . or squandering their teams' best efforts. —*from* SI, JUNE 18, 2001

AIRPLANE PILOT, tightrope walker, sword swallower, bomb-squad member, skydiver, closer. Success or failure in these jobs is absolute: You either do the job or you don't. The closer's job is the most clearly delineated one in sports. Most times he either gets a save—you need not dig too deep to hit the religious or heroic bedrock of the word—or a blown save, the cruelest, most negative stat ever invented. No middle ground. No safety net. Closers are the Flying Wallendas of baseball.

Trevor Hoffman fell off the high wire on May 27. Hoffman, 33, is the Padres' closer. He is the only active pitcher to have saved 30 games in each of the past six years. That afternoon the Padres gave the righthander a 4–2 lead to protect in the ninth inning against the Diamondbacks. The game took a total of two hours and 47 minutes, but Hoffman lost it in an eye blink: single, home run, fly out, single, home run. Drive home safely.

What Hoffman did in the wake of that defeat, when utter failure is a virus that attacks the immune system of confidence, reveals more about his staying power than his 53 saves in 1998. "To last in this job," Hoffman says, "you have to learn to take the good and the bad equally."

The results are brutally self-evident: You do or you don't. Many closers do (44 pitchers saved at least 30 games in a season over the past five years), but most don't for long. Just about any pitcher with good stuff, given the liberal nature of the save rule and the programmed use of closers by robotic managers, can save 30 games once. Mel Rojas, Heathcliff Slocumb and Billy Taylor proved as much in recent years—before they disappeared as quickly as they'd arrived.

Hoffman, one of the rare closers who endures, fought the virus after the Arizona defeat. He has developed a routine for such cases. First, while sitting alone in the dugout, he reflects on what happened; then, even after his worst outings, he goes to the clubhouse and fields questions from the media. "The people asking the questions are not responsible for the ball flying out of the park," he explains. Finally, alone, he finds something positive amid the despair. He won't leave the stadium until he is sure the virus is under control. This time Hoffman began the cleansing process at about 4:50 in the afternoon. He did not leave until nine o'clock that night.

"That's not normal, believe me—not that long," Hoffman says. "There were a lot of issues with that one. The first home run ran through my mind. A 2-and-2 pitch. I threw a fastball. It's easy to think, I ought to have thrown a changeup. Confidence is everything. If you start second-guessing yourself, you're bound to run into more bad [outings]. It took a while, but I got through it. It's a cliché, but it's true: It's better to have competed and lost than not to have competed at all. That's what I told myself. I battled. And I knew I'd be out there again."

ARMANDO BENITEZ fell off the high wire on May 11. Benitez, 28, is the Mets' closer. He is, with only one 30-save season on his résumé, a work in progress. Whether he turns out to be a Trevor Hoffman or a Mel Rojas will depend on nights like this, when he surrendered the game-winning hit to the Giants. The righthander's response, with the help of at least one other Met, was to demolish parts of the visiting dugout and clubhouse at Pacific Bell Park. The Giants sent the Mets a bill for $4,000 to cover repairs.

What did Hoffman say? Treat the good and the bad equally? How can any closer do that when, as Cardinals manager Tony La Russa put it, he has to endure "a maximum amount of pressure in a minimum amount of time"? How can he do it when success is so intoxicating and failure so debilitating?

Benitez is 6' 4" and listed at 229 pounds, with the shoulders of a linebacker and the scowl of a prison guard way too long on the job. He throws 96 mph worth of wicked fury on a pitching mound. The sensation of burying his heater past the best hitters in baseball—the fans standing, cheering and pleading, with the knowledge that he alone, not some scoreboard clock clicking off seconds, has the power to suck the last breath of life out of the opposition—that sensation has been known to make this bear of a man dance with joy like a pixie. He might quickly lift one knee, as if he had stepped barefoot on a hot sidewalk, or give a dismissive wave with his right hand. He knows that John Franco, his mentor, hates it when he reacts like that ("Never give the other guy extra incentive to beat your ass," Franco tells him), but such is the overwhelming power of the moment. . . .

HOFFMAN'S APPEARANCE on the mound puts a new slant on the game: He's converted more than 400 save opportunities.

1993 | A WHOLE flock of Blue Jays showed the way home for Joe Carter after his three-run walk-off homer against the Phillies won Game 6 — and the World Series — for Toronto in the SkyDome. | *Photograph by* CHUCK SOLOMON

1959 | A SPECIAL camera captured the ump's view of a fastball during spring training with the White Sox. | *Photograph by* JOHN G. ZIMMERMAN

1962 | WHITE SOX shortstop Luis Aparicio slid into third in a setup for a SPORTS ILLUSTRATED cover. | *Photograph by* MARK KAUFFMAN

ALL IS FORGIVEN

BY KEITH OLBERMANN

It took the death of his daughter and a very public plea from his son to end Jim Bouton's long exile from the Yankees.
—*from* SI, AUGUST 3, 1998

O F THE THOUSANDS OF words Jim Bouton used to describe his 28-year exile from the Yankees between the time of the publication of his controversial book, *Ball Four*, and his first Old-Timers' Day in the Bronx last Saturday, only four ultimately mattered to him: "Laurie made this happen."

Laurie was Bouton's 31-year-old daughter, killed nearly a year ago in an automobile accident. Her death inspired her brother Michael to try to do the seemingly impossible: put his father back in the good graces of a baseball establishment still holding a grudge over the diary Bouton published in 1970.

In a poignant first-person piece published in *The New York Times* on Father's Day, Michael asked George Steinbrenner to forgive his father and lift the unofficial ban that had kept him from the summer gatherings where Joe DiMaggio meets Darryl Strawberry and Whitey Ford crosses paths with Hideki Irabu. "Nobody told me Michael's letter was being printed," Bouton recalled last week. "That day my son David called and read me what Michael had written. I cried—joy, sadness, pride. The best Father's Day gift you could ever get."

Writing honestly and powerfully runs in the Bouton family. *Ball Four* certainly raised a few hackles. For the first time fans were told that baseball players—Mickey Mantle included—drank, fought and chased women. "I was maybe 14 when I read it, and it was like reading *Valley of the Dolls*," old-timer Dave Righetti said in the Yankees clubhouse. "I remember reading about them boring holes in the dugout walls to look up women's skirts, and using telescopes to look into hotel room windows." Bouton was accused by former teammates of violating the sanctity of the clubhouse, but after *Ball Four* those clubhouses would never again be thought of as sanctified places.

Michael's letter touched a nerve with the Yankees, though, and five weeks later there was Bouton, who in '63 and '64 won a total of 39 games for New York (plus two more in the '64 World Series), putting on a Yankees uniform just two lockers down from Moose Skowron and the old Marine, Hank Bauer. There were no dirty looks. There were no fights. There were no muttered epithets in Mantle's defense; Mantle and Bouton made their peace four years ago, when Bouton wrote a note of condolence after the death of Mantle's son Billy. As Bouton answered questions from a gaggle of writers never numbering fewer than 10, Bauer calmly read that day's sports pages, which were probably far more graphic and disillusioning than *Ball Four* seemed the day it rolled off the presses. "They asked me if it was O.K. with me to invite him," said Bauer. "I told them, 'I got nothing against Bouton; he didn't mention my name!'"

After a struggle to find a cap properly sized to re-create his trademark—the hat flying off his head as he delivered a pitch—Bouton finally made his way to the field. He ran out toward rightfield, pausing only to chat briefly with old Seattle Pilots teammate Tommy Davis, then visited with the fans in rightfield.

Any lingering tension lifted before the player introductions. "Jim's back, Jim's back," Joe Pepitone repeated again and again, mugging for the cameras. Bouton bantered with Bobby Murcer, Gene Michael and others of his era, and then sat in the dugout and visited with former teammate Mel Stottlemyre. The fan reaction, which Bouton had anticipated with some trepidation, was warm and supportive, and when he tipped his cap, the crowd fairly thundered.

As Bouton warmed up to face Jay Johnstone, the stadium scoreboard flashed, THANKS MICHAEL, LOVE, DAD—his own surprise for the son who had surprised him. Then came something unexpected. "Just as I was starting to pitch, I looked up in the stands and my daughters' friends held up a banner that read, WE LOVE LAURIE. I was overwhelmed."

On the first pitch his cap flew off, right on schedule. A breaking ball bounced well in front of the plate, a reminder that he is now 59 years old. Johnstone was retired on a grounder five pitches later, and Bouton's return from exile was over. "The whole experience was like a dream," he said. "What a variety of emotions. I feel like I just stepped off one of those paint-mixing machines."

The strongest of those emotions had followed not the applause nor even the appearance of the banner with his daughter's name; it had come in those brief moments with Stottlemyre. "Mel and I were talking about grief," he said. "He lost his son 11 years ago, and he understood. I wanted to know how to get through it. He told me you don't get over it, but it does get a little less painful each day. You don't want to forget her, you want her to be there with you always. Today it was as if she was here." A tear formed in Bouton's right eye, and he made no apology for it. "She was here." . . .

THE FLYING cap was a Bouton signature when he pitched; he had another reason for being hatless when he finally returned to Yankee Stadium.

1980 | DAVE PARKER lit it up in his third all-Star season for the Pirates, who were still smoking after winning the '79 Series. | *Photograph by* WALTER IOOSS JR.

1963 | CASEY STENGEL led the Yankees to 10 pennants and seven world titles in 12 years, then in '62 began four futile years with the Mets. | *Photograph by* NEIL LEIFER

> **Art of the Game**

Crate Expectations

Adapting the cheery style of orange-crate art but not shying from controversy, artist Ben Sakoguchi has created more than 100 paintings that constitute his "Unauthorized History of Baseball"

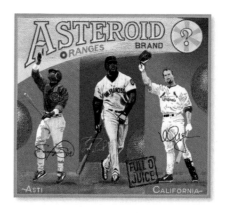

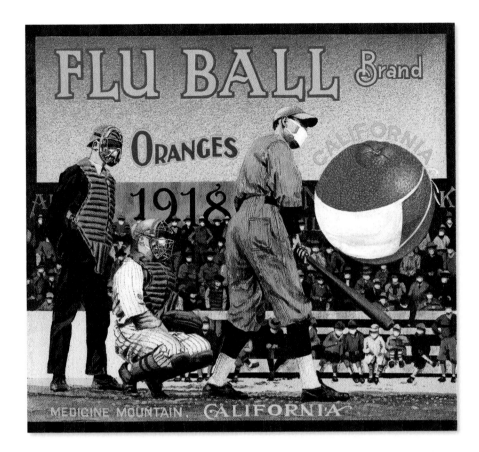

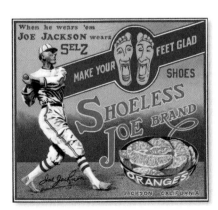

BALL STRIKE
OUT ● AT BAT
UMPIRES
PLATE ● BASE
LUCKY NUMBERS

		1 2 3 4 5 6 7 8 9 10
	PHILADELPHIA	0 0 1 1 0 1 2
	DETROIT	0 0 0 0 0 2
	BOSTON	0 0
	ST. LOUIS	0 0
	WASHINGTON	0 0 1 2 3 0
	CLEVELAND	0 0 0 0 3 1
	NEW YORK	0 1
	CHICAGO	0 0

BOSTON HERE · TUE

Shaving Troubles are OUT!

SCHICK INJECTOR
BLADES ARE BACK

1945 | AFTER FOUR years in the Army, Tigers slugger Hank Greenberg was happy to be battling Athletics ace Bobo Newsom. | *Photograph by* BETTMANN/CORBIS

1959 | WILLIE MAYS mesmerized San Francisco fans in a game against the Braves during the Giants' September pennant drive. | *Photograph by* HY PESKIN

JACK MORRIS, a five-time All-Star, won more games than any other pitcher during the decade (162), all of them for the Tigers.
Photograph by JOHN WEISS

>THE ALL-DECADE TEAMS

AMERICAN LEAGUE	NATIONAL LEAGUE
CATCHER *Lance Parrish*	CATCHER *Gary Carter*
FIRST BASE *Eddie Murray*	FIRST BASE *Keith Hernandez*
SECOND BASE *Lou Whitaker*	SECOND BASE *Ryne Sandberg*
SHORTSTOP *Cal Ripken*	SHORTSTOP *Ozzie Smith*
THIRD BASE *George Brett*	THIRD BASE *Mike Schmidt*
LEFTFIELD *Rickey Henderson*	LEFTFIELD *Tim Raines*
CENTERFIELD *Robin Yount*	CENTERFIELD *Dale Murphy*
RIGHTFIELD *Dwight Evans*	RIGHTFIELD *Tony Gwynn*
DESIGNATED HITTER *Don Baylor*	PINCH HITTER *Greg Gross*
STARTING PITCHER *Jack Morris*	STARTING PITCHER *Fernando Valenzuela*
RELIEF PITCHER *Dan Quisenberry*	RELIEF PITCHER *Lee Smith*

>DEBUT | FINALE<

1980 — FERNANDO VALENZUELA | WILLIE McCOVEY

1981 — CAL RIPKEN JR. | BOBBY BONDS

1982 — TONY GWYNN | WILLIE STARGELL

1983 — OREL HERSHISER | JOHNNY BENCH

1984 — ROGER CLEMENS | JIM PALMER

1985 — PAUL O'NEILL | ROD CAREW

1986 — BARRY BONDS | PETE ROSE

1987 — EDGAR MARTINEZ | REGGIE JACKSON

1988 — RANDY JOHNSON | STEVE CARLTON

1989 — KEN GRIFFEY JR. | MIKE SCHMIDT

>THE LEADERS

HITTING

BATTING AVERAGE*	WADE BOGGS	352
HOME RUNS	MIKE SCHMIDT	313
RBI	EDDIE MURRAY	996
AT BATS	DALE MURPHY	5,694
HITS	ROBIN YOUNT	1,731

SINGLES	WILLIE WILSON	1,292
DOUBLES	ROBIN YOUNT	337
TRIPLES	WILLIE WILSON	115
OBP*	WADE BOGGS	443
SLUGGING PCT.*	MIKE SCHMIDT	540
RUNS	RICKEY HENDERSON	1,122
STOLEN BASES	RICKEY HENDERSON	838
HIT BY PITCHES	DON BAYLOR	160

WALKS	RICKEY HENDERSON	962
STRIKEOUTS	DALE MURPHY	1,268
GAMES	DALE MURPHY	1,537

PITCHING

WINS	JACK MORRIS	162
LOSSES	JIM CLANCY	126
WINNING PCT.†	DWIGHT GOODEN	719
STRIKEOUTS	NOLAN RYAN	2,167

ERA†	DWIGHT GOODEN	2.64
INNINGS	JACK MORRIS	2,443⅔
WALKS	NOLAN RYAN	894
RUNS ALLOWED	JACK MORRIS	1,085
HOME RUNS ALLOWED	JACK MORRIS	264
SAVES	JEFF REARDON	264
SHUTOUTS	DAVE STIEB, FERNANDO VALENZUELA	27
COMPLETE GAMES	JACK MORRIS	133

* MINIMUM 2,500 PLATE APPEARANCES † MINIMUM 1,000 INNINGS

>HOT TICKETS 10 Games You Wish You'd Seen

Shea Stadium Oct. 27, 1986 Down to their last >
out in the Series, the Mets rally against the
Red Sox, scoring the game-tying run on a wild
pitch by Bob Stanley and the game winner on
a Mookie Wilson grounder that rolls through
the legs of first baseman Bill Buckner.

Dodger Stadium Oct. 15, 1988 Barely able to walk
because of injuries, NL MVP Kirk Gibson
delivers a pinch-hit, two-out, two-run home
run off Oakland's Dennis Eckersley in the
bottom of the ninth to give the Dodgers a
5–4 win in Game 1 of the World Series.

Riverfront Stadium Sept. 11, 1985 Cincinnati's
player-manager Pete Rose singles off Padres
pitcher Eric Show to pass Ty Cobb and become the major league career leader, ending
up with 4,292 hits. (Cobb's official total was
later amended to 4,189.)

Busch Stadium Oct. 14, 1985 A walk-off home
run by Cardinals shortstop Ozzie Smith's
against Dodgers reliever Tom Niedenfuer
gives St. Louis a 3–2 lead in the NLCS. It is
the switch-hitting Smith's first home run
from the left side of the plate after 3,411
plate appearances hitting southpaw.

Yankee Stadium July 24, 1983 Royals third baseman George Brett hits a two-out, two-run
ninth-inning home run off Yankees closer
Goose Gossage to give Kansas City a 5–4 lead.
But New York manager Billy Martin protests
that Brett's bat is illegal because there's pine
tar too far up the barrel. The umpires agree
and call Brett out. AL president Andy
MacPhail subsequently overturns the ruling
and orders the game completed on Aug. 18.
The Royals hold on to win 5–4.

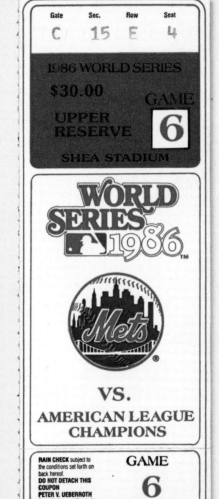

Fenway Park April 29, 1986 Red Sox righthander
Roger Clemens strikes out 20 Seattle
Mariners to break the major league record
that had been shared by Steve Carlton, Tom
Seaver and Nolan Ryan.

Municipal Stadium May 15, 1981 With tempera-
tures in the 40s in Cleveland, Indians righty
Len Barker throws the ninth perfect game in
baseball history, shutting down Toronto 3–0,
striking out 11 Blue Jays (all swinging) and
throwing 84 of his 103 pitches for strikes.

Wrigley Field Aug. 8, 1988 The Cubs, the last
team in the majors to install lights, face the
Phillies in the first night game at the Friendly
Confines. The game is rained out in the middle
of the third inning, postponing the first *official*
game under the Wrigley lights until the next
night, when the Cubs top the Mets 6–4.

Exhibition Stadium Sept. 14, 1987 The Blue Jays
set a major league record by hitting 10 home
runs against the Orioles in Toronto. Catcher
Ernie Whitt leads the onslaught with three
homers, Rance Mulliniks and George Bell
hit two each, and Lloyd Moseby, Rob Ducey
and Fred McGriff all had one in the Jays'
18–3 win.

Comiskey Park May 8–9, 1984 A home run by the
White Sox' Harold Baines mercifully puts an
end to a 25-inning contest between Chicago
and the Brewers. The score was 3–3 in the 21st
inning when Milwaukee's Ben Oglivie hit a
three-run homer, but Chicago then tied the
score. Although the game was suspended after
17 innings and completed the next day,
Baines's blast ended eight hours and six minutes of playing time in Chicago's 7–6 win.

BEST OF THE 1980s

TEAM	WINS	LOSSES	WIN PCT.
YANKEES	854	708	547
TIGERS	839	727	536
ROYALS	826	734	529
CARDINALS	825	734	529
DODGERS	825	741	527

ALAN TRAMMELL, TIGERS

WORST OF THE 1980s

TEAM	WINS	LOSSES	WIN PCT.
MARINERS	673	893	430
INDIANS	710	849	455
BRAVES	712	845	457
BREWERS	738	873	458
RANGERS	720	839	462

DALE MURPHY, BRAVES

1980s CULTURE

MUSIC: *Thriller* (Michael Jackson), *Born in the U.S.A.* (Bruce Springsteen), *The Joshua Tree* (U2), *Appetite for Destruction* (Guns 'n' Roses), *Purple Rain* (Prince)

MOVIES: *E.T. The Extraterrestrial, Raiders of the Lost Ark, Rambo: First Blood, Ghostbusters, Die Hard*

TELEVISION SHOWS: *The Cosby Show, Miami Vice, Cheers, Dallas*

BOOKS: *Beloved* by Toni Morrison; *Trump: The Art of the Deal* by Donald Trump; *A Perfect Spy* by John LeCarre; *White Noise* by Don DeLillo; *Jane Fonda's Workout Book* by Jane Fonda

ACHIEVEMENT: First permanent implant of a human heart is performed by Dr. William DeVries in Salt Lake City

INVENTION: Compact disc, CNN, a 24-hour news channel

SEX SYMBOLS: Bo Derek & Tom Selleck

VILLAIN: Captain Joseph Hazelwood, shortly after knocking back at least three vodkas, finds his ship, the *Exxon Valdez,* has run aground in Alaska's Prince William Sound, spilling 11 million gallons of oil.

PERSONALITY OF THE DECADE: Ronald Reagan

< BO DEREK

>NICKNAMES<

Steve [Bye Bye] Balboni ∧
Ozzie [the Wizard of Oz] Smith
Mike [Hit Man] Easler
Dennis [Oil Can] Boyd
Lenny [Nails] Dykstra
Fred [Crime Dog] McGriff
Will [the Thrill] Clark
Tim [Rock] Raines
Orel [Bulldog] Hershiser
Greg [Mad Dog] Maddux
Howard [HoJo] Johnson
Aurelio [Señor Smoke] Lopez
[Sweet] Lou Whitaker
Don [Donnie Baseball] Mattingly
William [Mookie] Wilson
Charles [Chili] Davis
Cecil [Big Daddy] Fielder
George [Storm] Davis
Steve [Bedrock] Bedrosian
Lonnie [Skates] Smith
Steve [Rainbow] Trout
Hensley [Bam Bam] Meulens

BORN		DIED	
Christina Aguilera	1980		John Lennon
Anna Kournikova	1981		Joe Louis
Prince William	1982		Grace Kelly
Kate Bosworth	1983		Gloria Swanson
LeBron James	1984		< Marvin Gaye
Jack Osbourne	1985		Orson Welles
Mary-Kate and Ashley Olsen	1986		James Cagney
Hilary Duff	1987		Jackie Gleason
Emily Browning	1988		Enzo Ferrari
Michelle Wie >	1989		Lucille Ball

> NEWS OF THE REAL WORLD

1980: Mount St. Helens erupts in Washington, killing 34 people, demolishing 178 homes and destroying hundreds of thousands of acres of timberland **1981:** 52 U.S. hostages released from Iran after 444 days **1982:** War breaks out between Great Britain and Argentina after the latter's invasion of the Falkland Islands **1983.** Terrorists bomb U.S. embassy and Marine barracks in Lebanon **1984:** Union Carbide Plant toxic gas leak in Bhopal, India, kills an estimated 1,750 **1985:** Palestinian terrorists hijack Italian cruise ship *Achille Lauro;* kill elderly American Leon Klinghoffer **1986:** Space shuttle *Challenger* explodes shortly after takeoff **1987:** U.S. military officials, including Lt. Col. Oliver North, testify before Congress on Iran-Contra affair **1988:** War between Iran and Iraq ends after eight years and 1.5 million casualties **1989:** U.S. troops invade Panama, arrest Gen. Manuel Noriega, later charged with drug trafficking and money-laundering

1966 | BROOKS ROBINSON was sky-high when the Orioles swept the Dodgers in the World Series. | *Photograph by* TSN ARCHIVES

1951 | AFTER HIS legendary shot won the pennant, Bobby Thomson and manager Leo Durocher paused outside the Giants clubhouse. | *Photograph by* BETTMANN/CORBIS

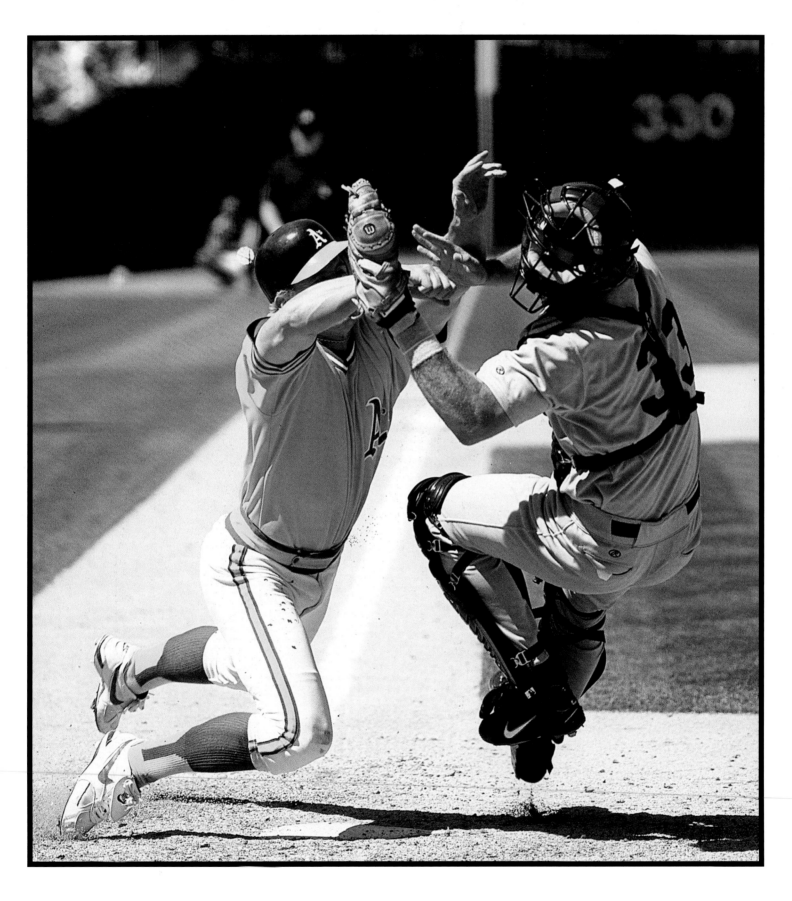

2002 | ON RETRO Day—A's in their '72 doubleknits, Rangers in '61 Senators duds—Bill Haselman slapped an old-fashioned tag on Eric Byrnes. | *Photograph by* BRAD MANGIN

2004 | DAVID ECKSTEIN needed flight insurance for his trip home over Devil Rays catcher Toby Hall. | *Photograph by* DONALD MIRALLE

THE RECORD ALMOST KILLED HIM

BY RICK TELANDER

With 61 homers in '61, Roger Maris bettered Babe Ruth, but got belted for doing it. Sixteen years later he found his bitter memories were finally getting a little sweeter. —*from SI, JUNE 20, 1977*

SUNDAY, OCT. 1, 1961, YANKEE Stadium, Bronx, N.Y. Bottom of the fourth, nobody on, one out, no score. Roger Maris of the Yankees steps to bat for the second time in the final game of the season. Tracy Stallard, a 24-year-old righthander for the Boston Red Sox, delivers a fastball—"a strike, knee-high on the outside of the plate," he would say later.

Maris swings and everybody knows the ball is gone. In the melee in the rightfield stands, Sal Durante, a teenager from Brooklyn, emerges with the home run ball and becomes a footnote to history. Maris slowly circles the bases to a standing ovation. Yogi Berra, the next batter, shakes his hand, as does the batboy and an ecstatic fan who has leaped out of the stands. Maris disappears into the dugout, comes out again, doffs his cap and smiles. On the last possible day he has broken Babe Ruth's "unbreakable" record and hit 61 home runs in a season.

Wednesday, March 23, 1977, Perry Field, Gainesville, Fla. Roger Maris, beer distributor and 42-year-old father of six, stands in the Yankees dugout watching his old team prepare to play a spring-training game against the University of Florida. George Steinbrenner, the Yankees owner, approaches. "Hey, Rog," he says, "where's the beer?" Maris laughs and shrugs. "You should have asked me earlier," he says.

Steinbrenner chuckles, but then his smile fades a bit. "You know, you're a hard guy to get a hold of, Roger," he says. "You're hard to get to New York for just one day."

There is a pause. Maris's smile continues, but it is artificial now, as though propped up with toothpicks. Steinbrenner is referring to the annual Old Timers' Game, an event Maris has never attended since he left the Yankees in 1966. Maris has refused to visit Yankee Stadium for any reason.

"Why don't you come?" Steinbrenner says in a softer voice. Maris stares out at the field. "They might shoot me," he says.

Steinbrenner's voice becomes solemn. "I'm telling you, Roger, you won't ever hear an ovation like the one you'd get if you'd come back to Yankee Stadium."

Maris looks at the ground. "Maybe," he says without conviction, and the conversation is over.

After all these years, the man who hit more home runs in a season than anyone else still has not recovered from the emotional turbulence of the summer of '61. Hounded ceaselessly by the sporting press and by fans, Maris proved himself inadequate to the vast demands of public relations. It is uncertain whether anyone could have been adequate.

At times, 50 or more reporters so packed the Yankee clubhouse to interview Maris that some of his teammates could not reach their lockers. When it became apparent that Maris had a real shot at Ruth's record, the barrage intensified. A hundred times a day he was asked if he thought he could break the record, how soon, what had he done to his swing, what did he think of all this. "You can believe me or not—I don't care—but I honestly don't know," he would answer, when thinking became unbearable.

Never a patient man, Maris told reporters that if they thought he was surly, it was too bad, because that was how he was going to stay. In one away game, angered by catcalls, he made obscene gestures to the crowd. In every road park, and frequently at Yankee Stadium, he was booed. He was, after all, chasing the immortal Babe.

He stopped smiling. His hair began to fall out. (His wife told him he looked like a molting bird.) A private person, Maris found he could never be alone, and his statements became less and less printable. In 1963 a reporter wrote that the trouble with Maris was that "he has proved to be such an unsatisfactory hero."

Since finishing his playing days in 1968, Maris has had little to do with baseball. He came to Perry Field this spring only because he has a few friends on the Yankees and because the team was now on his turf. "Baseball is just like a kid with a train," he told a reporter not long ago. "You got to outgrow it sometime." But there have been signs that Maris has not outgrown baseball, that very cautiously he is coming back to the game he never really wanted to leave. . . .

MARIS FOUND scant refuge from the constant onslaught of fans and the press during his pursuit of the Babe.

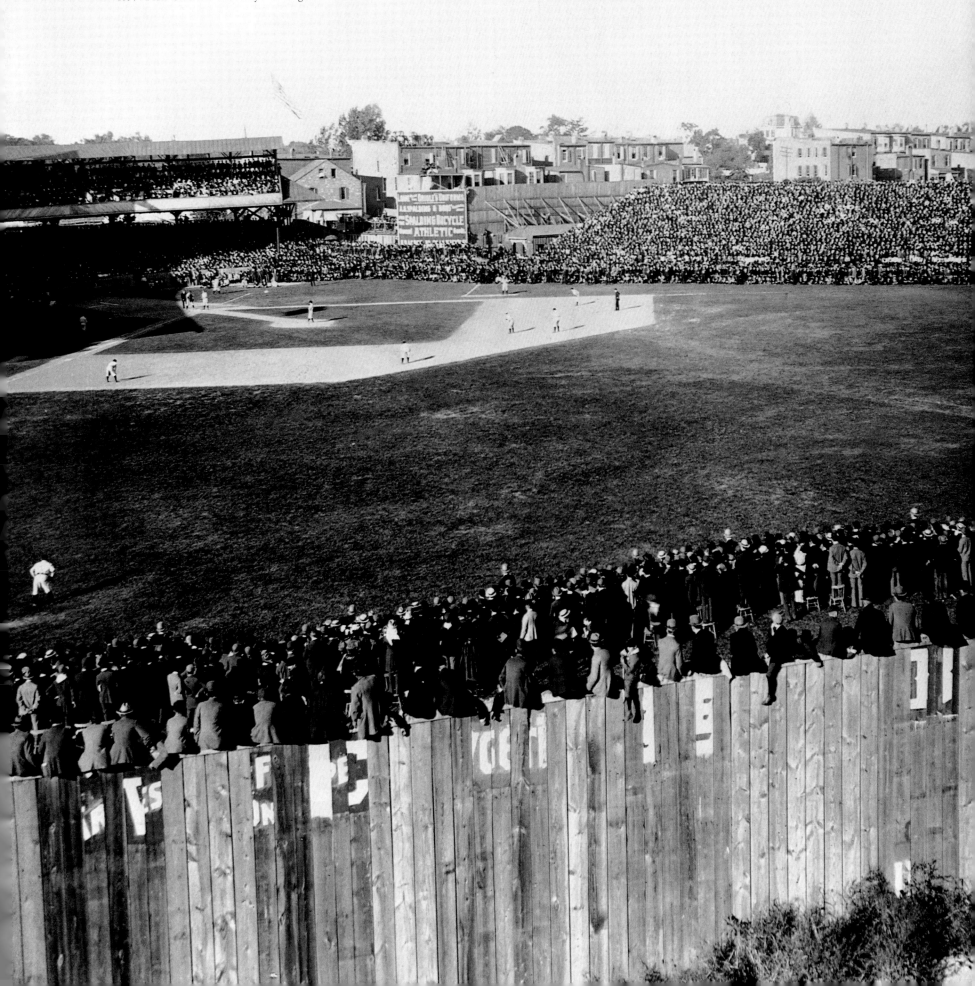

1987 | ORIOLES OUTFIELDER Ken Gerhart didn't have to worry about fan interference on this long fly in Baltimore. | *Photograph by* JERRY WACHTER

1897 | THE CROWD was really into the game—within a few feet of the action, in fact—when Boston took on Baltimore in the midst of a heated pennant race. | *Photograph by* CORBIS

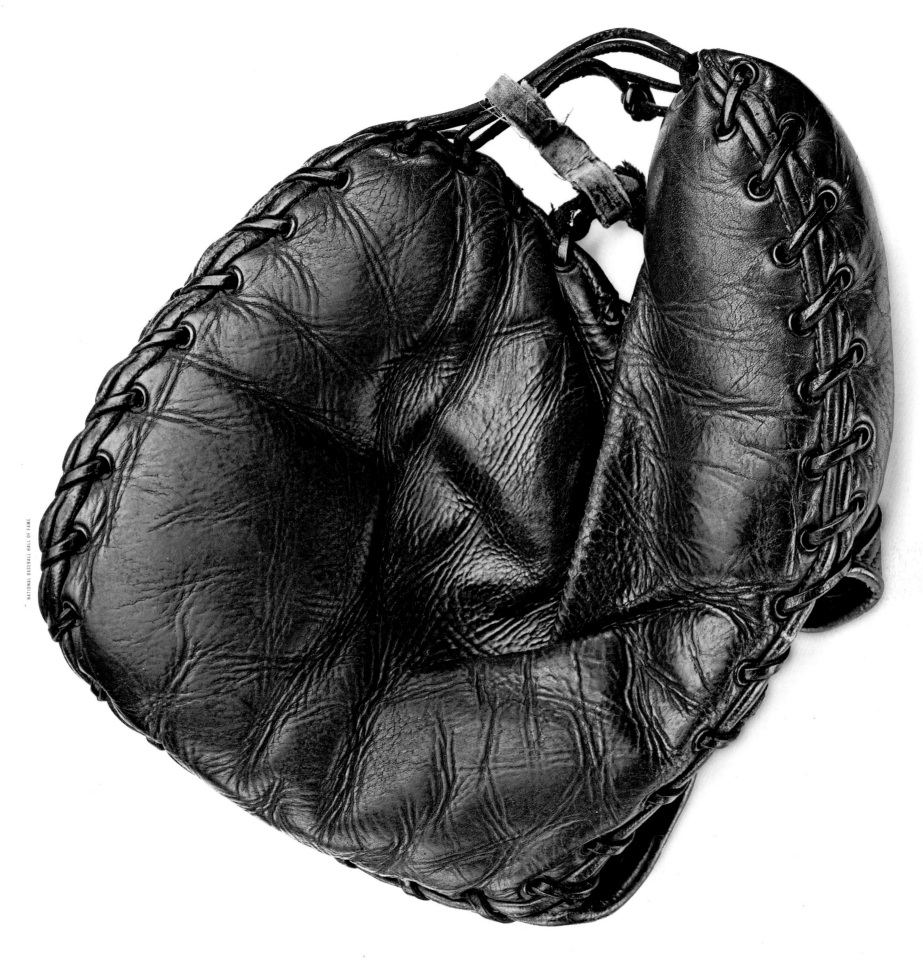

1936 | LOU GEHRIG was renowned for his power and productivity with a bat, but he also needed a good

glove to maintain his iron man status at first base for the Yankees. | *Photograph by* BETTMANN/CORBIS

ANDREW MORBITZER, A 38-YEAR-old marketing director from San Francisco, stood in line for beer and peanuts at a concession stand at AT&T Park as Barry Bonds took another shot at becoming only the second man in major league history to hit more home runs than Babe Ruth. This was four days after ESPN pulled the plug on its show *Bonds on Bonds*, largely because he'd been hitting home runs too infrequently for enough people to care. With one home run in his previous 66 plate appearances, Bonds could no longer keep people in their seats or in front of the TV the way he used to, but he proved with one flash of that familiar swing that he still has a sense of timing. In the final game of a home stand before a trip to Florida and New York, where more ambivalence and hostility would await, Bonds gave his loyal fans in San Francisco just what they wanted: career home run number 715.

It was 2:14 p.m. PDT when Bonds connected on a 90-mph fastball from righthander Byung-Hyun Kim of the Rockies. The baseball glanced off a fan's hands about 15 rows up in centerfield and fell onto a platform beyond the wall, eventually rolling off that and into the hands of the thirsty Morbitzer. For the first time since June 20, 1921, Ruth was third on the alltime home run list.

Bonds's teammates did not pour from the dugout to greet him as Hank Aaron's Atlanta teammates had done when Aaron passed Ruth in 1974. Giants principal owner Peter Magowan was out of the country. But the applause and cheers of 42,935 brought Bonds out of the dugout for two curtain calls, and in the clubhouse after the game the Giants gave Bonds a champagne toast and posed for pictures with him. "With all their support behind me and the fans of San Francisco, it can't get any better than this," he said.

Bonds, 41, entered this season needing only seven home runs to pass Ruth, but his pursuit of 715 was marked more by tedium than anticipation, largely because of the fallout from revelations of his alleged steroid use (Bonds has denied knowingly taking steroids) and because his home run rate (one every 16.3 at bats) was half what it had been in his glory years of 1999 through 2003—the years when, according to the book *Game of Shadows*, he engaged in a massive doping regimen. Said Giants manager Felipe Alou, "It looked like there was a lack of interest for 715 . . . even here." . . .

2006 | WITH THIS blast off the Rockies' Kim on May 28, Bonds passed the Babe on the alltime home run list. | *Photograph by* BRAD MANGIN

1957 | FUTURE HOME run king Hank Aaron was already taking the long view as the fourth of his 23 big league seasons began. | *Photograph by* JOHN ZIMMERMAN

1948 | JACKIE ROBINSON happily accommodated friendly fans during Dodgers spring training in the Dominican Republic. | *Photograph by* TSN ARCHIVES

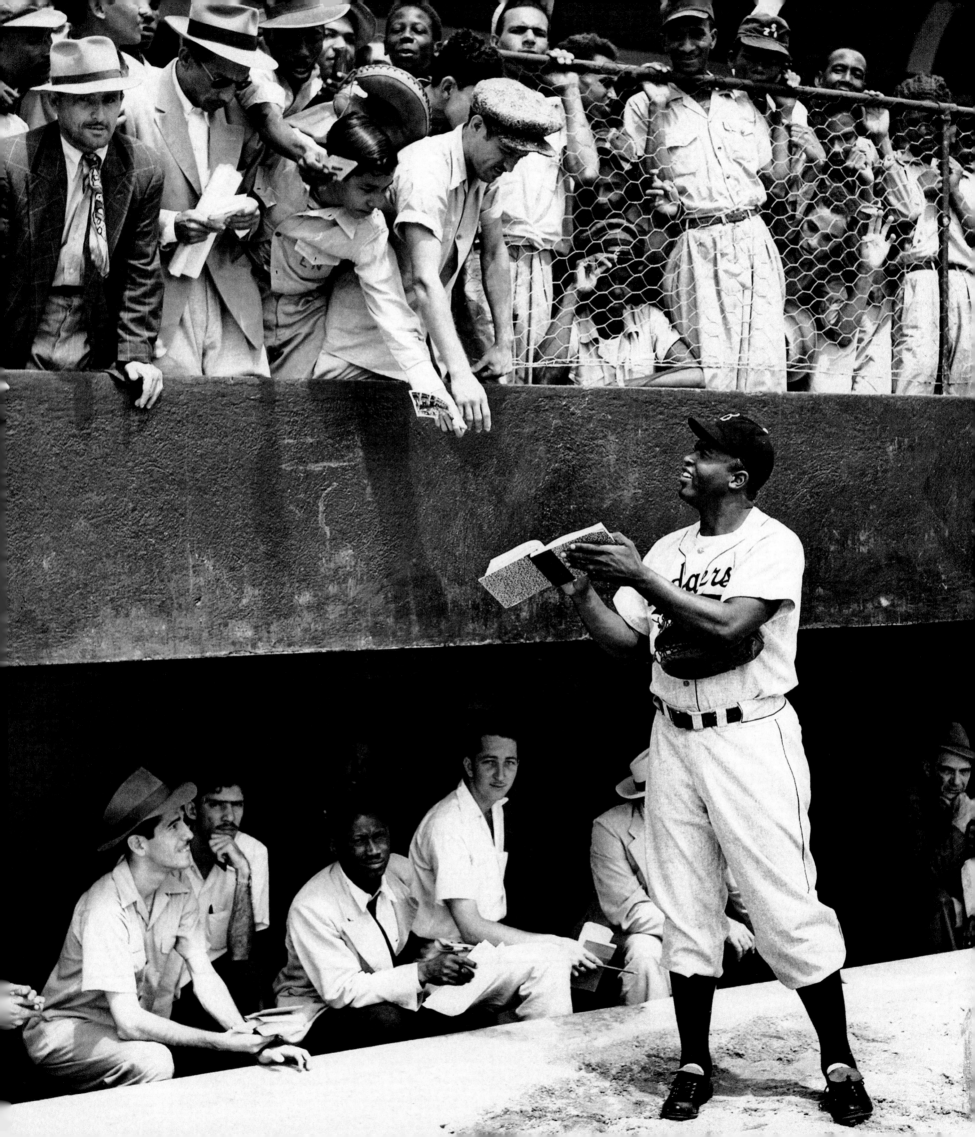

NO PLACE IN THE SHADE

BY MARK KRAM

Cool Papa Bell could run, hit, field and all that jazz, but for him and other players in the old Negro leagues, baseball was a bittersweet gig.
—*from* SI, AUGUST 20, 1973

IN THE LANGUAGE OF JAZZ, a "gig" is an evening of work; sometimes sweet, sometimes sour, take the gig as it comes, for who knows when the next will be. It means bread and butter first, but a whole lot of things have always seemed to ride with the word: drifting blue light, the bouquet from leftover drinks and most of all a sense of pain and limbo. For more than anything the word means *black*, down-and-out black, tired of-choppin'-cotton-gonna-find-me-a place-in-de-shade black.

Big shade fell on only a few. It never got to James Thomas Bell, or Cool Papa Bell as he was known in Negro baseball, that lost caravan that followed the sun. Other blacks would feel the touch of fame, or once in a while have the thought that their names meant something to people outside their own. But if you were black and played baseball, well, look for your name only in the lineup before each game.

Black baseball was a stone-hard gig. It was three games a day, sometimes in three different towns. It was the heat and fumes and bounces from buses that moved your stomach up to your throat and it was greasy meals at fly-papered diners at three a.m. and uniforms that were seldom off your back. "We slept with 'em on sometimes," says Papa, "but there never was 'nough sleep. We got so we could sleep standin' up or catch a nod in the dugout."

Only a half-mad seer—not any of the blacks who worked the open prairies and hidden ball yards in each big city—could have envisioned what would happen one day. The players knew a black man would cross the color line that was first drawn by the hate of Cap Anson back in 1883, yet no one was fool enough to think that some bright, scented day way off among the gods of Cooperstown they would hear their past blared out across the field and would know that who they were and what they did would never be invisible again.

When that time comes for Papa Bell, few will comprehend what he did during all those gone summers. The mass audience will not be able to measure him against his peers as they do the white player. The old ones like Papa have no past. They were minstrels, separated from record books, left as the flower in Grey's *Elegy* to "waste its sweetness on the desert air." Comparisons will have to do: Josh Gibson, the Babe Ruth of the blacks; Buck Leonard, the Lou Gehrig of his game; and Cool Papa Bell—who was he?

A comparison will be hard to find for Papa. His friend Tweed, whom Papa calls *the* Black Historian, says that you have to go all the way back to Willie Keeler for Papa's likeness. Papa's way was cerebral, improvisational; he was a master of the nuances that are the ambrosia of baseball for those who care to understand the game. Power is stark, power shocks, it is the stuff of immortality, but Papa's jewellike skills were the meat of shoptalk for 28 winters.

Arthritic and weary, Papa quit the circuit in 1950 at age 47, ending a career that began in 1922. During that time he had been the essence of black baseball, which had a panache all its own. It was an intimate game: the extra base, the drag bunt; a game of daring instinct, rather than one from the hidebound book. Some might say that it lacked discipline, but if so, it can also be said that never has baseball been played more artfully, or more joyously.

The yellow pages of Tweed's scrapbooks don't tell much about the way it was, and they don't reveal much about Papa, either; box scores never explain. They can't chart the speed of Papa Bell. "Papa Bell," says Satchel Paige, "why he was so fast he could turn out the light and jump in bed before the room got dark!" Others also embellish: he could hit a hard ground ball through the box and get hit with the ball as he slid into second; he was so fast that he once stole two bases on the same pitch. "People kin sure talk it, can't they?" says Papa.

Papa could run all right and he could hit and field as well. He played a shallow centerfield, even more so than Willie Mays when he broke in. "It doesn't matter where he plays," Pie Traynor once said. "He can go a country mile for a ball." As a hitter Bell had distance, but mainly he strove to hit the ball into holes; he could hit a ball through the hole in a fence, or drag a bunt as if it were on a string in his hand. Bell never hit below .308.

Papa Bell earned $90 a month his first year back in 1922. He would never make more than $450 a month, although his ability was such that later he would be on Jackie Robinson's all-time team in the same outfield with Henry Aaron and Willie Mays. Bill Veeck puts him right up there with Tris Speaker, Willie Mays and Joe DiMaggio. "Cool Papa was one of the most magical players I've ever seen," says Veeck. . . .

BELL, A star in the Negro leagues from 1922 till '50, never made it to the promised land of the majors but did reach the Hall of Fame.

> Artifacts

Leather and Lace

They've varied in shape and color over the years, but baseball shoes are all cutting-edge when it comes to spikes

c. 1905 | MYRON GRIMSHAW
First baseman, Boston Pilgrims

c. 1915 | WALTER JOHNSON
Pitcher, Washington Senators

1938 | BOB FELLER
Pitcher, Cleveland Indians

1971 | WILLIE MAYS
Centerfielder, S.F. Giants

1991 | RICKEY HENDERSON
Leftfielder, Oakland A's

1992 | JOE CARTER
Rightfielder, Toronto Blue Jays

1999 | CRAIG BIGGIO
Second baseman, Houston Astros

1973 | TWO-TIME Cy Young winner Bob Gibson, with a 2.91 ERA over 17 seasons, led the Cardinals to two world championships. | *Photograph by* WALTER IOOSS JR.

1971 | VIDA BLUE had a 24–8 record for the A's and won both the Cy Young and MVP awards. | *Photograph by* KEN REGAN

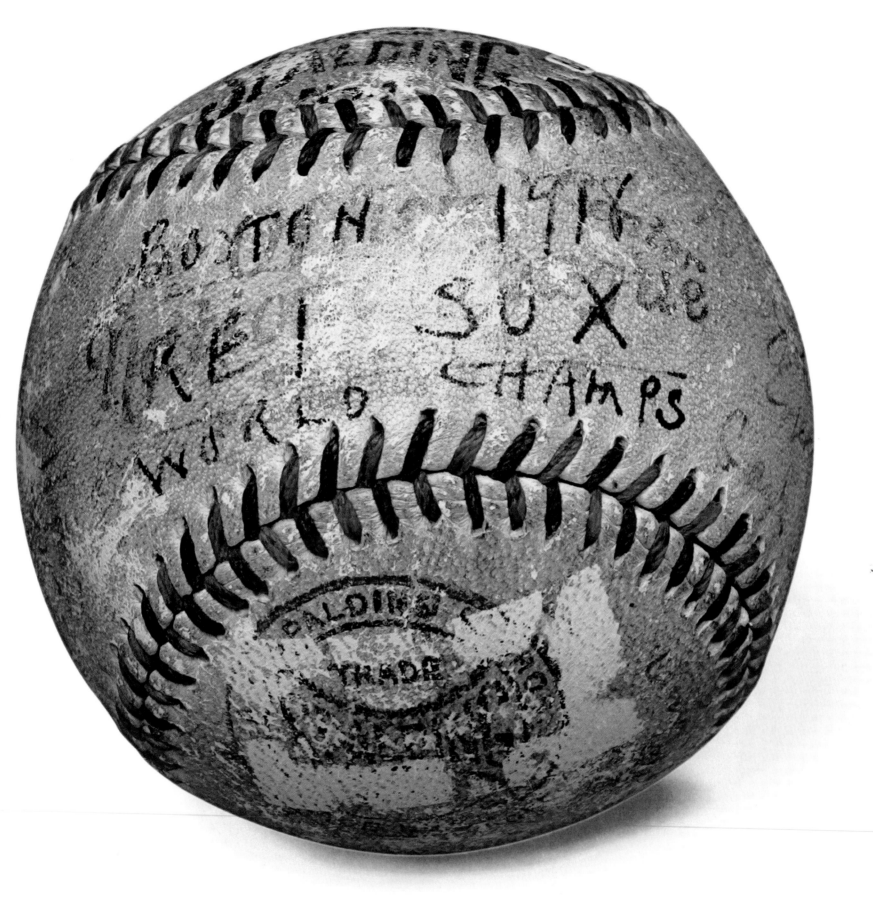

1918 | THE RED Sox won the World Series by riding the left arm of Boston pitcher Babe Ruth, who beat the Cubs twice. | *Photograph by* DAVID N. BERKWITZ

1919 | THE DOCUMENT that launched nearly a century of curses spelled out terms for the Bambino's transfer to the Yankees. | *Photograph by* MILO STEWART

UNIFORM AGREEMENT
FOR TRANSFER OF A PLAYER

TO OR BY A

Major League Club

NOTICE.—To establish uniformity in action by clubs when a player, released by a major league club to a minor league club, or by a minor league club to a major league club, refuses to report to and contract with the club to which he is transferred, the Commission directs the club securing him to protect both parties to the deal from responsibility for his salary during his insubordination by promptly suspending him.

Payment, in part or in whole, of the consideration for the release of such player will not be enforced until he is reinstated and actually enters the service of the purchasing club.

WARNING TO CLUBS.—Many contentions that arise over the transfer of players are directly due to the neglect of one or both parties to promptly execute and file the Agreement. The Commission will no longer countenance dilatory tactics, that result in appeals to it to investigate and enforce claims which, if made a matter of record, as required by the laws of Organized Base Ball, would not require adjustment. In all cases of this character, the complaining club must establish that it is not at fault for delay or neglect to sign and file the Agreement upon which its claim is predicated. (See last sentence of Rule 10.)

This Agreement, made and entered into this 26th day of December 1919

by and between _____Boston American League Baseball Club_____
(Party of the First Part)

and _____American League Base Ball Club of New York_____
(Party of the Second Part)

Witnesseth: The party of the first part does hereby release to the party of the second part the services of Player _____George H. Ruth_____ under the following conditions:

(Here recite fully and clearly every condition of deal, including date of delivery; if for a money consideration, designate time and method of payment; if an exchange of players, name each; if option to recall is retained or privilege of choosing one or more players in lieu of one released is retained, specify all terms. No transfer will be held valid unless the consideration, receipt of which is acknowledged therein, passes at time of execution of Agreement.)

By herewith assigning to the party of the second part the contract of said player George H. Ruth for the seasons of 1919, 1920 and 1921, in consideration of the sum of Twenty-five Thousand ($25,000.) Dollars and other good and valuable considerations paid by the party of the second part, receipt whereof is hereby acknowledged.

1993 | GREG MADDUX won four straight Cy Youngs (1992 to '95), including three as king of the hill for the Braves. | *Photograph by* RONALD C. MODRA

1966 | UMPIRES HAD to review some of the unique ground rules at the Astrodome before the Mets took on Houston. | *Photograph by* NEIL LEIFER

KEN GRIFFEY JR. was the AL
MVP with the Mariners in 1997, when he
hit .304 with 56 home runs and 147 RBI.
Photograph by CHUCK SOLOMON

> THE ALL-DECADE TEAMS

AMERICAN LEAGUE

CATCHER
Ivan Rodriguez

FIRST BASE
Frank Thomas

SECOND BASE
Roberto Alomar

SHORTSTOP
Alex Rodriguez

THIRD BASE
Wade Boggs

LEFTFIELD
Albert Belle

CENTERFIELD
Ken Griffey Jr.

RIGHTFIELD
Juan Gonzalez

DESIGNATED HITTER
Edgar Martinez

STARTING PITCHER
Roger Clemens

RELIEF PITCHER
Dennis Eckersley

NATIONAL LEAGUE

CATCHER
Mike Piazza

FIRST BASE
Jeff Bagwell

SECOND BASE
Ryne Sandberg

SHORTSTOP
Barry Larkin

THIRD BASE
Matt Williams

LEFTFIELD
Barry Bonds

CENTERFIELD
Steve Finley

RIGHTFIELD
Larry Walker

PINCH HITTER
Lenny Harris

STARTING PITCHER
Greg Maddux

RELIEF PITCHER
John Franco

> DEBUT   FINALE <

DEBUT		FINALE
FRANK THOMAS	1990	BILL BUCKNER
IVAN RODRIGUEZ	1991	DAVE PARKER
PEDRO MARTINEZ	1992	BERT BLYLEVEN
MANNY RAMIREZ	1993	NOLAN RYAN
ALEX RODRIGUEZ	1994	RICH GOSSAGE
DEREK JETER	1995	DAVE WINFIELD
ANDRUW JONES	1996	OZZIE SMITH
MIGUEL TEJADA	1997	EDDIE MURRAY
ROY HALLADAY	1998	PAUL MOLITOR
LANCE BERKMAN	1999	WADE BOGGS

> THE LEADERS

HITTING

BATTING AVERAGE*	TONY GWYNN	.344
HOME RUNS	MARK McGWIRE	405
RBI	ALBERT BELLE	1,099
AT BATS	RAFAEL PALMEIRO	5,848
HITS	MARK GRACE	1,754
SINGLES	TONY GWYNN	1,262
DOUBLES	MARK GRACE	364
TRIPLES	LANCE JOHNSON	113
OBP*	FRANK THOMAS	440
SLUGGING PCT.*	MARK McGWIRE	.615
RUNS	BARRY BONDS	1,091
STOLEN BASES	OTIS NIXON	478
HIT BY PITCHES	CRAIG BIGGIO	147
WALKS	BARRY BONDS	1,146
STRIKEOUTS	SAMMY SOSA	1,322
GAMES	RAFAEL PALMEIRO	1,526

PITCHING

WINS	GREG MADDUX	176
LOSSES	ANDY BENES	116
WINNING PCT.†	PEDRO MARTINEZ	682
STRIKEOUTS	RANDY JOHNSON	2,538
ERA†	GREG MADDUX	2.54
INNINGS	GREG MADDUX	2,394⅔
WALKS	RANDY JOHNSON	910
RUNS ALLOWED	JAIME NAVARRO	1,115
HOME RUNS ALLOWED	DAVID WELLS	233
SAVES	JOHN WETTELAND	295
SHUTOUTS	RANDY JOHNSON	25
COMPLETE GAMES	GREG MADDUX	75

* MINIMUM 2,500 PLATE APPEARANCES † MINIMUM 1,000 INNINGS

>HOT TICKETS 10 Games You Wish You'd Seen

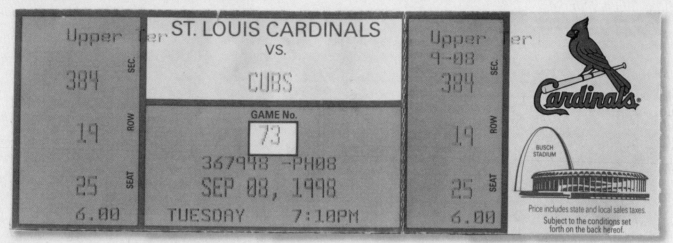

Camden Yards Sept. 6, 1995 Baseball crowns its new Iron Man when Cal Ripken Jr. plays in his 2,131st straight game, surpassing Lou Gehrig's "unbreakable" record for consecutive games.

∧ **Busch Stadium** Sept. 8, 1998 Cardinals first baseman Mark McGwire goes deep off Cubs pitcher Steve Trachsel for his 62nd home run of the season, surpassing the record set by Roger Maris in 1961. McGwire is congratulated by members of Maris's family seated next to the Cardinals dugout, and is embraced by Cubs rightfielder Sammy Sosa, who also spent the summer pursuing the record.

The Metrodome Oct. 27, 1991 Minnesota Twins righthander Jack Morris pitches a 10-inning, 1–0 shutout of the Atlanta Braves in Game 7 of the World Series, and pinch hitter Gene Larkin drives in the winning run in the 10th to give the Twins their second title in five years.

The SkyDome Oct. 23, 1993 Trailing by one run in the bottom of the ninth inning of Game 6 of the World Series, the Blue Jays' Joe Carter beats Phillies closer Mitch Williams for a Series-ending three-run home run, giving Toronto a second consecutive title.

Pro Player Stadium Oct. 26, 1997 Edgar Renteria singles off the Indians'

Charles Nagy with the bases loaded in the 11th inning of Game 7, giving the wild-card Marlins a world series championship.

Wrigley Field May 6, 1998 In only his fifth major league start, Cubs rookie Kerry Wood strikes out 20 Astros while pitching a one-hitter.

Oakland-Alameda County Stadium May 1, 1991 A's leadoff man Rickey Henderson proclaims himself "the Greatest" when he swipes third base against the Yankees and passes Lou Brock as baseball's alltime leading base stealer with 939.

Arlington Stadium May 1, 1991 At 44 Nolan Ryan becomes the oldest pitcher to throw a no-hitter when he blanks the Blue Jays 3–0 while striking out 16. The no-no is the record seventh of Ryan's career.

Dodger Stadium April 23, 1999 Cardinals third baseman Fernando Tatis sets a major-league record by hitting two grand slams in a single inning—the third—against Dodgers starter Chan Ho Park.

Jack Murphy Stadium June 3, 1995 Montreal's Pedro Martinez pitches nine perfect innings but, after the Expos take the lead in the top of the 10th, gives up a double to San Diego's Bip Roberts and is pulled for a reliever. Martinez gets the win.

BEST OF THE 1990s

TEAM	WINS	LOSSES	WIN PCT.
BRAVES	925	629	.595
YANKEES	851	702	.548
INDIANS	823	728	.531
WHITE SOX	816	735	.526
RED SOX	814	741	.523

BERNIE WILLIAMS, YANKEES

WORST OF THE 1990s

TEAM	WINS	LOSSES	WIN PCT.
DEVIL RAYS	132	192	.407
MARLINS	472	596	.442
TIGERS	702	852	.452
TWINS	718	833	.463
ROYALS	725	825	.468

EDGAR RENTERIA, MARLINS

1990s CULTURE

MUSIC: *The Bodyguard: Original Soundtrack* (Whitney Houston), *Nevermind* (Nirvana), *The Chronic* (Dr. Dre), *No Fences* (Garth Brooks), *Please Hammer, Don't Hurt 'em* (M.C. Hammer)

MOVIES: *Titanic, Forrest Gump, Jurassic Park, Sleepless in Seattle, The Silence of the Lambs*

TELEVISION SHOWS: *The Simpsons, Law & Order, Seinfeld, X-Files, Friends*

BOOKS: *The Bonfire of the Vanities* by Tom Wolfe; *Into Thin Air* by Jon Krakauer; *Men Are from Mars, Women Are from Venus*, by John Gray; *Harry Potter and the Sorcerer's Stone* by J. K. Rowling; *American Pastoral* by Philip Roth

ACHIEVEMENT: On Aug. 6, 1991 the World Wide Web, invented by British-born Tim Berners-Lee, became available, revolutionizing the dissemination of information.

INVENTIONS: Hubble space telescope, genetically engineered food, DVDs, Viagra

SEX SYMBOLS: Pamela Anderson & George Clooney

VILLAIN: Milwaukee's Jeffrey Dahmer was sent to prison in 1992 for killing 15 men and boys, having sex with the corpses and then cooking and eating them.

PERSONALITY: Bill Gates

< PAMELA ANDERSON

DIED

AVA GARDNER	1990	SAMMY DAVIS JR.
MILES DAVIS	1991	THEODOR ("DR. SEUSS") GEISEL
ALEX HALEY	1992	MARLENE DIETRICH
ARTHUR ASHE	1993	RUDOLF NUREYEV
BURT LANCASTER	1994	JACQUELINE KENNEDY ONASSIS
JERRY GARCIA	1995	HOWARD COSELL
CARL SAGAN	1996	TUPAC SHAKUR
MOTHER TERESA	1997	< DIANA, PRINCESS OF WALES
FRANK SINATRA	1998	BENJAMIN SPOCK
WILT CHAMBERLAIN >	1999	STANLEY KUBRICK

>NICKNAMES<

Andres [Big Cat] Galarraga ʌ
Randy [Big Unit] Johnson
Roger [Rocket] Clemens
Frank [the Big Hurt] Thomas
Juan [Gone] Gonzalez
David [Boomer] Wells
Rich [El Guapo] Garces
Jay [Bone] Buhner
[Everyday] Eddie Guardado
Ken [Junior] Griffey
Calvin [Pokey] Reese
Mariano [Mo] Rivera
Mark [Big Mac] McGwire
Gregory [Woody] Williams
Ivan [Pudge] Rodriguez
William [Buck] Showalter
Kenny [the Gambler] Rogers
Antonio [El Pulpo] Alfonseca
Mitch [Wild Thing] Williams
Jeff [the Barbarian] Conine
Leon [Bip] Roberts
Tom [Flash] Gordon

> NEWS OF THE REAL WORLD

1990: Anti-apartheid leader Nelson Mandela is freed after 27 years in South African prison **1991:** U.S.–led coalition drives Iraqi Army out of Kuwait in 41 days **1992:** Four days of riots rock Los Angeles after cops are acquitted of charges stemming from the videotaped beating of motorist Rodney King **1993:** Terrorists detonate bomb beneath World Trade Center—six dead, more than 1,000 injured **1994:** O.J. Simpson, charged with double-murder, leads police on low-speed chase in L.A. **1995:** Army vet Timothy McVeigh bombs Murrah Federal Building in Oklahoma City, 168 killed. **1996:** Tiger Woods wins third straight U.S. Amateur title, turns pro **1997:** Princess Diana killed in Paris car crash **1998:** Sex scandal hits White House as affair between President Clinton and White House intern Monica Lewinsky becomes public **1999:** Two students at Columbine High in Littleton, Colo., open fire at school, killing 13, then themselves

1955 | WHITEY FORD, an eight-time All-Star for the Yankees, won an AL–best 18 games in '55, then two more in the Series. | *Photograph by* HY PESKIN

1958 | EDDIE MATHEWS, the Braves' slugging third baseman, hit 512 homers in 17 seasons. | *Photograph by* JOHN G. ZIMMERMAN

1997 | A TRIFECTA for Reds manager Ray Knight: tossed in third inning for tossing third base and suspended for three games. | *Photograph by* AL BEHRMAN

1990 | REDS MANAGER Lou Piniella showed textbook form on his follow-through while arguing a call at first base. | *Photograph by* DAVID KOHL

THE SPIRIT OF ST. LOUIS

BY RICK REILLY

Cardinals play-by-play maestro Jack Buck didn't let a little thing like Parkinson's throw him. —*from* SI, MAY 7, 2001

PROMISE ME ONE THING. Promise that at the end of this you won't feel sorry for Jack Buck. As square as a pan of corn bread, as American as a red Corvette, Buck has been doing what he loves in the St. Louis Cardinals' radio booth for 47 years, which makes him just about the exact center of this country. The last thing he wants is sympathy.

Yeah, Buck has Parkinson's disease, which makes his hands tremble and his arms flail. He also has diabetes, which means poking needles into himself twice a day. He also has a pacemaker. And cataracts. And vertigo. And excruciatingly painful sciatica. And a box of pills the size of a toaster. But all that only gives him more material to work with.

"I wish I'd get Alzheimer's," he cracks. "Then I could forget I've got all the other stuff."

Luckily, you can still find the 76-year-old Buck at the mike during every St. Louis home game, broadcasting to the Cardinal Nation over more than 100 radio stations in 11 states. Herking and jerking in his seat, his face contorting this way and that, he still sends out the most wonderful descriptions of games you've ever heard.

"I've given the Cardinals the best years of my life," Buck says. "Now I'm giving them the worst."

That's a lie. Despite enough diseases to kill a moose, Buck has gotten even better lately. "I have no idea how," says his son and radio partner, Joe, "but his voice has been stronger lately. It's like he's pouring every ounce of energy God can give him into those three hours of the broadcast."

Yet Buck makes it all sound effortless, like talking baseball with the guy across the backyard fence. He's natural, simple and unforgettable. When Kirk Gibson hit his dramatic home run for the Los Angeles Dodgers and limped around the bases in the 1988 World Series, Buck, calling the game for CBS Radio, said, "I don't believe what I just saw!" When St. Louis's Ozzie Smith hit a rare lefthanded home run in Game 5 of the 1985

playoffs, Buck said, "Go crazy, folks! Go crazy!" When Mark McGwire hit No. 61 in 1998, Buck said, "Pardon me while I stand and applaud!"

Like thousands of other eight-year-old boys in Middle America in 1966, all I had of baseball most nights was Buck. If I fiddled enough with my mom's old radio in our kitchen in Boulder, Colo., I could pick up Buck doing the Cardinals' games on KMOX. Bob Gibson. Tim McCarver. Curt Flood. I worshipped Buck then. I respect him now.

He was a kid whose family couldn't afford toothpaste; who didn't go to the dentist until he was 15 (and immediately had five teeth pulled); who worked as a soda jerk, a newspaper hawk, a boat painter, a waiter, a factory hand; who was the first person in his family to own a car; who took shrapnel in an arm and a leg from the Germans in World War II; who danced in Paris on V-E Day.

This is a man who is coming up on his 10,000th game broadcast; who was in the stands the day that Joe DiMaggio's 56-game hitting streak ended; who called Stan Musial's five-home-run doubleheader; who ate dinner with Rocky Marciano in Havana; whom Jesse Owens called friend; who survived the Ice Bowl—and 16 years in the booth with Harry Caray.

I would eat a bathtub full of rubber chicken just to hear him emcee a banquet. He has more lines than the DMV. If an Italian woman wins the door prize, Buck says, "You know, I've always had a fondness for Italian women. In fact during World War II an Italian woman hid me in her basement for three months. [Pause.] Of course, this was in Cleveland."

If anything, Parkinson's has given Buck more banquet material. "I shook hands with Muhammad Ali recently," he says. "It took them 30 minutes to get us untangled."

This may be Buck's last year behind the mike, so he's savoring every inning. So should we. "This is his victory lap," says Joe. "This is him circling the outfield."

That lousy day is coming, of course, when he opens his mouth and the Parkinson's won't let anything come out. But don't feel sorry for him. "Hell, I've touched so many bases," says Buck, "I've got no quarrel with these last few."

So, on the day he quits, he'll have to pardon us while we stand and applaud. . . .

HITTERS AREN'T supposed to step in the bucket, but Jack Buck knew that was the only way to stay cool in the booth in St. Louis.

1927 | LOU ARCHER, an actor who appeared in *Babe Comes Home*, Ruth's second Hollywood feature, probably regretted having a slugger press his pants. | *Photograph by* JOHN SPRINGER COLLECTION

> Playback

Oddball Pitches

Pranks, put-ons and practical jokes have always come naturally to baseball players, even when they're not performing in the interest of public relations

1949 | IT WAS a banner year for Bobby Thomson, Whitey Lockman, Don Mueller and Willard Marshall.

c. 1960 | DON DRYSDALE (left) and Duke Snider reached out to two Dodgers fans.

1955 | CARDS PITCHER Frank Smith modeled his new neckwear for teammates.

1948 | JOE DiMAGGIO showed some AL umps how to make the call in West Palm Beach.

1978 | BOSTON PITCHER Bill Lee was known as Spaceman for his head, not his suit.

1951 | GIANTS PITCHER Sal Maglie lived, slept and sometimes ate baseball.

1971 | DERO AUSTIN, Indianapolis Clowns catcher, was big on the barnstorming circuit.

1938 | TARZAN HAD nothing on Indians ace Bob Feller when it came to monkeying around.

1938 | PHOTOGRAPHERS HAD the best seats in the house in D.C. for savoring the sweet swing of Joe DiMaggio. | *Photograph by* BETTMANN/CORBIS

LOVE, HATE AND BILLY MARTIN

BY FRANK DEFORD

His long history as a brawler jeopardized his career. But the record book proves that he could turn losers into winners.

—from SI, JUNE 2, 1975

IT WAS 18 YEARS AGO THIS spring that the Yankees got rid of Billy Martin. He was a bad influence, they said. Nobody saw him land a punch at the Copacabana nightclub when a bunch of his teammates got involved in a scrap with some fellows celebrating the end of their bowling season, but it was Martin's birthday party, and since he had a record for brawling, much of the blame landed on him. Then the next month he was in the middle of a big scuffle with the White Sox at Comiskey Park and was thrown out of the game. Three days later the Yankees sent him to Kansas City for Harry (Suitcase) Simpson. In the clubhouse Mickey Mantle cried. Casey Stengel told Martin, "Well, you're gone. You're the smartest little player I ever had."

In the cheerless cavalcade of the playing career that followed, Martin lasted no more than one season with any team: Detroit after K.C., then Cleveland, Cincinnati, Milwaukee and Minnesota. The late Jimmy Cannon wrote the foam about Martin that all the baseball people blew off their beers: "Now to Cincinnati in another league. And Billy Martin is positive he has come home at last. He always is."

A few years later, when Martin got a chance to manage, he won a division championship for the Twins and was fired, all in his first season. He won a division title with Detroit, but couldn't last out another year. Then Texas. He was Manager of the Year last season. This is his second full season with the Rangers. "It's been a truthful relationship here with everybody," says Martin, a man who prizes truth. "I have a real foundation here. I think I'll stay for the rest of my career." So now Texas. And Billy Martin is positive he has come home at last. He always is.

The problem is not just that Billy Martin gets in fights. Were he merely truculent he would have long since been cut loose from baseball. The problem is that he is a terribly complicated personality—not necessarily sophisticated-complicated, more ironic-complicated. He is a kind of Sir

Walter Scott knight errant cast loose into this strange modern world of compromise and convention, where duels are frowned upon and damsels in distress can be put on waivers. Despite all the donnybrooks, Martin is a man of sweet sentimentality. He believes in absolutes—some might say simplicities—and he is nurtured by the fundamental of chivalry, which he introduces into conversation as readily as he might order breakfast or argue with an umpire. Words such as loyalty, honor, truth, love, belief and pride surface regularly; and in his universe, where such absolutes rigorously figure, we should not be surprised that Martin also finds liars, back-stabbers, cowards, bullies and other blackguards lurking about, anxious to do him in. When in fact they do cross him, he does the only thing left for him to do in his well-defined world, which is to pop them in the chops or, where bosses are involved, to supply the lexical equivalent. Angels scout Frank Lane, a longtime general manager never known for being demure, admits that Martin is in a league all his own. "When I've talked like he does," Lane says, "I've always made sure I was talking on a five-year or seven-year contract."

Yet Martin also possesses powerful qualities of organization, inspiration, evaluation and attention to detail that make him nearly peerless among managers. Counting a minor-league season in 1968, he has taken four teams with losing records and turned them instantly into winners. This bespeaks more than a touch of genius. Since his abrasiveness draws attention, he also sells tickets, which managers and coaches almost never do, whatever the sport. The enraged citizenry of the Twin Cities and Detroit responded with classic organized American hysteria to his firings—printing up buttons and bumper stickers and indignantly registering their opinions on radio call-in shows. So we can be sure there will always be a home for Billy Martin.

Wherever he goes, Martin wants things his way, and he is not bashful. While it is politic for managers to utter platitudes about the managerial dependence upon the athletic talent at their disposal, and to allow that they can really only do a little bit here and there—a suicide squeeze twice a season, that sort of thing—Martin believes that the manager should be the force

about which the team revolves. Copernicus, you may recall, had similar public-relations difficulties with the Establishment over what revolves around what. "A manager can change the outcome in anywhere from 20 to 50 games," Martin proclaims heretically.

Twenty to 50? Why, you're talking about one out of almost every three games.

"Sure," says Martin. "That is, if he's the kind of guy I am, who handles everything himself. I'm not talking about the managers who just make out the lineup cards. *I call everything myself.* Infield in, halfway, back; all the pitchouts; whether to throw through or not. I call a lot of the pitches, too."

Charley Dressen failed to impress his players with a similar view of self-eminence: "Stay close, boys, and I'll think of some-

thing." But while Martin has quipped that the secret of his profession "is to keep the five players who hate you away from the four who are undecided," he has really been quite popular with his minions. What he did learn from studying Dressen— who once, furious and fully clothed, followed the naked Martin into a shower to get the last word—is that confidence need not be confused with majesty.

But if Martin picked up this or that from Dressen and some of the others he played for, Stengel, his patron, is the lone Influence. Indeed, on the days when a breeze blows, so that Martin's dark blue Ranger jacket billows in back above where he jabs his right hand into the rear pocket, a man can take off his glasses, and it seems once more that it is the bandy-legged old man going out to lift Lopat for Page, not merely his favorite protégé about to lift Bibby for Foucault. . . .

MARTIN, WHO instantly turned four losing teams into winners, believed a manager like him could change the outcome of 50 games a year.

1967 | IT WAS a Triple Crown season for Carl Yastrzemski, a Hall of Famer who played 23 seasons with the Red Sox. | *Photograph by* ART SHAY

1967 | JIM FREGOSI debuted at short for the expansion Angels in '61, became their manager in '78 and led them to their first title in '79. | *Photograph by* WALTER IOOSS JR.

1960 | ROBERTO CLEMENTE (21) had a hit in every game of the Pirates' seven-game win over the Yankees in the World Series. | *Photograph by* NEIL LEIFER

1963 | LONG BEFORE Joe Torre was a manager he was a tough out—a .297 hitter over 18 seasons with the Braves and three other teams. | *Photograph by* NEIL LEIFER

THE STUFF OF LEGEND

BY STEVE WULF

The Hall of Fame was built in Cooperstown upon a foundation of fable, but from its bogus beginnings has come a nearly sacred shrine in an almost perfect setting. —*from* SI, JUNE 12, 1989

I T'S AN UGLY LITTLE THING that looks more like a fossilized chaw of tobacco than a baseball. The cross seams on one side of it have come apart, revealing some kind of cloth stuffing that resembles dirty yarn. Hard to believe anybody saved the thing in the first place. This is the so-called Doubleday ball, supposedly used by Abner Doubleday and the boys 150 years ago and most certainly used 100 years later to foster the belief that baseball was created in Cooperstown, N.Y., in 1839.

We all know by now, of course, that Abner Doubleday was the man whom baseball invented, and not the other way around. Historians tell us that Cooperstown has no better claim to being baseball's birthplace than Brooklyn or Hoboken, N.J., or Murray Hill in Manhattan, to name just a few sites where baseball was played in its earliest days. In 1839, the year Doubleday is alleged to have conceived the game in Cooperstown, he was a first-year cadet at West Point, confined to post.

So how can something so wrong be so right? As the National Baseball Hall of Fame and Museum celebrates its 50th anniversary this summer baseball fans should give thanks to the solons of the game who had the bad sense and good taste to make Cooperstown home plate. Maybe the game didn't begin in Cooperstown, but it's nice to think that it began in some small town when some boy named Abner drew a diamond in the dirt. And after the great players have touched 'em all, they can find no warmer greeting than the one they get when they cross the plate there on the shores of Otsego Lake.

"It's something like going to heaven," Charlie Gehringer (Class of '49) said of his induction. He could have been speaking of Cooperstown (pop. 2,300), which is the stuff of picture postcards, or of the state of grace that comes with joining the likes of Babe Ruth and Lou Gehrig and Christy Mathewson.

Once you begin to appreciate the Hall of Fame then you should go back and take another look at Cooperstown's Ex-hibit A, that ugly little Doubleday ball. It's not just stuffed with cloth but also with the dreams of boys and the sweat of men. Pardon the mush, but it's the perfect symbol of a game bursting at the seams with 150 years of history and lore. Out of that homely ball, which is the oldest physical evidence of the game anywhere, have sprung all of the thousands of other artifacts in Cooperstown. And, pardon the anthropomorphism, each one of those relics has a story to tell.

There's the resin bag that Ralph Branca used to get a grip on the ball he threw to Bobby Thomson in 1951. The shoes of Shoeless Joe Jackson. The glove Brooks Robinson used to make all those plays in the 1970 World Series. Cool Papa Bell's sunglasses, themselves the essence of cool, worn when he starred in the Negro leagues. There's Ruth's 60th home run ball and Roger Maris's 61st. Maury Wills's 104th stolen base from 1962. The bat with which Ted Williams, in his last at bat, homered. Joe DiMaggio's locker, which had also been used by Mickey Mantle. There's Wally Pipp's glove. The medal that catcher and spy Moe Berg was awarded for his CIA work during World War II. A huge trophy inscribed: PRESENTED TO DENTON T. YOUNG, THE KING OF PITCHERS—call it Cy Young's award. The helmet rack from Connie Mack Stadium. Jocko Conlan's whisk broom. Ty Cobb's sliding pads. The Babe's bowling ball. . . .

Tom Heitz, the head librarian for the Hall of Fame, naturally favors the treasures found in archives, correspondence and old newspapers. His latest find is a yearbook for the 1910 Chicago Giants Base Ball Club, a Negro league team in an era about which little is known. In the guide is a profile of hitherto unsung star Joseph (Cyclone) Williams, a pitcher who went 115-31-1 from 1905 to 1909. "If you have ever witnessed the speed of a pebble in a storm you have not even then seen the equal of the speed possessed by this wonderful Texan Giant," says the guide.

Also in Heitz's possession is a letter from *The Sporting News,* canceling the subscription of one "Abner Doubleday, Main St., Cooperstown, N.Y." And while the Doubleday myth may indeed have been canceled by cruel fact, the notion that baseball began in Cooperstown still survives. Why, just the other day Heitz received a most intriguing letter from Hugh MacDougall, a village trustee. While doing some unrelated research, MacDougall found this item in the June 6, 1816, issue of the *Otsego Herald,* under the title *Village Ordinances*: "Be it ordained, That no person shall play at Ball in Second or West street in this village, under a penalty of one dollar, for each and every offence."

Does that mean that 23 years before Doubleday didn't invent baseball, Cooperstown youths were creating a nuisance playing ball at what is now the corner of Main and Pioneer Streets, right at the flagpole, 50 yards from the steps of the museum? It couldn't have been football or basketball, which had not yet been invented. Why, Cooperstown just might be the right place, after all. . . .

THE BALL that started it all, including the Hall: the famous 1839 Abner Doubleday ball, which allegedly proved that he had invented baseball.

2001 | IT WAS a rocky moment for L.A.'s Paul Lo Duca when the Colorado catcher Ben Petrick scored at Dodger Stadium. | *Photograph by* JOHN W. MCDONOUGH

2003 | CUBS RIGHTFIELDER Sammy Sosa had his flaps up and landing gear down as he prepared for arrival at third base in Wrigley. | *Photograph by* BOB ROSATO

Assault and Battery

The storied rivalry between the Dodgers and Giants turned bloody at Candlestick Park in San Francisco when Juan Marichal used his bat as a weapon and set off baseball's ugliest brawl.

1965 | After knocking down two Dodgers, Marichal came to bat anticipating retaliation; following Sandy Koufax's first pitch, the return throw to the mound by Johnny Roseboro came too close to Marichal, who jawed with the catcher, then clubbed him on the head. Dodgers pitcher Bob Miller tackled Marichal before Roseboro, bloodied but not seriously injured, was led off by Willie Mays (above).

Photographs by NEIL LEIFER

A DAY OF LIGHT
AND SHADOW

BY JONATHAN SCHWARTZ

A profoundly—almost perversely—devoted Red Sox fan recounts the ecstasy and foreboding in the days and weeks before the one-game playoff between Boston and New York in 1978.
—*from* SI, FEBRUARY 26, 1979

IN THE KITCHEN IN UPPER Manhattan, Luis Tiant appeared to be in charge of the Red Sox' 162nd game of the year. Boston had widened a small lead over Toronto to five runs, and Tiant's impeccable control compelled even the restless woman roaming through the apartment to stop at the kitchen door and admire his performance, as one would admire an exquisitely bound volume of dense theological writing in another language.

In the bedroom, the Yankees had fallen well behind Cleveland and were hitting pop-ups, always a sign late in the game that things are out of hand.

The woman was restless because her quiet Sunday afternoon was being assaulted by the babble of baseball and by what she perceived as yet another increase in my furious tension. She had retreated to the living room to sit sullenly among the Sunday editions of *Newsday, The Washington Post* and two New York papers. She had been told that this was positively *it*; that there was *no* chance that the Red Sox would advance past this Sunday afternoon; that the baseball season would be over by sundown. She had been told that there would *never* be a repetition of my impulsive flight to Los Angeles after the Yankees' four-game Fenway Park sweep three weeks before. I had simply up and left the house during the seventh inning of the last humiliating defeat. I had taken nothing with me but a Visa card and $50. I had called home from Ontario, Calif., having pulled my Avis Dodge off the road leading to the desert, though I realized it was well after midnight in New York. "I am filled with regret," I said from a phone booth without a door.

"Over what?" I was asked.

Her question meant this: Was I filled with regret because the Red Sox had lost four consecutive games, or was I filled with regret because I had up and left without explanation and had not bothered to call until the middle of the night—and if you want this relationship to work you're going to have to work at it?

I replied above the roar of traffic from the San Bernardino Freeway that I was regretful about leaving, and about my insensitivity and my inability to put baseball in perspective. "A trip of this kind," I said severely, "will *never* happen again."

The truth: I was regretful because the Red Sox had lost four consecutive games, had blown an enormous lead and had handed the championship of the Eastern Division of the American League to the Yankees.

Three weeks later, the phone rang for an hour after the Sunday games were over. Congratulations! From California—Palm Springs, Brentwood, San Francisco. From Stamford, Conn., and Bridgehampton, N.Y. From 73rd Street and 10th Street in Manhattan. Congratulations!

Returning from oblivion, the Red Sox had tied for first place on the last day of the season, forcing a playoff game in Boston the next afternoon. Somehow this development had moved people to seek me out with warm feelings, as if my control had been as superb as Tiant's and had contributed to the unexpected Red Sox comeback. My control, of course, had vanished after Labor Day, leaving me infuriated and melancholy. And yet I accepted congratulations that Sunday afternoon as if my behavior during September had been exemplary. In fact, I had wept and raged. Had participated in two fistfights, had terminated a close friendship and had gone out in search of a neighborhood 15-year-old who had written red sox stink in orange crayon on the back window of my car. I had set out after him with vicious intent, only to return home in a minute or so, mortified. The psychiatrist, whom I immediately sought out, said to me, "This is *not* what a 40-year-old should be doing with his time. *Comprenez-vous?*"

On the triumphant Sunday evening, I drank Scotch and talked long distance. I was asked, "Are you thrilled?" I was thrilled. "Can they do it?" I doubted they could. "Are you going to the game?" Well, maybe.

I had actually thought of trying to use my connections as a radio broadcaster to round up some kind of entrée to Fenway Park for the next afternoon, but the prospect of tracking down people in their homes on a Sunday night was depressing. And

there would be the scramble for the air shuttle, an endless taxi ride in a Boston traffic jam, no ticket or pass left at the press window as promised, and a frantic attempt to reach Bill Crowley, the Red Sox' cantankerous p.r. man on the phone—"Bill, the pass was supposed to have been . . . and no one's seen it and they can't . . . and is there any possibility that I could. . . . "

No. I would watch at home, alone. I would stand in the bedroom doorway and watch with the sound off to avoid Yankee announcer Phil Rizzuto's ghastly shrieking. At home, in the event of a Red Sox victory, I would be able to accept congratulatory calls, this time for the real thing. "To me, it's the division championship that means the most," I had often said to whoever would listen. "After the division it's all dessert."

And yet. Had there been a more significant athletic event held in this country during my lifetime than the Yankee–Red Sox playoff? It occurred to me that perhaps there had been one—the Bobby Thomson game of 1951. The circumstances had been similar: a playoff involving intense rivals home-based in relative proximity; personalities that occupied the mind at four in the morning; and startling rallies through August and September, the '51 Giants having wiped away a 13½-game Dodger lead and the '78 Yankees having fought from 14 back of the Red Sox. The difference seemed to be a small one: for the Dodgers and Giants it had been the third of a three-game playoff; for the Red Sox and Yankees it would be one game, sudden death. . . .

LIGHT-HITTING Yankees shortstop Bucky Dent blasted the shocking homer that beat the Red Sox in a one-game playoff for the division title.

> **Artifacts**

There's Always a Catch

Mitts have evolved from defensive measures, to protect the hands, into instruments of defensive prowess

1883 | FINGERLESS GLOVE

1884 | FINGERS SEWN ON GLOVE

c. 1891 | PILLOW-STYLE MITT

c. 1895 | CLOTH CATCHER'S MITT

c. 1903 | PADDED-HEEL GLOVE

1910 | WEBBED FIELDER'S GLOVE

c. 1925 | WALLY PIPP'S GLOVE (1B)

c. 1950 | PHIL RIZZUTO'S GLOVE (SS)

2006 | JOHNNY DAMON'S GLOVE (OF)

1955 | IN SPRING training, these Cards were all in play (from left): Bill Virdon, Harry Elliott, Rip Repulski, Wally Moon and Stan Musial. | *Photograph by* MARK KAUFFMAN

THE 2000s

ICHIRO SUZUKI hit .350, stole 56 bases and played a brilliant rightfield for the Mariners in '01, earning AL MVP honors in his first U.S. season. | *Photograph by* DARREN CARROLL

>THE ALL-DECADE TEAMS

AMERICAN LEAGUE	NATIONAL LEAGUE
CATCHER	CATCHER
Ivan Rodriguez	*Jason Kendall*
FIRST BASE	FIRST BASE
Jason Giambi	*Todd Helton*
SECOND BASE	SECOND BASE
Alfonso Soriano	*Jeff Kent*
SHORTSTOP	SHORTSTOP
Miguel Tejada	*Edgar Renteria*
THIRD BASE	THIRD BASE
Alex Rodriguez	*Scott Rolen*
LEFTFIELD	LEFTFIELD
Manny Ramirez	*Barry Bonds*
CENTERFIELD	CENTERFIELD
Johnny Damon	*Andruw Jones*
RIGHTFIELD	RIGHTFIELD
Ichiro Suzuki	*Vladimir Guerrero*
DESIGNATED HITTER	PINCH HITTER
David Ortiz	*Mark Sweeney*
STARTING PITCHER	STARTING PITCHER
Mike Mussina	*Randy Johnson*
RELIEF PITCHER	RELIEF PITCHER
Mariano Rivera	*Trevor Hoffman*

>DEBUT   FINALE<

DEBUT		FINALE
JOHAN SANTANA	2000	DWIGHT GOODEN
JUAN PIERRE	2000	ALBERT BELLE
ALBERT PUJOLS	2001	CAL RIPKEN JR.
ICHIRO SUZUKI	2001	TONY GWYNN
CARL CRAWFORD	2002	TIM RAINES
JAKE PEAVY	2002	DAVID JUSTICE
DONTRELLE WILLIS	2003	RICKEY HENDERSON
JASON BAY	2003	DAVID CONE
RYAN HOWARD	2004	EDGAR MARTINEZ
JEFF FRANCOEUR	2005	LARRY WALKER

>THE LEADERS

HITTING

BATTING AVERAGE* TODD HELTON	.344
HOME RUNS ALEX RODRIGUEZ	281
RBI ALEX RODRIGUEZ	763
AT BATS MIGUEL TEJADA	3,834
HITS TODD HELTON	1,157
SINGLES ICHIRO SUZUKI	902
DOUBLES TODD HELTON	295
TRIPLES CRISTIAN GUZMAN	64
OBP* BARRY BONDS	533
SLUGGING PCT.* BARRY BONDS	779
RUNS ALEX RODRIGUEZ	752
STOLEN BASES JUAN PIERRE	267
HIT BY PITCHES CRAIG BIGGIO	120
WALKS BARRY BONDS	881
STRIKEOUTS PAT BURRELL	886
GAMES MIGUEL TEJADA	970

PITCHING

WINS RANDY JOHNSON, BARTOLO COLON	103
LOSSES LIVAN HERNANDEZ	77
WINNING PCT.† PEDRO MARTINEZ	.726
STRIKEOUTS RANDY JOHNSON	1,679
ERA† PEDRO MARTINEZ	2.58
INNINGS LIVAN HERNANDEZ	1,417⅓
WALKS RUSS ORTIZ	576
RUNS ALLOWED LIVAN HERNANDEZ	683
HOME RUNS ALLOWED ERIC MILTON	179
SAVES MARIANO RIVERA	250
SHUTOUTS RANDY JOHNSON	12
COMPLETE GAMES LIVAN HERNANDEZ	31

* MINIMUM 2,500 PLATE APPEARANCES †MINIMUM 1,000 INNINGS; STATISTICS THROUGH 2005

>HOT TICKETS 10 Games You Wish You'd Seen

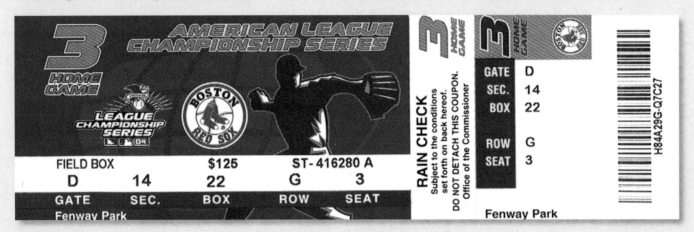

∧ Fenway Park Oct. 17, 2004 With the Red Sox trailing the Yankees three games to none and 4–3 in the ninth inning, pinch runner Dave Roberts steals second and scores the game-tying run. David Ortiz's walk-off home run in the 12th inning extends the Red Sox season.

Bank One Ballpark Nov. 4, 2001 Hitting against Mariano Rivera, Diamondbacks leftfielder Luis Gonzalez bloops a single over a drawn-in Yankees infield to score Jay Bell with the winning run giving Arizona its first world championship and Randy Johnson, who came in relief in the eighth, his third win of the Series.

Yankee Stadium Oct. 16, 2003 The Yankees Aaron Boone hits a series-ending solo home run off Boston's Tim Wakefield to lead off the bottom of the 11th and send the Yankees to the World Series.

Pac Bell Park Oct. 5, 2001 San Francisco's Barry Bonds hits his 71st and 72nd home runs of the season, against the Dodgers, surpassing Mark McGwire's single-season record, which was set in 1998. Bonds finishes the season with 73 HRs.

Yankee Stadium June 13, 2003 After being stuck on 299 career wins for three starts, Roger Clemens beats the Cardinals for his 300th. In the second inning of the game Clemens fans Cardinals shortstop Edgar Renteria for the 4,000th strikeout of his career.

Miller Park May 23, 2002 Dodgers rightfielder Shawn Green sets a major league record by racking up 19 total bases against the Brewers. In six at bats, Green has a single, a double and four home runs for seven RBIs in the Dodgers' 16–3 win.

Safeco Field Oct. 1, 2004 Seattle's Ichiro Suzuki gets his 257th and 258th hits of the year, to tie and then pass George Sisler's 84-year-old major league record for hits in a season. He finishes with 262.

Yankee Stadium June 11, 2003 After starter Astros Roy Oswalt is taken out in the second inning because of a pulled groin, five relievers (Pete Munro, Kirk Saarloos, Brad Lidge, Octavio Dotel and Billy Wagner) hold the Yankees hitless for the remaining eight innings, giving Houston the only six-pitcher no-hitter in history.

Safeco Field July 10, 2001 In his final All Star Game, Baltimore third baseman Cal Ripken Jr. unexpectedly starts at shortstop, switching places with Texas shortstop Alex Rodriguez. Ripken hits a home run to lead off the third inning and is named MVP of the midsummer classic for the second time in his career.

Yankee Stadium Oct. 21, 2000 In Game 1 of the New York Subway Series, the Yankees win 4–3 over the Mets with a 12th inning single by former Met Jose Vizcaino.

BEST OF THE 2000s (THROUGH 2005)

TEAM	WINS	LOSSES	WIN PCT.
YANKEES	582	386	.601
CARDINALS	575	397	.592
BRAVES	571	399	.589
ATHLETICS	571	400	.588
GIANTS	548	422	.565

ALBERT PUJOLS, CARDINALS

WORST OF THE 2000s

TEAM	WINS	LOSSES	WIN PCT.
TIGERS	386	585	.398
DEVIL RAYS	386	583	.398
ROYALS	401	571	.413
BREWERS	413	558	.425
PIRATES	417	553	.430

DMITRI YOUNG, TIGERS

2000s CULTURE

MUSIC: *The Eminem Show* (Eminem), *Get Rich or Die Tryin'* (50 Cent), *Elephant* (The White Stripes), *No Strings Attached* ('N Sync); *Oops!. . . I Did It Again* (Britney Spears)

MOVIES: *The Lord of the Rings, Capote, Harry Potter, Million Dollar Baby, Napoleon Dynamite*

TELEVISION: *American Idol, 24, Survivor, The Sopranos, Desperate Housewives, The Daily Show, The West Wing*

BOOKS: *The Tipping Point* by Malcolm Gladwell; *The Da Vinci Code* by Dan Brown; *It's Not About the Bike* by Lance Armstrong; *The Kite Runner* by Khaled Hosseini; *The World Is Flat* by Thomas L. Friedman

ACHIEVEMENT: Mapping of the human genome, a project started in 1990, was completed, with the help of supercomputers, by scientists from 18 nations

INVENTIONS: iPod, Segway, satellite radio, self-contained artificial heart.

SEX SYMBOLS: Angelina Jolie & Brad Pitt

VILLAIN: Osama Bin Laden, head of the terrorist network al-Qaeda and mastermind of the Sept. 11 attacks.

(SPLIT) PERSONALITY OF THE DECADE: Paris Hilton/Dick Cheney

< ANGELINA JOLIE

>NICKNAMES<

David [Big Papi] Ortiz ∧
Alex [A-Rod] Rodriguez
Larry [Chipper] Jones
Orlando [El Duque] Hernandez
Luis [Gonzo] Gonzalez
Travis [Pronk] Hafner
Kevin [Shrek] Mench
Francisco [K-Rod] Rodriguez
Dontrelle [D-Train] Willis
Kenji [Jo Mama] Johjima
Pat [the Bat] Burrell
Covelli [Coco] Crisp
Barry [Planet] Zito
Joe [Cupcakes] Blanton
Dmitri [Da Meat Hook] Young
Carlos [El Caballo] Lee
Ryan [Mad Dog] Madson
Hideki [Godzilla] Matsui
Gary [Little Sarge] Matthews
[Super] Joe McEwing
Ernest [Junior] Spivey
Aubrey [Huff Daddy] Huff

DIED

ALEC GUINNESS	2000	TOM LANDRY
STEVE ALLEN	2000	CHARLES M. SCHULZ
DALE EARNHARDT	2001	GEORGE HARRISON
JOHN LEE HOOKER	2001	KEN KESEY
ROONE ARLEDGE >	2002	SAM SNEAD
MILTON BERLE	2002	JOHNNY UNITAS
BOB HOPE	2003	KATHARINE HEPBURN
IDI AMIN	2003	DAVID BRINKLEY
YASSER ARAFAT	2004	< RAY CHARLES
ROSA PARKS	2005	JOHNNY CARSON

> **NEWS OF THE REAL WORLD** **2000:** U.S. Presidential election hung up by chads in Florida; Bush declared winner after Supreme Court fight **2001:** Terrorists crash planes into Twin Towers, Pentagon on Sept. 11—nearly 3,000 killed. **2002:** Three-week sniper spree terrorizes the Washington, D.C., area until police capture John Allen Muhammad and Lee Boyd Malvo, both later convicted of murder; Justice Department confirms an ongoing investigation of criminal activity in the collapse of energy giant Enron **2003:** Claiming threat of weapons of mass destruction, U.S. invades Iraq; the space shuttle *Columbia* disintegrates over east Texas and Louisiana as it reenters Earth's atmosphere; SARS epidemic spreads from China, infecting more than 8,000, killing hundreds worldwide **2004:** Tsunami devastates Indian Ocean basin—thousands in Indonesia, Sri Lanka, India and Thailand die **2005:** Hurricane Katrina floods Gulf Coast, devastates New Orleans

1990 | ROYALS OUTFIELDER Bo Jackson showed questionable bat control against the A's in Oakland. | *Photograph by* BRAD MANGIN

1983 | GEORGE BRETT was a little hot when his game-winning homer against the Yanks was disallowed because of excessive pine tar on his bat. | *Photograph by* BETTMANN/CORBIS

FROM THE HILL TO THE HALL

BY HERBERT WARREN WIND

As spring training opened, Yogi Berra loomed larger than ever as one of baseball's great personalities. —*from* SI, MARCH 2, 1959

IT IS PLEASANT TO CONTEMPLATE the good fortune that has come the way of Lawrence Peter Berra. If it is coming to any athlete, he has it coming to him. Aside from being a person of unusual decency and natural charm, he has, from a fairly inauspicious beginning in the big leagues, achieved over the last dozen years a place among the memorable players in the long history of the game. Over and above this, Berra is a personality of such original force and magnetism that sometimes it has even obliterated his stature as a player. He is, quite possibly, the last of the glorious line of baseball's great characters.

In this age where ballplayers have kept growing taller and more statuesque until the breed is now in appearance a combination of the stroke on the college crew and the juvenile lead in summer stock, Berra adheres to the classic blocky dimensions of the oldtime catcher. He stands 5' 8" and weighs about 192 and looks even chunkier (especially in a baseball uniform) than these figures would augur, for he has the broad and wide-set shoulders of a much taller man, a barrel chest and enormous arms. Unlike most men of similar musculature, Berra is very lithe, very loose—in fact, there is such friskiness in his movements (except when he is catching the second game of a doubleheader) that, as he approaches 34, he still conjures up the picture of a beknickered boy of 13 or 14. Berra's build is quite deceptive in other ways, or at least it has led a number of observers into glib deductions that are strikingly wayward. For example, nearly everyone decided years ago that a man with his non-missile dimensions would *ipso facto* have to be a slow runner. Only in recent years has it been generally appreciated that Yogi has always been extremely fast, one of the Yankees' best base runners in fact. Even stranger is that ivied slice of myopia which depicts Berra as all awkwardness at bat, a man who busts the ball out of the park by sheer brute strength. This is simply not correct. While there is assuredly little esthetic splendor about the way Yogi bunches himself at the plate, he handles the bat beautifully, with a delicacy and finesse which few place hitters approach and which is rarer still for a power hitter. In the 1955 World Series—not the '56 Series, in which he hit three home runs and drove in 10 runs, but the '55 Series in which he batted .417—Yogi put on one of the finest demonstrations of straightaway hitting in modern times, meeting the ball right between the seams again and again and lining it like a shot over the infield, very much in the fashion of Paul Waner and Nap Lajoie. "There's no one more natural or graceful than Yogi when he's taking his cut," Phil Rizzuto said not long ago. "He's all rhythm up there, like Ted Williams."

Williams and Berra are alike in one other respect: They are talkative men. As splendidly endowed as Williams is in this department, he is simply not in Berra's class. In truth no player in the annals of baseball has been. Stationed behind the plate Berra has a steady flow of new faces to ask how things are going, and during lulls between batters there is always the umpire. Early this year, Casey Stengel, a fairly articulate man himself, had a few words to say about Berra's verbosity. Asked if he considered Berra to be the best late-inning hitter in the game, a claim many have made for him, Casey replied that he didn't know about that. "He could be the best late-inning hitter in baseball because he's got to hit sometime during a game, and he is a very bad early-inning hitter. Sometimes Mr. Berra allows himself to go careless. He forgets to start the game with the first inning. He's out there behind the plate saying hello to everybody in sight. Oh, Mr. Berra is a very sociable fellow. He acts like home plate is his room."

In all of Yogi's actions on the ball field there is a beguiling spontaneity and a total lack of affectation. Beyond this, a tide of friendliness comes pouring through, and it communicates itself in a wondrous way not only to the people within earshot of his gravelly banter but also to the outlanders perched in the deep recesses of the stadium. You just sense you like that guy.

Berra has an abiding love of sports, and it explains the man directly. It is extraordinary to find an experienced professional athlete whose youthful affection for his game has not withered. Once he enters the dressing room, that spirit of the young boy, all eagerness for the game, clutches him wholly. He loves to play ball like other men like to make money or work in the garden. And this is what makes Berra the ballplayer he is. . . .

YOGI BERRA, seen here hitting in Game 2 of the 1960 World Series against the Pirates, was a great talker on and off the field.

> **Artifacts**

Tools of the Trade

First used to market tobacco in the 1880s, baseball cards soon evolved into iconic—and sometimes priceless—collectibles

JOHN WARD, S. S. N. Y's.
COPYRIGHTED BY GOODWIN & CO., 1887.
CIGARETTES
GOODWIN & CO. N. Y.

C. 1911

JAMES O'NEIL
Champion Base-Ball Batter

1888

PLANK—Pitcher

C. 1910

1887

TY YOUNG, Cleveland

1911

LEROY "Satchell" PAIGE

1949

SPEAKER BOSTON AM.

1911

GEORGE HERMAN (BABE) RUTH
BIG LEAGUE CHEWING GUM

1933

REULBACH, Brooklyn - Nationals

1914

Matthewson, p. N. Y. Nat'l

1910

1953

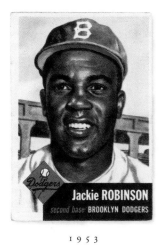

1911

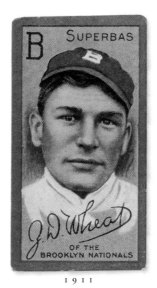

1911

1933

PHILLIPS, 1st base, BROOKLYN.

C. 1885

C. 1909

1911

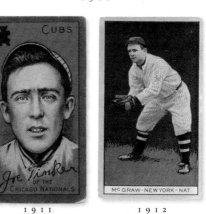

1911   1912

OLD JUDGE CIGARETTES Goodwin & Co., New York.

C. 1888

ROBERTO CLEMENTE

1955

RAPID ROBERT
CAN STILL BRING IT

BY FRANK DEFORD

Like his legendary heater, Bob Feller comes at you fast and hard—
and he's got a lot on his mind. —*from* SI, AUGUST 8, 2005

IT IS DIFFICULT TO IMAGINE now what a marvel Bob Feller was when he burst upon the scene in 1936, a callow youth of 17. Many athletes are great. Bob Feller was seminal. In that long-ago time, unlike nowadays, it was unheard of for teenagers to succeed in the big top of athletics. Perhaps in all the world only Sonja Henie had previously excelled at so young an age in any sport that mattered, and, after all, she was but a little girl wearing tights and fur trim, performing dainty figure-eights. Feller dressed in the uniform of the major league Cleveland Indians, striking out American demigods. In his first start Bobby Feller struck out 15, one short of the league record. Then, later in the season, he broke the mark, fanning 17, one for each year of his life, in the only professional team sport that mattered then in the United States.

He led the league with 240 strikeouts when he was still a teenager, in 1938. The next year he was best with 24 wins when he was still not old enough to drink. Six times he had the most wins, seven times the most strikeouts, and both of those totals might well have been in double figures had he not spent the heart of his career on a battleship. In 1940 he threw baseball's only Opening Day no-hitter, then went on to earn the pitchers' triple crown: most wins, most strikeouts, best ERA.

Cleveland, of course, took him to its bosom. "I don't think anything had ever happened like Feller," says Bob August, his contemporary and a native of the city who grew up to be a distinguished journalist there. "It was the Depression, and things were pretty bad here, and then this amazing kid came along. What a lift it gave us all. People today who don't know exactly what he did still seem to sense how special Bob Feller was to Cleveland."

To the nation, he was as much a sensation as a curiosity. The press called him Master Feller, and General Mills hired the phenomenon to endorse its cereals in tandem with the only minor more famous than he, Shirley Temple. Dutifully he went back to high school after his rookie season. The next spring he made the cover of Time magazine, and at a time when radio meant as much as television does now, NBC radio covered live, in its entirety, his graduation from Van Meter (Iowa) High.

Feller was raised Roman Catholic. One day the parish priest upbraided Bill Feller for allowing his son to play on Sabbath afternoons. Bob still remembers. His father said this to the priest: "I'll never see you again." Thereupon he turned heel, and the Fellers started worshipping on Sunday mornings as Methodists, so that Bob might play on Sunday afternoons without sanctimonious censure from the clergy.

The bidding for Feller's services began. The family chose the Indians mostly because they were comfortable with Cleveland's scout, Cy Slapnicka, a no-nonsense Iowan like themselves. The following year, when there was some dispute about whether the Indians had observed the legal arcana in signing the prodigy, Judge Landis, the commissioner, was inclined to void the contract and put the lad on the open market. Now understand: Aided by the fact that he even looked like a wrathful Jehovah, Kennesaw Mountain Landis had put the fear of God into everybody in baseball for 15 years. Well, to his face, the farmer from the Raccoon River told the commissioner: Do that, mister, take my boy away from where he wants to play, and I'll haul baseball into court. Landis backed down. Feller never played with anybody but the Indians all his life. His statue now stands outside the team's park. "Bill Feller was one smart Iowa farmer," Bob Feller declares.

And so the tree was bent. Almost from the moment he arrived in the majors, Feller was known for speaking his mind, doing it his way. He got a pilot's license at the age of 20, when that was risky business. He was the first major leaguer to enlist in the service after Pearl Harbor. When the fleet admiral wanted him to leave the war zone and go on shore duty in Hawaii, where all he had to do was pitch for the Navy team, Chief Petty Officer Feller said no thanks, he wouldn't leave his ship.

After the war he battled owners about his right to run barnstorming troupes in the off-season. He struck out Jackie Robinson and told everyone that the black guy would never make it because he was too musclebound to handle a high hard one—and it doesn't faze Feller in the least that he still hasn't heard the end of that. He was the highest-paid player in the game and the

first president of the players' association, fighting for what little they could get then: telephones in the clubhouse, toilets in the bullpen, penny-ante stuff like that.

But then, when the games were over for Feller, everything crumbled because of something he couldn't control. It drove him batty, but there wasn't anything he could do, and all the big money he had made as the highest-paid player in the game, all his rainy-day security, drip-dripped away until about all Rapid Robert had left was that mythical arm. So he would travel the country, flying his own plane, driving rental cars, working the sticks—*Bob Feller Pitches Tonight!*—a lounge act, tossing up a few to tank-town anchormen and politicians before minor league games, signing autographs, even working the dank clubhouses, trying to peddle insurance policies to the bush leaguers. For more than three decades he did

this, 80 or 90 dates in his best years. He flew 10,000 hours, he says, not giving up his license till he was 75 years old.

Meanwhile his superstar contemporaries—and there were only three of them mentioned in the same breath as Rapid Robert—had, each in his way, become comfortable aristocracy, certified as icons. DiMaggio: always in his sleek, silvery suits, Mr. Coffee, and . . . nation's Most Famous Widower. Williams: fishing, bloviating, doing as he damn well pleased, and the devil take the hindmost. Musial: Stan the Doyen of St. Louis, holding court at his restaurant, the National League grandee. And then there was Feller, alone with his arm, on the road, playing all the places he never had to work as a pro, because then he had been the child prodigy and come straight to the top. In some ways he had to live his life backward, the bushes after the big time. . . .

FELLER LED the league in strikeouts seven times for the Indians, despite missing prime years serving in the Navy in World War II.

FRANCIS MILLER

1967 | JIM LONBORG almost lost his shirt after beating the Twins at Fenway to clinch the pennant for the Red Sox. | *Photograph by* WALTER IOOSS JR.

1960 | BILL MAZEROSKI ran into a little traffic at third after his Game 7 homer in the bottom of the ninth beat the Yankees. | *Photograph by* AP IMAGES

TIGER TALES

BY LEIGH MONTVILLE

As the day approached when Tiger Stadium would fall to the wrecking ball, it was clear that a lot of sweet memories would go with it.   —*from* SI, JULY 12, 1999

THE MANAGER SCRATCHES sometimes at the blue paint on the walls and posts and ceiling of the home dugout. How can he not? The paint looks soft, inviting, almost as if it had been applied to cardboard, or papier-mâché. It is the final layer on top of years and years of paint jobs. The manager gets a fingernail in there and scratches a little bit, and flecks of history fall into his hand. "You see the different colors," Tigers manager Larry Parrish says. "You have the dark blue at the top, and then you get other shades of blue from other years, then shades of green and then some other colors and then, well, you're at the wood. You're back at the beginning."

The beginning was 1912. "I saw Ty Cobb when I was a kid," 86-year-old Arthur Brooks says. "My grandfather had a deal with the Tigers: Whenever it snowed he would hitch up the horses and plow our lumberyard, then plow all around the stadium. The Tigers gave him four tickets to every game for that. The best player I ever saw was Charlie Gehringer, second base. He was just smooth. He made everything look easy. At the plate—this was before all of this home run stuff, all these lunkheads with all their money—he was a place hitter. Is that a term you know? Nobody does it now. He was a place hitter. All line drives."

The lumberyard is still in business beyond rightfield: Brooks Lumber, run by Arthur Brooks's descendants. Baseball has been played at the corner of Michigan and Trumbull avenues since 1896, first at Bennett Park, built over the cobblestones of an old haymarket, then at the present stadium, opened on April 20, 1912, the same week the *Titanic* sank. The lumberyard has been the Tigers' neighbor almost from the beginning. "There's a lot of Brooks lumber in that stadium," Arthur says. "There's been a lot of changes through the years. Do you know that the clubhouse used to have one shower for the entire team? The place smelled so bad that pitchers didn't want to be taken out of games because they didn't want to go to the clubhouse."

A FORMER player—no names, please—made a sentimental visit to Tiger Stadium a year ago. Wearing his business suit, he wandered through the cramped and unchanged locker room, talked with the current occupant of his old locker, then traveled through the long tunnel toward the dugout and the playing field. As he approached the dugout, he stopped at a small sink in the tunnel. He unzipped his fly. "You'd always do this during a game," he said to a local sportswriter as he whizzed into the sink. "Saved you from going back to the clubhouse."

The modern player still walks where the long-ago player walked. The sink is still an option. The extra bats, balls and uniforms are still stored in the ceiling of the clubhouse, brought down by a clubhouse attendant on a ladder every day. The manager's office still has no bathroom. The lockers are still small and crowded together. The footsteps and voices of the past still provide the directions to be followed. "I can strike out, go into the tunnel and bang on the same wall that Ty Cobb banged on," says Tigers third baseman Dean Palmer. "Except he didn't strike out as much as me."

THE WORDS that have flowed from the Tiger Stadium press box have described the exploits of most players in the American League for 87 years. They have described the work of 11 hometown Hall of Famers, from the fierce Cobb to the hard-working Mickey Cochrane to the graceful Al Kaline. They have described six of the Tigers' nine World Series, the last in 1984. The words have also described troubled teams and troubled times. "This is not the original press box," says *The Detroit News* columnist Joe Falls. "The old press box burned down during the winter of '77. Jim Campbell, the general manager, said he wished the fire'd happened 'five months from now.' He was asked why. 'Because then all of [the writers] would have been in there.'"

THE BEST seats in baseball are still at Tiger Stadium, maybe 10,000 of them that put the spectator closer to the game than he would be at any other ballpark. The worst seats in baseball, too many to count and all with obstructed views, are also here. The front row of the upper deck in right overhangs the field by about 10 feet, catching fly balls and turning them into home runs. The eye can still see the transformer on the light tower that Reggie Jackson hit with his monster home run in the 1971 All-Star Game. The ear can still hear the four-man list of players who hit homers over the roof in left: Harmon Killebrew, Frank Howard, Cecil Fielder and Mark McGwire. The mind can still remember Mark (the Bird) Fidrych talking to the baseball on the mound in 1976.

The future awaits only a mile away, where the $290-million Comerica Park is being built. The Tigers' press guide details the wonders to come: the chair seats and suites; the dramatic view of the Detroit skyline; the beer garden on the third base side and the food court on the first base side, which will feature a carousel. The old park simply sits there. One day closer to its fate. . . .

TIGER STADIUM had some of the best seats in all of major league baseball (close to the field)—and some of the worst (obstructed views).

1960 | BASEBALL'S FABLED geometry could be glimpsed through the girders of Yankee Stadium. | *Photograph by* NEIL LEIFER

1958 | EVEN BEFORE Opening Day, the Dodgers' move to L.A. occasioned a parade that included Carl Furillo (6) and Pee Wee Reese. | *Photograph by* RICHARD MEEK

Acknowledgments

THE WORDS AND PICTURES COLLECTED HERE are the work of writers, photographers and editors who have covered baseball for SPORTS ILLUSTRATED since its launch more than 50 years ago. But this book would not have been possible without the tireless efforts of many current members of the SI staff: Linda Verigan, Ed Truscio, Chris Hercik, Keir Novesky, Stephen Skalocky, Geoffrey Michaud, Bob Thompson, Dan Larkin, Annmarie Modugno-Avila, Joy Birdsong, Natasha Simon, Ted Menzies, Karen Carpenter, George Amores, Scott Schild, Nina Prado, Richard Demak, Gabe Miller and Rebecca Plevin. The Baseball Hall of Fame provided invaluable expertise and special access to its treasures, and we are indebted to the Cooperstown team, especially Jeff Idelson, Scot Mondore, Sean Gahagan, Ted Spencer, Jim Gates, Pat Kelly, Sue MacKay, Peter Clark, Marty Bellew, Brad Horn, Milo Stewart, Erik Strohl and Doug Walden. Aaron Goodman's rendering of SI's alltime all-stars owes much to the painstaking preparation by Allyson Vieira and Michael Gross. Peter Capolino and Lynn Bloom at Mitchell & Ness helped make the magic of the Dream Team photo possible by supplying the vintage jerseys, and M&N's historian, Jared Wheeler, helped ensure their authenticity. A tip of the cap, too, to Dustin Hockensmith and St. John's University for the use of their dugout, and to Gary Cypres and Mark Rucker for items from their collections.

Finally, special thanks to SPORTS ILLUSTRATED managing editor Terry McDonell for giving us the green light and the resources to swing for the fences.

Grateful acknowledgment is also, made to the following for permission to reprint copyrighted material:

Aches and Pains and Three Batting Titles Copyright © 1966 by Myron Cope
The Benching of a Legend Copyright © 1960 by Roger Kahn
A Day of Light and Shadow Copyright © 1979 by Jonathan Schwartz
Final Twist of the Drama Copyright © 1974 by George Plimpton
"Everyone Is Helpless and in Awe" Copyright © 1974 by Roy Blount Jr.

Photo Credits

Historic artifacts courtesy of the National Baseball Hall of Fame

COVER CREDITS: *FRONT* (Top to bottom, from left): Jeff Carlick/MLB Photos/Getty Images; National Baseball Hall of Fame/MLB Photos/Getty Images; Brian Bahr/Getty Images; Focus on Sport/Getty Images; Christain Peterson/Getty Images; Tom Dipace; Diamond Images/Getty Images; Tony Tomsic/MLB Photos/Getty Images; James Drake; Diamond Images/Getty Images; Jim Mone/AP Images; Marvin E. Newman; Donald Miralle/Getty Images; F. Carter Smith/AP Images; Heinz Kluetmeier; James Drake; Tom Dipace; Jim Mone/AP Images; Manny Millan; John Dominis/Time Life Pictures; Heinz Kluetmeier; Ronald C. Modra; Jed Jacobsohn/Getty Images; Focus on Sport/Getty Images; *BACK* (Top to Bottom, from left): Tom Dipace; Gary Caskey/Reuters; Neil Leifer; V.J. Lovero; Mark Goldman/Icon SMI; Linda Kaye/AP Images; Walter Iooss Jr.; Chuck Rydlewski/Wireimage.com; David Durochik/MLB Photos/Getty Images; National Baseball Hall of Fame/MLB Photos/Getty Images; Neil Leifer; Walter Iooss Jr.; Neil Leifer; Walter Iooss Jr.; US Presswire; Josh Merwin/BEImages; Robert Beck; Tom Dipace; Mark Kauffman; Sue Ogrocki/Reuters; AP Images; Hank Walker/Time Life Pictures; Stephen Dunn/Getty Images; Kidweiler Collection/ Diamond Images/Getty Images; *FRONT FLAP* (Top to Bottom, from left): William R. Smith; Manny Rubio; AP Images; Neil Leifer; Art Shay; Jonathan Daniel/Getty Images; Diamond Images/Getty Images; Ron Vesely/MLB Photos/Getty Images; *BACK FLAP* (Top to Bottom, from left): Jamie Squire/Getty Images; AP Images; Bettmann/Corbis; Ronald C. Modra; Focus On Sport/Getty Images; Ken Leblanc/Wireimage.com; Brad Mangin; Ron Vesely/MLB Photos/Getty Images; *SPINE* (Top to Bottom, from left): Bryan Yablansky/Sportschrome; Scott Jordan Levy/Time Life/Getty Images; National Baseball Hall of Fame/Getty Images; Andy Hayt/Getty Images

TABLE OF CONTENTS (Top to Bottom from left): Hy Peskin; Walter Iooss Jr; John G. Zimmerman(2); Walter Iooss Jr. James Drake, Sheedy & Long; Neil Leifer; Walter Iooss Jr.(2); Neil Leifer; James Drake; Bernie Fuchs; Walter Iooss Jr.

ARTIFACTS: Bret Willis: 1, 6, 7, 48(7), 72, 80-81(4), 90-91, 142,183 (8),199, 229, 236-237, 265, 273(7), 282-283(8), 293; Susan Einstein/Gary Cypres Collection: 58-59(3), 273(1), 282-283(5); David N. Berkwitz: 48 (I), 80-81(8), 240; Milo Stewart: 48(I), 49, 105, 273(I), 292; Trancendental Graphics: 282-283(7).; Everett Collection: 58-59(8); John Stuart: 81(I); Gladstone Collection of Baseball Art: 282-283 (I); Michael Heape: 183(I), 241.

PICTURES: TSN/ICON SMI: 9,26,52,100; Getty Images: 10-11, 65, 104, 140, 152-153, 203, 223, 289; MLB Photos/ Getty Images: 25; NY Herald Tribune / N.Y Times/ AP Images: 12; Chicago Tribune/AP Images: 124; Time Life /Getty Images: 14, 45, 134 143, 255,206; AP Images: 32, 64, 96,112, 124(4), 129,250, 251; Corbis: 254; New York Daily News: 17; SportPics: 88-89; TSN Archives/ZUMA Press: 82-83, 87, 170, 221, 233; Rich Clarkson & Associates: 106-107; UPI: 252; Reuters: 124(2).

GATEFOLD: Aaron: Ozzie Sweet; Bench: Rich Pilling/MLB Photos/Getty Images; Berra: Tony Triolo; Clemens: David Walberg; Cobb: Charles M. Conlon/TSN/Icon SMI; Dimaggio: AP Images; Eckersley: Don Smith/MLB Photos/Getty Images; Gehrig:Bettmann/Corbis; Grove: Photofile/Getty Images; Hornsby: Charles M. Conlon/TSN/Icon SMI; Koufax :MLB Photos/Getty Iamges; Mantle: George Silk/Time Life Pictures/Getty Images; Mathewson: Charles M. Conlon/TSN/Icon SMI; Mays: Neil Leifer; McCarthy: Charles M. Conlon/TSN/Icon SMI; McGraw: Underwood & Underwood/Corbis; Musial: Photofile/Getty Images; Rivera: Kathy Willens/AP Images; Robinson: Bettmann/Corbis; Rodriguez: Otto Greule/Getty Images; Ruth: Time Life Pictures; Schmidt: John W. McDonough; Spahn: Bettmann/Corbis; Stengel: Pictorial Parade/Getty Images; Wagner: Charles M. Conlon/TSN/Icon SMI; Williams: AP Images; Young: National Baseball Hall of Fame/MLB Photos/Getty Images; Johnson: Charles M. Conlon/TSN/Icon

DECADES: PRE 1920 *DEBUT* (Top to Bottom) National Baseball Hall of Fame/MLB Photos/Getty Images; Charles M. Conlon/TSN/Icon SMI; Durant Collection; AP Images; National Baseball Hall of Fame/MLB Photos/Getty Images; National Baseball Hall of Fame/MLB Photos/Getty Images;Underwood & Underwood/Corbis; Bettmann/Corbis; Underwood &Underwood/Corbis (2); *FINALE* (Top to Bottom):

Lou Gehrig's license plate reflected his status in New York, even a year after his death in 1941.

National Baseball Hall of Fame/MLB Photos/Getty Images; Photo File/Getty Images; National Baseball Hall of Fame (2): Underwood &Underwood/Corbis (2);AP Images; National Baseball Hall of Fame/MLB Photos/Getty Images; Bettmann/Corbis; AP Images.

1920: *DEBUT* (Top to Bottom): Bettmann/Corbis; Underwood & Underwood/Corbis; Underwood & Underwood/Corbis; AP Images; AP Images; National Baseball Hall of Fame; AP Images; Charles M. Conlon/TSN/Icon SMI; TSN/Icon SMI; Bettmann/Corbis; *FINALE* (Top to Bottom): Underwood &Underwood/Corbis; Bettmann/Corbis (2);Underwood & Underwood/Corbis (2); Bettmann/Corbis; National Baseball Hall of Fame/MLB Photos/Getty Images, AP Images; AP Images; Bettmann/Corbis.

1930 *DEBUT* (Top to Bottom): Charles M. Conlon/TSN/Icon SMI; National Baseball Hall of Fame/MLB Photos/Getty Images; International News Photo; National Baseball Hall of Fame/MLB Photos/Getty Images; AP Images; National Baseball Hall of Fame; National Baseball Hall of Fame; AP Images; National Baseball Hall of Fame/MLB Photos/Getty Images; Charles M. Conlon/TSN/Icon SMI; *FINALE* (Top to Bottom): Acme Photo; National Baseball Hall of Fame/MLB Photos/Getty Images (2); AP Images (2); Tom Sande/AP Images; Bettmann/Corbis; AP Images; Bettmann/Corbis; National Baseball Hall of Fame/MLB Photos/Getty Images (2).

1940 *DEBUT* (Top to Bottom):Corbis; National Baseball Hall of Fame/MLB Photos/Getty Images; Getty Images; Bettmann/Corbis; AP Images; Kidwiler Collection/Diamond Images/Getty Images; AP Images. Hulton Archive/Getty Images;Marty Lederhandler/AP Images; Getty Images; *FINALE* (Top to Bottom): Bettmann/Corbis; MLB Photos/Getty Images; Bruce Bennett Studios/Getty Images; National Baseball Hall of Fame/ MLB Photos/Getty Images; Underwood& Underwood/Corbis, Bettmann/Corbis, Olen Collection/Diamond Images/Getty Images, National Baseball Hall of Fame/MLB Photos/Getty Images; National Baseball Hall of Fame/MLB Photos/Getty Images (2).

1950 *DEBUT* (Top to bottom) Harry Harris/AP Images;William C. Greene/TSN Archives/Icon SMI; AP Images; UPI; Hy Peskin; Heinz Kluetmeier; John G. Zimmerman; Pictorial Parade/Getty Images; AP Images; James Drake; *FINALE* (Top to Bottom): Bettmann/Corbis, National Baseball Hall of Fame/MLB Photos /Getty Images; AP Images, Bettmann/Corbis; Louis Requena/MLB Photos/Getty Images; Kidwiler Collection/Diamond Images/Getty Images; AP Images; Kidwiler Collection/Diamond Images/Getty Images; Diamond Images/Getty Images; Bettmann/Corbis.

1960 *DEBUT* (Top to Bottom) Lee Balterman; AP Images; Herb Scharfman (2); Louis Requena/MLB Photos/Getty Images; John G. Zimmerman; Fred Kaplan; Walter Iooss Jr.; AP Images; Marvin E. Newman; *FINALE* (Top to Bottom): Phil Bath; Kidwiler Collection/Diamond Images/Getty Images; AP Images; Rich Clarkson; Bettmann/Corbis; John G. Zimmerman; Bettmann/CORBIS; AP Images (2); TSN/Icon SMI.

1970 *DEBUT* (Top to Bottom): James Drake; Bettmann/Corbis; Louis Requena/MLB Photos/Getty Images; Ronald C. Modra (2); MLB Photos/Getty Images; Ronald C. Modra; Bettmann/Corbis; MLB Photos/Getty Images; Mickey Pfleger, *FINALE* (Top to Bottom): Bettmann/Corbis; Tony Triolo; Focus On Sport/Getty Images; Richard Meek; Sheedy & Long; Wil Blanche; Neil Leifer; Walter Iooss Jr.; Neil Leifer; Ozzie Sweet.

1980 *DEBUT* (Top to Bottom): Rich Pilling/MLB Photos/Getty Images; Jerry Wachter; Al Tielemans; Mark Duncan/AP Images; Ronald C. Modra; Ron Vesely/MLB Photos/Getty Images; Icon SMI; AP Images; Ronald C. Modra (2); *FINALE* (Top to Bottom) Michael Zagaris/MLB Photos/Getty Images; AP Images; Walter Iooss Jr; Ronald C. Modra; Bettmann/Corbis; Walter Iooss Jr.; AP Images; Chuck Rydlewski/Wireimage.com; Anthony Neste; AP Images.

1990 *DEBUT* (Top to Bottom): Chuck Solomon (2); John Iacono; David Liam Kyle; Chuck Solomon (2); John Biever; Jeff Carlick/Getty Images; Vincent Laforet/Getty Images; Bob Rosato; *FINALE* (Top to Bottom) Jerry Wachter; Otto Greule Jr/Getty Images; Gerry Thomas; Chuck Solomon; John Iacono; Al Tielemans (2); V.J. Lovero; Brad Mangin (2).

2000 *DEBUT* (Top to Bottom): Victor Baldizon; Todd Warshaw/Getty Images; Chuck Solomon; Brad Mangin; Chuck Solomon; Robert Beck; Jeffery A. Salter; MLB Photos/Getty Images; Al Tielemans; John Biever; *FINALE* (Top to Bottom) Chuck Solomon; AP Images; Robert Beck; John W. McDonough; Bob Rosato; John Cordes/Icon SMI; Jeff Gross/Getty Images; Heinz Kluetmeier; John Iacono; Chuck Solomon.

TIME INC. HOME ENTERTAINMENT PUBLISHER, Richard Fraiman; EXECUTIVE DIRECTOR, MARKETING SERVICES, Carol Pittard; DIRECTOR, RETAIL & SPECIAL SALES, Tom Mifsud; MARKETING DIRECTOR, BRANDED BUSINESSES, Swati Rao; DIRECTOR, NEW PRODUCT DEVELOPMENT, Peter Harper; ASSISTANT FINANCIAL DIRECTOR, Steven Sandonato; ASSISTANT GENERAL COUNSEL Dasha Smith Swin; PREPRESS MANAGER, Emily Rabin; BOOK PRODUCTION MANAGER, Jonathan Polsky; MARKETING MANAGER, Danielle Radano; ASSOCIATE PREPRESS MANAGER, Anne-Michelle Gallero; SI DIRECTOR, NEW PRODUCT DEVELOPMENT, Bruce Kaufman

Sports Illustrated